Revisiting Landmark Cases in Medical Law

Is it lawful for a doctor to give a patient life-shortening pain relief? Can treatment be lawfully provided to a child under 16 on the basis of her consent alone? Is it lawful to remove food and water provided by tube to a patient in a vegetative state? Is a woman's refusal of a caesarean section recommended for the benefit of the fetus legally decisive? These questions were central to the four focal cases revisited in this book.

This book revisits nine landmark cases. For each, a new leading judgment is attributed to an imagined judge, Athena, who operates within the constraints of the legal system of England and Wales. Her judgments accord with an innovative legal theory, referred to as 'modified law as integrity', and are linked as a line of precedent. The result is a re-spinning of extant judicial threads into a web of legal principles with a greater claim to coherence and defensibility than those in the original cases.

The book will be of great interest to scholars and students of medical law, criminal law, bioethics, legal theory and moral philosophy.

Shaun D. Pattinson is Professor of Medical Law and Ethics and was the founding Director of Durham CELLS (Centre for Ethics and Law in the Life Sciences) at Durham University, UK. His publications include two sole authored books, *Influencing Traits Before Birth* (Ashgate, 2002; reissued 2017) and *Medical Law and Ethics* (5th edn Sweet & Maxwell, 2017), and a book co-edited with Patrick Capps, *Ethical Rationalism and the Law* (Hart Publishing, 2017). He is a member of the Nuffield Council on Bioethics, which is the UK's leading bioethics committee, Fellow of both the Royal Society of Arts and Royal Society of Biology, and a Senior Fellow of the Higher Education Academy.

Biomedical Law and Ethics Library

Scientific and clinical advances, social and political developments and the impact of healthcare on our lives raise profound ethical and legal questions. Medical law and ethics have become central to our understanding of these problems, and are important tools for the analysis and resolution of problems – real or imagined.

In this series, scholars at the forefront of biomedical law and ethics contribute to the debates in this area, with accessible, thought-provoking, and sometimes controversial, ideas. Each book in the series develops an independent hypothesis and argues cogently for a particular position. One of the major contributions of this series is the extent to which both law and ethics are utilised in the content of the books, and the shape of the series itself.

The books in this series are analytical, with a key target audience of lawyers, doctors, nurses, and the intelligent lay public.

Series Editor: Sheila A.M. McLean
Professor Sheila A.M. McLean is Professor Emerita of Law and Ethics in Medicine, School of Law, University of Glasgow, UK.

Available titles:

The Umbilical Cord Blood Controversies in Medical Law
Karen Devine

The Fetus as a Patient
A Contested Concept and its Normative Implications
Edited by Dagmar Schmitz, Angus Clarke and Wybo Dondorp

Health Research Governance in Africa
Law, Ethics, and Regulation
Cheluchi Onyemelukwe-Onuobia

Revisiting Landmark Cases in Medical Law
Shaun D. Pattinson

For more information about this series, please visit:
www.routledge.com/Biomedical-Law-and-Ethics-Library/book-series/CAV5

Revisiting Landmark Cases in Medical Law

Shaun D. Pattinson

LONDON AND NEW YORK

First published 2019
by Routledge
2 Park Square, Milton Park, Abingdon, Oxon OX14 4RN

and by Routledge
52 Vanderbilt Avenue, New York, NY 10017

Routledge is an imprint of the Taylor & Francis Group, an informa business

© 2019 Shaun D. Pattinson

The right of Shaun D. Pattinson to be identified as author of this work has been asserted by him in accordance with sections 77 and 78 of the Copyright, Designs and Patents Act 1988.

All rights reserved. No part of this book may be reprinted or reproduced or utilised in any form or by any electronic, mechanical, or other means, now known or hereafter invented, including photocopying and recording, or in any information storage or retrieval system, without permission in writing from the publishers.

Trademark notice: Product or corporate names may be trademarks or registered trademarks, and are used only for identification and explanation without intent to infringe.

British Library Cataloguing-in-Publication Data
A catalogue record for this book is available from the British Library

Library of Congress Cataloging-in-Publication Data
Names: Pattinson, Shaun D., author.
Title: Revisiting landmark cases in medical law / Shaun D. Pattinson.
Description: Abingdon, Oxon [UK] ; New York, NY : Routledge, 2018.
| Series: Biomedical Law and Ethics Library | Includes bibliographical references and index.
Identifiers: LCCN 2018024122 | ISBN 9781138808331 (hardback)
Subjects: LCSH: Medical laws and legislation—England—Case studies. | Medical ethics—England—Case studies.
Classification: LCC KD3395 .P39 2018 | DDC 344.4203/21—dc23
LC record available at https://lccn.loc.gov/2018024122

ISBN: 978-1-138-80833-1 (hbk)
ISBN: 978-1-315-75065-1 (ebk)

Typeset in Galliard
by Swales & Willis Ltd, Exeter, Devon, UK

Contents

Preface   viii
Acknowledgements   ix

1   The rationale and method of revisiting medical law cases   1

1.1 Introduction 1
    1.1.1 Some contextual issues 3
    1.1.2 Overview of this chapter 5
1.2 An interpretative account of adjudication 6
    1.2.1 Law as integrity 7
    1.2.2 Criticism of law as integrity 10
1.3 Law as a moral judgment 12
    1.3.1 The dialectically necessary argument for the PGC 13
    1.3.2 Dialectically contingent arguments for the PGC 16
    1.3.3 Direct applications of the PGC 18
    1.3.4 Indirect applications of the PGC 21
1.4 Modified law as integrity 23
1.5 Crafting judgments 25

2   *Adams*: life-shortening pain relief   28

2.1 Introduction 28
2.2 Legal developments 30
2.3 The principle of double effect 34
2.4 Devlin J's principle and the principle of double effect 38
    2.4.1 Other jurisdictions 40
2.5 Application of the PGC 41
2.6 Options available to Athena J 43
2.7 Idealised judgment: Attorney-General's
    Reference (No 1 of 1958) *(CA, Crim) 48*

vi *Contents*

3 *Gillick*: consent from a child 54

3.1 Introduction 54
3.2 The decision in Gillick *55*
   3.2.1 The capacity test 56
   3.2.2 Parental rights 58
   3.2.3 Criminality 60
3.3 Gaps and legal developments 61
   3.3.1 Refusal of medical treatment 62
   3.3.2 *Gillick* v the MCA test 66
   3.3.3 16- and 17-year-olds 68
   3.3.4 Other jurisdictions and international instruments 72
3.4 Application of the PGC 74
   3.4.1 Relational autonomy 74
   3.4.2 Competence 77
3.5 Options available to Lady Athena 82
3.6 Idealised judgment: Gillick v West Norfolk
   and Wisbech AHA *(HL) 85*

4 *Bland*: patients in a vegetative state 92

4.1 Introduction 92
4.2 Tensions and developments 93
   4.2.1 Legal fictions 93
   4.2.2 The best interests of patients in PVS and MCS 97
   4.2.3 The five safeguards 99
   4.2.4 Other jurisdictions 101
4.3 Application of the PGC 103
4.4 Options available to Lady Athena 106
4.5 Idealised judgment: Airedale NHS Trust v Bland *(HL) 108*

5 *Re MB*: refusal of treatment in late pregnancy 115

5.1 Introduction 115
5.2 Legal principles on capacity and refusal of treatment in late
   pregnancy 116
   5.2.1 The capacity test 116
   5.2.2 The assisted suicide issue 122
   5.2.3 The interests of the fetus 123
   5.2.4 Best interests 126
   5.2.5 Procedural safeguards 128
5.3 Other jurisdictions 130
5.4 Application of the PGC 131
   5.4.1 Capacity 131
   5.4.2 The weight of the rights of the fetus 133

Contents vii

5.5 *Options available to Lady Athena 136*
5.6 *Idealised judgment:* Re MB (Medical Treatment) *(CA) 138*

6   Conclusion: revisiting five further cases   146

6.1 *Introduction 146*
6.2 *The role of precedent and judgment writing 148*
   6.2.1 Some idiosyncrasies of appellate judgments 151
6.3 *Legal principles identified and applied in the idealised*
   judgments 152
   6.3.1 The principles 153
6.4 *Revisiting five further cases 153*
   6.4.1 *Re A*: lethal separation of conjoined twins 154
   6.4.2 *U*: undue influence 156
   6.4.3 *Quintavalle*: cloning and interpreting legislation 160
   6.4.4 *Burke*: advance requests for life-prolonging
   treatment 164
   6.4.5 *Yearworth*: property in sperm 168
6.5 *Concluding remarks 172*

Bibliography   173
Index   187

Preface

It is a trite truism that it is easier to criticise than create. Legal researchers and law students spend much of their time reading and criticising appellate judgments. We are often quick to dismiss a case as not well reasoned and conclude that the judge has misunderstood or overlooked a powerful reason for deciding a point another way. Yet, few have considered how their alternative approach could have been written as a judgment and what it would have meant for the law if that judgment had been the ratio decidendi of the court.[1] This book takes on that task. It examines landmark cases in medical law and offers a *new judgment* for each. A chapter is dedicated to each of four focal cases and five additional cases are examined in the concluding chapter. It will be argued that even when the outcome reached on the facts was defensible, the underlying reasoning for these cases was inadequate. *Uniquely*, the rewritten judgments in this book will be linked as if comprising a line of precedents. The new judgments will be presented as if written by an appellate judge who shares much with Ronald Dworkin's Hercules, but gains the support of a grounded moral theory and (to reject the mistaken suggestion that an ideal judge is a male judge) is a woman.[2]

Some say that before you criticise someone, you should walk a mile in their shoes; that way when you criticise them, you are a mile away and have their shoes. My judge travels on paths overlooked by contemporary judges. My aim is not just to argue that there were lost opportunities for the appeal courts to put the law onto a more defensible path; I also want to provide a method for the exploration of alternative paths in other areas of law and even other common law systems. My judge operates within the constraints of the legal system of England and Wales, but judges in other jurisdictions and other areas of law face similar challenges and may utilise many of the same tools. The principal purpose of this book is thus ambitious: *to articulate and apply a new legal method for judicial reasoning.*

---

1 Exceptions are those who have contributed rewritten judgments to edited collections, such as Balkin 2007, Hunter et al 2010a, Brems 2012, and Smith et al 2017.
2 See Dworkin 1978, esp ch 4; 1986, esp ch 7; and the first chapter of this book.

Acknowledgements

Over four years have passed between submission of the book proposal and submission of the manuscript to the publisher. I have benefited from innumerable discussions during that period, and indeed over the course of my academic career, and cannot now recall all my debts. I will therefore restrict myself to thanking those who have commented on early drafts of one or more chapters (in alphabetical order): Nathalie Barbosa de la Cadena, Deryck Beyleveld, Roger Brownsword, Patrick Capps, Emma Cave, Zoe Gounari, Gleider Hernández, William Lucy, Aoife O'Donoghue and Clayton Ó Néill. I am grateful to Mary Donnelly for drawing my attention to some of the literature on *Gillick*. I would also like to thank those studying on the 'Law and Medicine' module at Durham who were kind enough to offer comments on early drafts of three chapters, particularly Georgia McDonnell, Janie Hui and Lily Malcolm-Watts.

I would like to offer special thanks to Liz McElwain, who has been an exceptional copy-editor.

I dedicate this book to my dearest Zoe and our beautiful boy, Orion.

SDP

1 The rationale and method of revisiting medical law cases

1.1 Introduction

This book revisits four landmark cases in English medical law in depth and five more briefly in the concluding chapter. These are cases that have shaped and continue to shape the direction of the law addressing medical activities in England and Wales. But such a claim would capture dozens, perhaps even hundreds of cases. The late Ken Mason, one of the founders of medical law as an academic discipline, once gave a lecture in which he sought to identify the five most significant UK medical law cases of the past 30 years[1] and only two of those cases are also selected here.[2] In 2015, Herring and Wall published an edited collection addressing 15 landmark cases in medical law, which included only three of Mason's five and only four of this book's nine cases.[3] Readers may therefore legitimately ask how my leading cases have been selected. They may also ask why I have selected cases from a single jurisdiction.

I must start by explaining what my 'revisiting' involves. An *idealised judgment* is to be provided for each case. These cases are to be examined chronologically so that the idealised judgments may coherently build on the principles set down in the earlier idealised judgments. Each will therefore be written as if it were a judgment of a contemporary appeal court and treated as if it were the majority view, which necessitates the selection of cases from a single jurisdiction. *Other approaches in the literature do not attempt to link idealised judgments for medical law cases together as a line of precedent.*[4] This book's approach differs from, for example, Fuller's famous article on the case of the Speluncean Explorers, which presents five imaginary judgments addressing the fictional facts of a single case in

---

1 See Mason 1998. For discussion see Laurie 2006.
2 Mason's selection: *Re B* [1981] 1 WLR 1421, *Gillick v Norfolk and Wisbech AHA* [1986] AC 112, *Re MB* [1997] 2 FCR 541, *A-G's Reference (No 3 of 1994)* [1998] AC 245, and *R v Cox* (1992) 12 BMLR 38. The shared cases are *Gillick* and *Re MB*.
3 Herring & Wall 2015. All three of us have selected *Gillick* and *Re MB*.
4 See eg Balkin 2007 (which rewrites judgments for a single case), Hunter et al 2010a and Brems 2012 (which do not focus exclusively on medical law or link the rewritten judgments as a line of precedent), Herring & Wall 2015 (which does not provide rewritten judgments) and Smith et al 2017 (which does not link the rewritten judgments as a line of precedent).

2 The rationale and method

a hypothetical legal system.[5] My revisiting will seek to show how someone akin to Dworkin's Hercules, sitting as an appeal judge in actual cases occurring over about 40 years, might have attempted to weave a 'seamless web' of legal principle in English medical law.[6] My judge will be called *Athena* and will apply a modified version of Dworkin's 'law as integrity'. But here I am getting ahead of myself. The point is that if this enterprise is to elicit any new insights, the judges in the selected cases must have missed opportunities to aid the development of coherent and justifiable legal doctrine by reliance on clear principles.

My selection of cases is also driven by the goal of providing English medical law with a core set of legal principles. This has led me to select four focal cases concerned with the value of human life and/or patient autonomy:

(1) *R v Adams*[7] – on the administration of life-shortening pain relief;
(2) *Gillick v West Norfolk and Wisbech AHA*[8] – on the treatment of children under 16 years of age;
(3) *Airedale NHS Trust v Bland*[9] – on removal of nutrition and hydration from a patient in a vegetative state; and
(4) *Re MB (Caesarean Section)*[10] – on the refusal of treatment in late pregnancy.

For convenience, these will be referred to as (1) *Adams*, (2) *Gillick*, (3) *Bland* and (4) *Re MB*. Each case will be the subject of a chapter in this book. These focal cases are cases where it seems to me that, despite the decision/direction made on the facts being largely defensible, the reasoning leaves issues unaddressed, creates avoidable confusion and invites moral critique. In short, these are cases where the reasoning adopted left a problem of explanation and justification – the very issues at the core of modified law as integrity.

Five additional cases are revisited in the conclusion:

(5) *Re A (Children) (Conjoined Twins: Surgical Separation)*[11] – on the lethal separation of conjoined twins;
(6) *U v Centre for Reproductive Medicine*[12] – on undue influence in the context of medical treatment;
(7) *R (Quintavalle) v Secretary of State for Health*[13] – on the interpretation of legislation in the face of unanticipated developments in medical science;

---

5 See Fuller 1949.
6 See Dworkin 1978, esp ch 4, and 1998, esp ch 7.
7 [1957] Crim LR 365 (Crown Ct, 1957).
8 [1986] AC 112 (HL, October 1985).
9 [1993] AC 789 (HL, February 1993).
10 [1997] 2 FLR 426 (CA, February 1997).
11 [2001] Fam 147 (CA, September 2000).
12 [2002] EWCA Civ 565 (CA, April 2002).
13 [2003] UKHL 13 (HL, March 2003).

The rationale and method **3**

(8)   *R (Burke) v GMC*[14] – on advance requests for life-prolonging treatment; and
(9)   *Yearworth v North Bristol NHS Trust*[15] – on property in human sperm.

For convenience, these will be referred to as (5) *Re A*, (6) *U*, (7) *Quintavalle*, (8) *Burke* and (9) *Yearworth*. These five additional cases are, perhaps, not as obviously landmark cases, but revisiting provides the opportunity to further expand the core principles of English medical law and articulate the method of modified law as integrity. Revisiting *Re A* enables explication of how the principles from the rewritten judgments in *Adams* and *Bland* can be woven together to address a very different set of facts. Revisiting *Quintavalle* enables application of the method to statutory interpretation. *U* and *Burke* are cases for which modified law as integrity challenges both the reasoning and the conclusions reached on the facts. *Yearworth* enables the articulation of principles beyond those in the other revisited cases.

This book does not revisit many otherwise significant cases for which revisiting the reasoning would offer little new insight into how the law could have been placed on a more coherent footing. Into this group I would place the principal cases on the standard of care in medical negligence.[16] An appeal court judge operating within the courts of England and Wales could not, of course, be this selective with regard to the cases on which she sits. The method of this book is, however, applicable to *any* case. The purpose of this chapter is not just to examine the nine selected cases, but to lay down the method by which they are to be addressed. Before detailing this method, this introduction will briefly explore some contextual issues in relation to the development of English medical law.

1.1.1 Some contextual issues

The project of revisiting landmark cases with the aim of offering idealised judgments is, by its nature, one focussed on argument from the judges' viewpoint. It is also directed towards those 'hard' cases for which the settled rules and rulings do not give decisive guidance on the dispute/question before the court.[17] That is not to suggest that judges are the only or even the most important participants in the legal enterprise. Nor is it to suggest that hard cases, addressed by appeal courts, are representative of the legal enterprise as such. Legal practice in a modern polity involves many officials and professionals. Indeed, law as a social enterprise affects the lives of us all. Similarly,

---

14 [2005] EWCA Civ 1003 (CA, July 2005).
15 [2009] EWCA Civ 37 (CA, February 2009).
16 *Bolam v Friern Hospital Management Committee* [1957] 1 WLR 582 and *Bolitho v City and Hackney HA* [1998] AC 232. I am tempted by the view that greater coherence could be provided by reinterpreting medical negligence in terms of corrective justice: see Beever 2007. In any event, it seems to me that the rights of those affected by medical mistakes would be better protected by the development of alternative patient safety and redress systems.
17 See Dworkin 1978, 81. cf Adams & Brownsword (2006, 102) who prefer to call these 'difficult cases', reserving the term 'hard case' for those where the judge believes the settled rules and rulings are clear but has significant reservations about applying them.

4   The rationale and method

the mainstay of most lawyers' work is (in lawyer-speak) non-contentious. The courts are not, for example, involved with the routine business of drafting wills or conveying land. In those rare cases where the courts are involved, the vast majority are dealt with by plea or default, or hinge on contested questions of fact; and in such cases, the settled rules and rulings are considered decisive.[18]

Montgomery, Jones and Biggs point out that a wide range of 'hidden' law-making now underpins the development of law on controversial issues of medical ethics.[19] Legislative interventions in the field have established many bodies with significant regulatory and advisory powers, such as the Human Fertilisation and Embryology Authority (HFEA),[20] Human Tissue Authority (HTA)[21] and the various professional regulators.[22] Subsequent Parliamentary intervention has typically given legislative force to policy decisions made by these bodies. Notable examples can be found in the Human Fertilisation and Embryology Act 2008. To note just one, this Act modified the legislative requirement that assisted reproductive treatment services should only be provided to women where account has been taken of the welfare of the resulting child.[23] This changed the requirement that attention be given to the need of that child for a *father*, to one directed to the need of that child for *supportive parenting*. The HFEA had, however, already marginalised that focus on the prospective father by giving it only passing attention in its Code of Practice. In a sense, the legislation was merely catching up with the operation of the law in practice. Legal change brought about by regulatory bodies in this way is not strictly hidden, as is suggested by Montgomery and his co-authors' phrase 'hidden law-making', but it has not received the same degree of attention as received by legislative law-making.

Another mechanism behind legal change considered by Montgomery and his co-authors could be called strategic activism. As I have pointed out elsewhere, pressure groups have increasingly sought to give effect to their views through the judicial process.[24] In some cases, the courts have accepted submissions from groups and individuals who were not parties to the action. This includes a case to be revisited in the final chapter: in *Re A*, the Court of Appeal allowed submissions from the Archbishop of Westminster and the ProLife Alliance. A further trend has been for such groups and individuals to bring cases themselves. I know of no case where a group or individual with a 'genuine and legitimate interest'[25] has been denied standing by the courts to challenge the legality of the decision of a public body on a topic of medical controversy. *Gillick*, another of my landmark cases,

---

18 See Beyleveld & Brownsword 1987, 669.

19 See Montgomery et al 2014.

20 Established by the Human Fertilisation and Embryology Act 1990.

21 Established by the Human Tissue Act 2004.

22 See Montgomery et al 2014, 348.

23 Human Fertilisation and Embryology Act 1990, s 13(5). For discussion see Pattinson 2009b, 275; 2017b, 281. Other examples concern sex selection and donor selection ('saviour siblings'): see Pattinson 2009b, 291–294; 2017b, 298–302 and Montgomery et al 2014, 352.

24 See Pattinson 2006, 20–21; 2017b, 21–22.

25 Sir Thomas Bingham MR in *Re S* [1996] Fam 1, 18.

The rationale and method 5

was a challenge to a Department of Health circular that had not, at the time, had any direct impact on the applicant or her four daughters. The ProLife Alliance and Comment on Reproductive Ethics (CORE), led by the Quintavalles,[26] were particularly active in this regard in the 2000s. In one week in 2003 the appeal courts decided two separate cases against the Quintavalles and they had already lost a case in the House of Lords only a month earlier.[27] One of those cases is revisited in the final chapter: *Quintavalle.*

The selection of cases to bring, or in which to intervene, is rarely random. As Montgomery, Jones and Biggs put it:

> In such cases, the individual dispute can be said to be secondary to the issue of principle and it is likely that suitable cases are selected by the sponsors of the litigation to maximise the possibility that the case will lead to their preferred result. This selection process is rarely transparent and its ability to shape the opportunities presented to judges may be significant.[28]

Awareness of such practices raises many questions about limits to third party interventions and the granting of leave in medical law cases. A further question that is directly relevant to the enterprise of this book is: how may the courts counter distortions and distractions presented by the applicant's selection of a test case? Perhaps, for example, the situation raised by a test case is atypical and could thereby encourage undue emphasis on principles that are not applicable to more commonplace facts.

These questions are not evoked by all my landmark cases. Significant cases are sometimes not immediately recognised as such by the courts, academics or pressure groups. Only later is it recognised that cases such as *Adams* gave voice to important principles. Montgomery and his co-authors note that its reliance on the principle of 'double effect' was not the focus of the judge's own account of that case (which 'concentrates on issues of evidence and the approaches taken by the police and lawyers'), nor was its significance initially recognised by all leading academics or the Church of England.[29]

1.1.2 Overview of this chapter

This chapter will be divided into four further sections. The first will outline an interpretative account of adjudication and explain that this book seeks to further

---

26 Josephine Quintavalle and her son Bruno Quintavalle.
27 The relevant cases were: *R (Pro-Life Alliance) v BBC* [2003] UKHL 23, *R (Josephine Quintavalle) v HFEA* [2003] EWCA Civ 667, and *R (Bruno Quintavalle) v Secretary of State for Health* [2003] UKHL 13. See Pattinson 2017b, 21–22.
28 Montgomery et al 2014, 358. Judges have also played a role in case selection: see Robertson 1998, ch 5, on the role of Lord Griffith in *Pepper v Hart* [1993] AC 593.
29 See Montgomery et al 2014, 359. The judge's own account of the case took the form of a book: Devlin 1985.

6 *The rationale and method*

English medical law by seeking the most coherent and justifiable interpretation of past decisions. The second section will defend a moral account of law. The third section will bring together the first and second sections by offering a modified version of Dworkin's law as integrity. The fourth section will situate Athena within the context of the English legal system.

1.2 An interpretative account of adjudication

In his book *Contract Theory*, Smith distinguishes four accounts of any area of law: (1) historical, (2) prescriptive, (3) descriptive, and (4) interpretative.[30] According to Smith:

> Interpretative theories aim to enhance understanding of the law by highlighting its significance or meaning . . . [T]his is achieved by explaining why certain features of law are important or unimportant and by identifying connections between those features—in other words, by revealing an *intelligible order* in the law, so far as such order exists.[31]

This project is interpretative in this sense, but it is also historical, descriptive and prescriptive.[32] There is an unavoidable historical element to 'revisiting' past cases and presenting idealised judgments as if they were made at the time. But, in contrast to a typically historical approach to the selected cases, this book is not about explaining what motivated judges to do what they did or otherwise focussed on the law's causal history. Such revisiting is also unavoidably descriptive and prescriptive. The existing rules and rulings provide data for interpretation and the idealised judgments are clearly meant to be prescriptive. Smith's distinction between (2) and (3), however, implies that law can be properly described non-prescriptively (that is, what counts as law is different from what ought to count as law). It thereby assumes legal positivism (which holds that legal validity is distinct from moral validity) over legal idealism (which holds that moral validity is a condition of legal validity). In contrast, the specific interpretative account used in this book, and defended below, understands law as a *moral* enterprise. Here, I use the word 'moral' to refer to *prescriptive* requirements that are *other-regarding* in the sense of requiring furtherance of the interests of others and *categorical* in the sense of overriding other demands and one's desires/inclinations.[33]

The interpretative account of this book seeks the most coherent and morally justifiable interpretation of past decisions, thereby revealing intelligible order in

---

30 See Smith 2004, 4–6.
31 Smith 2004, 5 (emphasis in original).
32 Smith (2004, 5–6) accepts that 'nearly all' interpretative accounts involve historical, prescriptive and descriptive elements. As explained below, for the interpretative account to be defensible it will need all of these elements.
33 See Gewirth 1978, 1, and Pattinson 2017b, 568–569.

the law. The idealised judgments will seek principles to support the conclusions reached in the cases selected for revisiting, even when those principles are not part of the reasoning of judges in earlier decisions.

It is an account that shares much with a 'constructive interpretation' of legal reasoning, according to which 'our law consists in the best justification of our legal practices as a whole, that it consists in the narrative story that makes of these practices the best they can be'.[34] Dworkin presents an imaginary super-judge, Hercules, who decides cases by finding and applying the principles that best explain and justify the existing rules and rulings within that jurisdiction. My account of law departs from aspects of Dworkin's legal theory. It places an additional constraint upon the judge by requiring conformity to the direct and indirect requirements of a specific moral principle. But I am, once again, getting ahead of myself. Let me first present a more detailed summary of Dworkin's theory, before seeking to challenge and revise aspects of that theory.

1.2.1 Law as integrity

Dworkin's theory is presented in its most systematic form in his book *Law's Empire* (1986), which was preceded by two collections of essays: *Taking Rights Seriously* (1977) and *A Matter of Principle* (1985). Interpretation of Dworkin's work is hindered by his use of different vocabulary in each book to convey similar ideas and by his generally elusive style. Indeed, in *Law's Empire*, he goes so far as to declare that he makes no effort 'to discover how far this book alters or replaces positions I defended in earlier works'.[35]

In *Taking Rights Seriously*, Dworkin presents his theory of adjudication as 'the Rights Thesis'.[36] He identifies legal positivism as the view that 'valid legal rules' are exhaustive of 'the law', which means that judges must go beyond the law when dealing with a 'hard case', where 'no settled rule disposes of the case'.[37] Dworkin concludes that legal positivism implies a theory of hard cases in which 'unelected' judges exercise unconstrained discretion and thereby 'make law' by retrospective legislation.[38] The implication is that legal positivism fails to explain adjudication in hard cases and leads to procedural immorality by undermining democracy and the rule of law.

In response, Dworkin advances a theory of adjudication in which law includes not only formal rules and rulings, but also those *principles* that underlie those rules and rulings. Dworkin fleshes out his theory using his ideal judge Hercules, who seeks out the best justification of the rules and rulings within that jurisdiction

---

34 Dworkin 1986, vii.
35 Dworkin 1986, viii.
36 See Dworkin 1978, esp ch 4.
37 Dworkin 1978, 17 and 81. Legal rules are thereby distinguished from non-legal 'standards' (such as principles and policy): ibid, 22.
38 See Dworkin 1978, ch 4, esp 81 and 84.

8 *The rationale and method*

according to fit (with existing rules and rulings) and justification (moral defensibility).[39] Hercules is permitted, according to a 'theory of mistakes', to treat some previous precedents as mistaken.[40] There is, Dworkin maintains, a 'right answer' for Hercules to find, even in hard cases.[41] He further connects 'principles' to 'rights' and holds that the most 'fundamental' right is the 'right to equal concern and respect'.[42] But, he insists, this does not commit him to 'some transcendental strongbox' theory of law, which he dismisses as 'nonsense'.[43] Hercules' best justifying theory is not one premised on objective/universal moral principles; rather it is grounded in 'those moral principles that underlie the community's institutions and laws'.[44]

Dworkin distinguishes between morality in the 'anthropological sense' and in the 'discriminatory sense'.[45] The former refers to the moral views that are held or dominant in a community. The latter, to which he seeks to adhere, refers to a moral position that is free from '[p]rejudices, rationalizations, matters of personal aversion or taste, arbitrary stands, and the like'.[46] This requires, Dworkin elaborates, that reasons be given for a moral position. Four types of response are excluded:[47]

(a) prejudice – taking account of considerations excluded by the community's conventions;
(b) mere emotional reaction – personal feeling without reason or justification;
(c) rationalisation – appeal to false or irrational beliefs, or citing evidence not plausibly connected to their conclusions or not generally regarded as sufficient by that person; and
(d) parroting – mere citation of the beliefs of others.

Further, a discriminatory moral position must be held sincerely, be consistent with that person's other moral beliefs and not be presented as self-evident when it is controversial.[48] This specification of 'discriminatory morality' notably relies on the 'anthropological morality' that it is meant to replace. This is most clearly the case with regard to Dworkin's rejection of prejudice, defined as 'postures of judgment that take into account considerations our conventions exclude'.[49] This is question-begging: Dworkin relies on anthropological morality ('our conventions') to justify an alternative to anthropological morality.

39 See Dworkin 1978, 105ff.
40 See Dworkin 1978, 118–121.
41 See Dworkin 1978, ch 13.
42 Dworkin 1978, xii and ch 6.
43 Dworkin 1978, 216.
44 Dworkin 1978, 79.
45 See Dworkin 1978, 248–253.
46 Dworkin 1978, 248.
47 See Dworkin 1978, 249–251.
48 See Dworkin 1978, 251–252.
49 Dworkin 1978, 249.

The rationale and method   9

In *Law's Empire*, Dworkin explains and develops his theory using a new vocabulary. Dworkin maintains that the debate between legal positivism and 'natural law' must be about how to best interpret legal practice.[50] Otherwise, he argues, it is no more than an empty linguistic dispute about the meaning of words (which he calls the 'semantic sting'). Interpretation of a social practice, text or work of art is said to be 'constructive'.[51] A 'constructive interpretation' involves imposing a purpose on the object or practice (on the 'pre-interpretative data'), whereby the interpreter derives a general justification to 'fit' that data and portray it in its best light.[52] Applied to law, Dworkin identifies the pre-interpretative data as the rules, rulings, etc of positive law and views portrayal of that data in its best light in terms of its best moral or political light.

Perhaps not surprisingly, Dworkin holds that the best constructive interpretation of law is his own, now called 'law as integrity'. This is contrasted with 'conventionalism' (legal positivism) and 'legal pragmatism' (American realism).[53] *Conventionalism* holds that judges are constrained by those rights and responsibilities that are explicit in past rules and rulings, but when the force of those materials is spent, judges are free to 'make' law.[54] *Legal pragmatism* rejects the need for fit with past rules and rulings, and thereby denies that people have legal rights. Instead, 'judges do and should make whatever decisions seem to them best for the community's future'.[55] *Law as integrity* holds that rights and responsibilities flow from previous rules and rulings 'not just when they are explicit in these decisions but also when they follow from the principles of personal and political morality the explicit decisions presuppose by way of justification'.[56] Law as integrity is thereby presented as avoiding the need for judges to make law according to their own lights, either when cases go beyond extant explicit rules and rulings (as per conventionalism) or irrespective of those existing rules and rulings (as per legal pragmatism). Given Dworkin's definitions of conventionalism and legal pragmatism, both must be rejected by anyone attempting a constructive interpretation of legal practice.

Dworkin maintains that his ideal judge[57] will decide hard cases 'by trying to find, in some coherent set of principles about people's rights and duties, the best constructive

---

50 See Dworkin 1986, 31–46. He uses the label 'natural law' to refer to legal idealism based on an objective morality, eg 35.

51 See Dworkin 1986, chs 2 and 3.

52 This has three stages (the pre-interpretative, interpretative and post-interpretative): see Dworkin 1986, 65–66.

53 eg Dworkin 1986, esp 94–96 and 225.

54 See Dworkin 1986, 95.

55 Dworkin 1986, 95.

56 Dworkin 1986, 96.

57 This remains Hercules (Dworkin 1986, 230), but is now sometimes Hermes (when interpreting statutes: ibid, 317) or Siegfried (when considering a judge operating in a wicked, Nazi-type legal system: ibid 105).

10 The rationale and method

interpretation of the political structure and legal doctrine of the community'.[58] He will seek out a principle that 'both *fits* and *justifies* some complex part of legal practice' and thereby provides 'the consistency of principle' required by integrity.[59] This first step involves Hercules examining the existing formal legal materials, which Dworkin explains using the metaphor of the chain novel.[60] If a novelist writes the first chapter of a book, then another novelist writes the second and yet another writes the third chapter, and so on, the resulting manuscript will only make a coherent novel if each writer seeks to place his or her chapter within the framework set by the previous writers. Like a chain writer, Hercules cannot ignore previous landmark decisions. However, Dworkin says, it is more important that he should fit what judges did than what they said.[61] Hercules will frequently find more than one interpretation capable of fitting the 'bulk' of the previous materials and will then move to the justifiability stage.[62] This will involve examining the interpretative options by reference to the background moral principles of his community. The aim, remember, is to put together a coherent set of rights and responsibilities that provide the best overall interpretation of the legal materials of the community. Hercules will thereby find 'right answers' in 'most hard cases' using reason and imagination.[63] Dworkin does not claim that the right answers to questions of law can always be demonstrated as such, or that another lawyer or judge will find the same route and destination as Hercules.[64] He rejects the 'absurd claim' that the right answers obtained by integrity are 'objective' in the sense of 'located in some "transcendental reality"'.[65] Rather, he avers, they are right in the sense that the judge cannot avoid considering them as right.[66]

1.2.2 Criticism of law as integrity

Dworkin's 'right answer' thesis has given rise to considerable academic discussion. Finnis questions the whole idea of a right answer being available to Hercules. He declares:

> An ideal human judge, no matter how 'superhuman' his powers, could not sensibly search for a uniquely correct legal answer to a hard case . . . . For in such a case, the search for the one right answer is particularly incoherent and senseless, in much the same way as a search for the American novel which meets the two criteria 'most romantic and shortest' (or 'best and funniest'; or 'most American and most profound').[67]

---

58 Dworkin 1986, 255.
59 Dworkin 1986, 228 (emphasis added).
60 See Dworkin 1986, ch 6, esp 228ff.
61 See Dworkin 1986, 248.
62 See Dworkin 1986, esp 245.
63 Dworkin 1986, viii–ix and 412.
64 See Dworkin 1986, 412.
65 Dworkin 1986, 83.
66 See Dworkin 1986, esp 235–237.
67 Finnis 1990, 8.

The rationale and method 11

Finnis goes on to argue that there is incommensurability between Dworkin's dimensions of 'fit' (coherence with existing legal materials) and 'justifiability' (moral soundness). He claims that Dworkin does not offer a suitable account of how these dimensions are to be weighed and balanced.[68] Freeman offers a different criticism. He draws attention to Dworkin's recognition that different judges will use their own convictions to reach their own conclusions and asks how we are to respond to a citizen who is told that another judge 'could equally well have come to a different conclusion and that too would have been right in the eyes of that second judge'.[69]

Interpreting Dworkin's argument in its best light,[70] he has at least a partial response to these criticisms. Finnis does not consider Dworkin's denial that Hercules has access to some transcendental reality of uniquely correct answers to hard cases. Nor does Finnis demonstrate any incommensurability between fit and justifiability by merely showing that Dworkin has not satisfactorily accounted for how these two dimensions are to be weighed and balanced. Similarly, Freeman's rhetorical question only poses a problem for Dworkin if citizens cannot be shown why they must regard a judge's conclusion as providing the right answer. Such partial answers will be developed into full answers below. Accordingly, it will be argued, a 'right answer' is one that strikes the best *moral* balance between 'fit' and 'justification' *in the light of the conditions under which a judge is to adjudicate.* Those conditions include the artificial nature of legal reasoning and the imperfect nature of knowledge. An answer generated by a morally justified procedure is to be regarded as the right answer, because no better answer could be provided. The development below will, however, go beyond Dworkin's theory by appealing to a specific theory of universal morality.

As presented, Dworkin's method is *question-begging* against rival conceptions of law.[71] I do not mean this in the lay sense of raising questions, but in the philosophical sense of illegitimately assuming the very thing that it is meant to prove (ie the *petitio principii*).[72] If the debate between rival concepts of law is not to be illegitimately loaded against rival theories, then it must be characterised as a debate over a neutral referent (starting point for discussion) upon which all protagonists can agree and the derivation of the concept of law governed by similarly neutral rules.

As Beyleveld and Brownsword point out, Dworkin's constructive interpretation rejects the is/ought distinction that is central to legal positivism, because it explicitly incorporates a necessary moral element.[73] This is, indeed, an essential feature of the second stage of his method. Consider Dworkin's application of constructive interpretation to the classic dispute over whether wicked Nazi rules are legally valid rules:

---

68 See Finnis 1990, 9.
69 Freeman 2014, 604.
70 A 'principle of charitable interpretation' would require that we interpret those we criticise so as to render what they say as rational as possible: see Beyleveld & Pattinson 2010, 271–272, and ch 6 of this book (6.5).
71 The following owes much to Beyleveld & Brownsword 1986; 1987.
72 See further Toddington 1993, 92–93.
73 See Beyleveld & Brownsword 1987, 666–667.

12 *The rationale and method*

> We need not deny that the Nazi system was an example of law, . . . because there is an available sense in which it plainly was law. But we have no difficulty in understanding someone who does say that Nazi law is not really law . . . . For he is not using 'law' in that sense; he is not making that sort of preinterpretative judgement but a skeptical interpretative judgment that Nazi law lacked features critical to flourishing legal systems whose rules and procedures do justify coercion. His judgement is now a special kind of political judgment.[74]

A legal positivist could accept the first step of this method, which purports to identify what is law without any necessary moral element. A legal positivist will not, however, accept ground rules for choosing a conception of law that includes this second step. According to legal positivism, whether or not Nazi law can be provided with a plausible moral interpretation (as 'a special kind of political judgment') is irrelevant to its status as law. Dworkin has not shown why a legal positivist must accept constructive interpretation as a methodological thesis.

Dworkin similarly begs the question against a legal idealist who is also a moral objectivist. For Dworkin, his method of constructive interpretation seeks to ground justifiability in the moral values of the community, thereby assuming that objectivist legal idealism is wrong. To put it another way, why must we accept Dworkin's criteria for moral evaluation? His reliance on 'discriminatory morality', when construing existing rules and rules within a community in their best moral light, already assumes that we accept the force of a refined version of the conventional morality of that community. Similarly, even if we question Finnis' claim that 'fit' and 'justifiability' are incommensurable, Finnis is right that Dworkin has not shown how we are to weigh and balance these dimensions. How are we to resolve conflict between these dimensions? Appeal to the conventions of the community can provide no answer where those conventions conflict.

1.3 Law as a moral judgment

In their book *Law as a Moral Judgment* (1986), Beyleveld and Brownsword present an account of law in which legal validity consists of the exercise of morally legitimate power. Unlike Dworkin, they do not invoke the critical moral values of the community, but rely on Gewirth's argument for a universal moral principle. They avoid begging the question on the debate between legal positivism and legal idealism by addressing it in terms of different conceptions of a neutral starting point, which is 'the enterprise of subjecting human conduct to the governance of rules'.[75] This enterprise, they argue, can only be understood in terms of the reasons that individuals have for complying with those rules, which is to say that the law must be viewed as an affair of practical reason. If practical reason can be shown to presuppose moral

---

74 Dworkin 1986, 103–104.
75 See eg Beyleveld & Brownsword 1986, 120, citing Fuller 1969.

reason, it would follow that the legal enterprise is necessarily a moral enterprise. This is what follows if Gewirth's argument for a supreme principle of morality is sound.

1.3.1 The dialectically necessary argument for the PGC

In *Reason and Morality* (1978), Gewirth argues that the Principle of Generic Consistency (PGC) is the supreme principle of morality. He employs what he calls the 'dialectically necessary method'. It is 'dialectical' in the sense that it is conducted from claims made within the first-person perspective of an agent.[76] It is 'necessary' in the sense that all the steps of the argument follow logically (thus necessarily) from premises that cannot be coherently denied within this perspective (thus necessary premises).

Imagine Anna (here representing any agent), who considers whether she has any moral duties to anyone else. By this, Anna is considering whether she is required to further the interests of others, regardless of whether she wants to or is culturally expected to do so.[77] Anna cannot coherently deny that she is (among other things) an agent, which is to say that she must recognise that she is able to voluntarily choose whether to act in the interests of others. Gewirth's argument seeks to show that Anna must accept the PGC as a strict implication of her understanding of what it is for her to be an agent. This means that 'Gewirth doesn't demonstrate that the PGC is true in an agent-independent sense, but only that it has to be accepted by each agent just by virtue of being an agent'.[78] Gewirth's argument is that it is dialectically necessary for agents to accept that all agents have the generic rights, understood as rights to the conditions of acting for any and every chosen purpose.

Gewirth's argument has three stages.[79] The *first stage* seeks to establish that Anna instrumentally ought to defend and pursue her possession of those conditions that are necessary for her to act at all or with general chances of success (that is, the 'generic conditions of agency'). The *second stage* seeks to show that this commits Anna to claiming rights to the generic conditions of agency (that is, the 'generic rights'). The *third stage* of the argument seeks to establish that Anna must accept that all agents have the generic rights (that is, the PGC).

In *stage one*, Anna considers what it means when she voluntarily chooses to pursue (or intends to pursue) a purpose. It must mean that she attaches a positive value to her chosen purpose sufficient to motivate her to pursue it. Even if Anna happens to think that her purpose has a negative value on some other ground, she

---

76 An agent is a being able to act for voluntarily chosen purposes and, thus, an intelligible subject and object of prescriptive claims.
77 Remember that 'moral' was defined above to refer to *prescriptive* requirements that are *other-regarding* and *categorical*; see also Gewirth 1978, 1.
78 Claassen & Düwell 2013, 506.
79 A full analysis and defence of the argument can be found in Beyleveld 1991. My summary here draws on my previous summaries (Pattinson 2002a, ch 1; Pattinson 2017b, ch 16; Capps & Pattinson 2017b, 3–5) and Beyleveld 2012.

14   *The rationale and method*

must still value it proactively, otherwise she would not be *voluntarily* choosing to pursue it.[80] By way of example, once Anna chooses to see the latest *Star Wars* movie, she regards being able to see that movie as valuable for her, even if she generally favours more cerebral movies or later regrets her decision.[81]

Since she must proactively value her purpose, Anna must attach instrumental proactive value to anything that is necessary for her to achieve that purpose. That is to say, Anna denies that she is an agent if she does not accept that she ought to be motivated to pursue whatever is necessary to achieve her purpose or abandon that purpose. This follows from Anna reasoning according to the principle of instrumental reason, which she must accept in order to understand what it is for her to be an agent.[82] This means that it is dialectically necessary for Anna to accept that she 'categorically instrumentally' ought to pursue the 'generic conditions of agency'.

This stage does not require Anna to value her agency as an end in itself.[83] She may (without contradiction) consider it permissible to do things that damage or risk damage to her agency. It is, in other words, only dialectically necessary for Anna to accept: 'Unless I am willing to accept generic damage to my capacity to act, I categorically ought to pursue and defend my possession of the generic conditions of agency'.[84]

In *stage two*, Anna recognises that she needs to have the generic conditions in order to pursue and defend her possession of them. Now consider Bob (representing any other agent), who could affect Anna's possession of the generic conditions. Anna must be against Bob interfering with her possession of the generic conditions against her will. For the same reason, she must also be in favour of Bob helping her to secure possession of the generic conditions, when she wishes to have his help and is unable to secure them without help. Thus, Anna must claim that Bob categorically ought not to interfere with her having the generic conditions *against her will*, and ought to aid her to secure them when she cannot do so by her own unaided efforts, *if she so wishes*. Rephrased in the terminology of a rights claim, it is dialectically necessary for Anna to claim that she has negative and positive rights to have the generic conditions of agency. In other words, she must claim the 'generic rights' for herself.

Stage three involves the move from Anna's (dialectically necessary) claim that she has the generic rights to the (dialectically necessary) claim that Bob has the generic rights. To do this Gewirth invokes the 'logical principle of universalisability'.[85] According to this logical principle, *if* Anna's possession of Q provides her with a

---

80 This argument does not require Anna to have free will. All that is required for her action to be voluntary in the sense required for the argument is that Anna *feels like* she is the self-cause of her behaviour: see further Pattinson 2002a, 5–6 (n 9); Beyleveld 2012, 4 (n 6), and ch 3 (3.4.1).

81 See also Claassen & Düwell 2013, 505.

82 According to which 'if I wish to pursue a chosen purpose and having X, or doing Y, is necessary to achieve that purpose, then I ought to pursue/defend having X, or doing Y, or give up pursuing that purpose': see further Beyleveld 2012, 4, and Beyleveld & Bos 2009, esp 16–18.

83 See Beyleveld 2012, 5.

84 Beyleveld 2012, 5.

85 See Gewirth 1978, 105.

The rationale and method 15

sufficient reason to hold that she possesses P, *then* Bob's possession of Q provides Anna with sufficient reason to hold that Bob also possesses P. It applies here if and only if it is dialectically necessary for Anna to accept: 'It is merely *because* I am an agent that I have the generic rights'.

Anna must indeed accept this. If Anna were to deny it, she would by implication assert that she has the generic rights *because* she has a property that is not necessarily possessed by all agents (such as being called Anna, being human, being female, etc). However, this implies that if she lacked this property she would not have the generic rights, which contradicts the previously established statement, made on the basis of her claim to be an agent, that she has the generic rights. Thus, it is dialectically necessary for Anna to claim that she has the generic rights because she is an agent. Gewirth terms this the 'Argument from the Sufficiency of Agency' (the ASA).[86]

Applying the principle of universalisability now, Anna must accept that Bob also has the generic rights. In other words, it is dialectically necessary for Anna to accept that all agents have the generic rights equally. Since Bob must reason in the same way from his own perspective, it follows that he denies that he is an agent if he does not accept that Anna has the generic rights. Thus, it is dialectically necessary for every agent to accept that all agents have the generic rights. This is the Principle of Generic Consistency – the PGC for short.

In a more recent paper, Beyleveld has argued that the dialectically necessary argument requires acceptance of only three propositions: (a) the principle of instrumental reason; (b) there are generic conditions of agency; and (c) dialectically necessary commitments are not merely distributively universal, but also collectively universal.[87] Dialectically necessary commitments are 'distributively universal' if Anna's dialectically necessary claim to X for herself implies that it is dialectically necessary for Bob to claim X for himself. Dialectically necessary commitments are 'collectively universal' if Anna must act in accord with the dialectically necessary commitments of all agents. Beyleveld's new argument for (c) should be of interest to those who accept stage one, but not stages two and three, of the above argument.

Few readers will have failed to recognise that, if successful, the argument for the PGC has radical implications. As Beyleveld and Brownsword point out, it requires agents to consider the PGC to be the supreme principle of morality, law and all other purposive activities. The soundness of this argument for a supreme principle of all practical reason would refute the amoralist who denies the need to reason morally at all. Yet, Gewirth's dialectically necessary argument has been greeted with widespread academic scepticism.[88]

---

86 See Gewirth 1978, 110.
87 Beyleveld 2017a, 239–241 and 252–254, responding to Westphal 2017.
88 For response to the vast majority of published criticisms see Beyleveld 1991. For collected papers criticising and defending the argument, see Regis 1984, Boylan 1999, Bauhn 2016a, and Capps & Pattinson 2017a.

16 The rationale and method

1.3.2 Dialectically contingent arguments for the PGC

To evade scepticism of the dialectically necessary argument,[89] Beyleveld has devised several dialectically contingent arguments for the PGC. These arguments incorporate (contingent) premises that can be coherently denied, but happen to attract widespread support. Two of these arguments will be summarised here.

The first proceeds dialectically from the contingent assumption that humans have rights.[90] If Anna were to recognise that Bob has rights to anything, to avoid contradicting this recognition she must accept that Bob has rights to the necessary means of exercising those rights. This requires Anna to grant Bob rights to the generic conditions of agency, as the necessary conditions for exercising any rights irrespective of their specific content. Also, since only agents can meaningfully exercise a right, agents must be the relevant subjects and recipients of these rights. Thus, if Anna grants any rights to Bob, she is logically required to recognise the PGC as the supreme principle of morality.

The argument from the acceptance of rights only works if those rights are understood as justifiable claims imposing correlative duties, the benefits of which are waivable by the rights holder. That is to say, Anna must accept that Bob has claim-rights according to the *will conception* of rights.[91] It does not work if Anna merely accepts that Bob has rights according to the *interest conception*, whereby the duties she owes to Bob track his interests, but not necessarily some aspect of his freedom and are not thereby automatically waivable by Bob.[92]

Beyleveld and Brownsword have argued that human rights instruments, such as the European Convention on Human Rights, 'operate centrally with the will conception of rights'.[93] They claim that the fact that such instruments 'do not outlaw boxing, mountain-climbing, and other dangerous activities, and do not require persons to vote, etc, shows that the will conception . . . is to be applied to at least some of the rights'.[94] This, they argue, implies adherence to the will conception, because the will and interest conceptions are 'conceptions of rights as such'.[95] Beyleveld and Brownsword have not, however, done all that is required to link the permissibility of consensual activities to the will conception. The interest conception allows Bob to waive the benefit of those rights that serve to protect some aspect of his freedom,

---

89 There are works supporting the argument: see Pattinson 2002a, 9 (n 12) (which lists works by 17 supporters). Additional supporters: Beyleveld & Bos 2009, Bielby 2008, Brown 2004, B Capps 2017, P Capps 2009, Clucas 2006, Dobson 2006, Düring & Düwell 2017, Hübenthal 2016, Montaña 2016, Olsen 2017, Rodrigues & van den Berg 2012, Samar 2016, Spence 2006, Stevenson 2016, Tang & Yen 2016, Townend 2017 and Walters & Morley 2016.
90 See Beyleveld 1996 and Beyleveld & Brownsword 2001, 79–82.
91 This is recognised by Beyleveld & Brownsword 2001. On claim-rights see the seminal work of Hohfeld 1923. The 'will' conception is also known as the 'choice' conception: see eg Hart 1955.
92 Also known as the 'benefit' conception of rights: see eg MacCormick 1977.
93 Beyleveld & Brownsword 2001, 82.
94 Beyleveld & Brownsword 2001, 81.
95 Beyleveld & Brownsword 2001, 81.

but denies that this is a feature of all his rights. The Strasbourg court therefore did not contradict itself when it declared that:

> the nature of some of the rights safeguarded by the Convention is such as to exclude a waiver of the entitlement to exercise them, but the same cannot be said of certain other rights.[96]

Thus, this first dialectically contingent argument operates from an assumption that is neither widely accepted nor implied by acceptance of the European Convention on Human Rights.

Beyleveld has more recently presented a second dialectically contingent argument, which cannot be evaded by appeal to the interest conception of rights.[97] This alternative argument draws out the implications of acceptance of (a) stage one of the dialectically necessary argument and (b) the view that all human beings are equal in dignity and rights. This thereby combines the least controversial stage of the dialectically necessary argument with an ethical view that is both widely accepted and presupposed by most human rights instruments.

Stage one of the dialectically necessary argument requires Anna to accept (as dialectically necessary) that she categorically instrumentally ought to defend and pursue the generic conditions of agency. Plugging in the assumption that Bob is equal in dignity and rights, it follows that Anna must consider Bob's claim to his generic conditions of agency as equal to her own. It follows that if Anna is to avoid either denying this impartiality or denying that she is an agent, she must accept that she categorically ought to pursue/defend Bob's generic conditions of agency, in accordance with his will. That is to say, she must recognise that Bob has the generic rights. It further follows that Anna is required to accept that all agents have the generic rights. In other words, Anna is logically required to accept the PGC as the supreme principle of morality.

The assumption made by this second argument has a greater claim to being implied by human rights instruments. Consider, for example, the Universal Declaration of Human Rights 1948 (UDHR). Article 1 states that '[a]ll human beings are born free and equal in dignity and rights' and Article 2 adds that '[e]veryone is entitled to all the rights and freedoms . . . without distinction of any kind'. The UDHR is no more than a declaration, but the preamble to the European Convention on Human Rights states that it aims to secure 'the universal and effective recognition and observance of the Rights' in the UDHR. Article 14 of the Convention goes on to assert that the rights and freedoms granted by its provisions are to be secured 'without discrimination on any ground'. It is those Convention rights that are given 'further effect' by the Human Rights Act 1998, according to its preamble. The view that all humans

---

96 *Albert and Le Compte v Belgium* (App Nos 7299/75, 7496/76) (1983) 5 EHRR 533, [35] and *H v Belgium* (App No 8950/80) ECHR 30 November 1987, [54].

97 Beyleveld 2012. See also the other dialectically contingent arguments in Beyleveld 1996.

18 *The rationale and method*

are equal in dignity and rights can therefore be understood as capturing the essence of Dworkin's 'discriminatory morality', as reflected in his appeal to the 'right to equal concern and respect'.

1.3.3 Direct applications of the PGC

Gewirth distinguishes between the 'direct' and 'indirect' application of the PGC.[98] For the purposes of this book, direct applications will be understood as deductive determinations as to whether actions are compatible with the generic rights of agents. For various reasons, to be explained below, some matters cannot be dealt with directly. The PGC therefore requires certain procedural mechanisms in its application, which indirectly apply the PGC.

Anyone seeking to apply the PGC must first understand the content of the generic rights. When Anna claims rights to the generic conditions of agency, she claims rights to whatever she *needs* to act or act successfully, regardless of her specific purpose. Those needs vary in degree.[99] To act at all, she has *basic needs*, such as her life. To act successfully, she has *nonsubtractive needs* to those things required for her to maintain her current level of purpose-fulfilment and *additive needs* to those things required to increase her current level of purpose-fulfilment. There is therefore a hierarchy of generic need (and, correlatively, generic harm), which can be measured by the 'criterion of degrees of needfulness for action'.[100] It follows that the generic rights are to be ranked hierarchically in descending order: basic, nonsubtractive, then additive generic rights. Anna must therefore recognise that knowingly acting contrary to Bob's will so as to kill him (depriving him of a basic need) is worse than breaking a promise to him (depriving him of a nonsubtractive need), which is worse than denying him an opportunity to learn a new skill (depriving him of an additive need).

Remember that Anna must recognise generic rights that are both negative and positive. The positive generic rights are limited by two provisos.[101] *First,* Anna has a duty to aid Bob to secure his generic conditions only where he is unable to do so by his own unaided effort. This is because all rights claims made within the dialectically necessary argument derive from the agent's categorically instrumental need for the generic conditions, and the assistance of another agent is not so needed where he can achieve his purposes without assistance. I will refer to the limitation that Bob is unable to self-assist as the 'own unaided effort'

---

98 See Gewirth 1978, chs 4 and 5, respectively. Gewirth distinguishes between the requirements of the PGC that are imposed on the 'interpersonal actions of individual persons' and those that are 'imposed on various social rules that govern multiperson activities and institutions': ibid, 200.

99 See Gewirth 1978, 53–63.

100 See Gewirth 1996, 45–46. See also Gewirth 1978, esp. 53–58 (using the previous label of 'criterion of degrees of necessity for action').

101 See Gewirth 1978, 217–230. Variants of these provisos are common to most moral theories: see Pattinson 2009a.

The rationale and method 19

proviso. *Secondly*, Anna only has a duty to aid Bob to secure his generic features when her doing so does not deprive her of the same or more important generic capacities, as measured by the degree of needfulness for action. This is because Anna must first recognise the dialectical necessity of her own claim to the generic rights before recognising the dialectical necessity of Bob's equal generic rights. I will refer to the limitation that Anna faces only a reasonable burden as the 'comparable cost' proviso. It follows that Anna should not remain wilfully silent as Bob unwittingly walks into the path of a car, but she is not required to place herself immediately between him and the car. Bob's generic rights are will-rights, so he may release Anna from the positive duties she owes to him. But she must not be too eager to infer such release (by, for example, his mere failure to ask for help) nor too willing to assume that he requires assistance when she is able to simply ask him.[102] Since assisting those in need often requires coordinated collective action, in practice the discharge of many positive duties will fall primarily on the state and its institutions.[103]

Up to this point Bob has represented any other agent, but recognising another as an agent is not as straightforward as it might appear. Agency involves a special kind of self-awareness, namely, reflective purposivity. This means that Anna can know directly that she is an agent, but she cannot know this directly of anyone other than herself. Imagine Otto (who behaves as if he is an agent) and Maram (who is a newborn baby and so does not behave as if she is an agent).[104] Anna cannot directly experience the pains, pleasures, feelings or thoughts of either Otto or Maram. She can perceive their characteristics and behaviour, and she can draw inferences from what she perceives. Anna might consider it perfectly natural to infer agency from Otto's agency-like behaviour and, by a similar process, conclude that Maram is capable of feeling pleasure and pain but not capable of reflective purposivity, so is only partially or potentially an agent.[105] But these inferences depend on unverifiable metaphysical assumptions. She has no way of eliminating the possibility that Otto is merely a very cleverly programmed automaton without a mind, or ruling out the

---

102 Beyleveld 2012, 5 (n 9).

103 See Gewirth 1996, 59, Beyleveld 2012, 14, and Bauhn 2016b, 222–225.

104 This book is devoted to medical law, which concerns human subjects. I therefore do not discuss non-humans who behave like agents (eg the androids in films such as *Blade Runner* and *Bicentennial Man*), non-human animals with greater or fewer apparent capacities than Maram (eg chimpanzees and bacteria) or non-humans without any apparent agency-like capacities (eg bricks or tables). The argument presented has application to all these, but not in the way assumed by some critics: cf Holm & Coggon 2008 and Beyleveld & Pattinson 2010.

105 Gewirth's own application of the PGC involves him making these very inferences. He simply assumes that (anyone represented by) Otto is an agent and (anyone represented by) Maram is a partial or potential agent ('marginal agent'). He therefore grants the generic rights to Otto directly. Gewirth argues that the 'Principle of Proportionality' operates to extend the population to which the PGC applies in the abstract and concludes that Maram has partial generic rights (see eg Gewirth 1978, 120–124). Unfortunately, the Principle of Proportionality cannot operate on the PGC in this way: see Beyleveld & Pattinson 2000a and Pattinson 2002a, ch 2. Gewirth's reasoning on 'marginal agents' has also been criticised by Hill 1984 and Pluhar 1995, ch 5.

20   *The rationale and method*

possibility that Maram is a locked-in agent with whom she is not (yet) able to interact fully. Now, let's consider Otto and Maram separately.[106]

Remember that Anna cannot strictly know whether or not Otto is an agent. She can treat Otto as if he is an agent, because he behaves like an agent. If she were to treat him as an agent and act in accordance with his presumed generic rights, she could be making a mistake and would thereby be unnecessarily restricting her own freedom of action. But if she were to treat Otto as a non-agent, she could be making a mistake and would thereby fail to respect his generic rights, despite being able to do so. This is worse because it directly violates the PGC. Since the PGC is categorically binding, it can never be justifiable to run the risk of violating it where this can be avoided. Therefore, it is dialectically necessary for Anna to treat Otto as an agent and act in accordance with his (presumed) generic rights.[107] Remember that Otto represents anyone who displays sufficient agency-like behaviour to make it possible for Anna to treat them as agents (that is, those who are analogically or ostensibly agents). So, it is dialectically necessary to treat others who are *ostensible agents* in this way as agents.[108] This reasoning also establishes that agency-like characteristics and behaviour must, under moral precaution, be considered evidence of agency.

Anna also cannot strictly know that Maram is not an agent. Neither can she treat Maram as an agent, because she does not behave like one. She cannot coherently treat Maram as if she is able to exercise the generic rights. It is, however, possible and meaningful for Anna to guard against mistakenly treating Maram as a non-agent by acting towards her in ways that would respect her generic rights should she (unknowably) happen to be an agent.[109] It is therefore dialectically necessary for Anna to grant Maram 'duties of protection' tracking her (presumed) generic interests. This means that Anna has a duty not to kill, inflict pain or otherwise harm Maram in ways that would violate her generic interests if she were a locked-in agent, and duties to provide appropriate assistance to prevent harm to her presumed generic interests. If we want to express this in terms of rights, Maram is to be treated as having rights according to the interest conception (interest-rights) and Otto as having rights according to the will conception (will-rights).

---

106   The substance of the following argument, for the dialectical necessity of moral precaution, was seminally presented in Beyleveld & Pattinson 1998 and 2000a.

107   With one proviso: see Pattinson 2002a, 24.

108   There is a danger that the label 'ostensible agent' could be misinterpreted as suggesting that the relevant other is seemingly *but not actually* an agent (as opposed to seemingly but not necessarily an agent). Unfortunately, this danger is not removed by an alternative label. 'Apparent agent', which is used synonymously in Beyleveld & Pattinson 2010, could, for example, be misinterpreted as suggesting that the relevant other is *clearly* an agent or is *seemingly but not actually* an agent. Precautionary reasoning operates because the need not to violate the categorical PGC requires such others to be treated as agents, given that it is impossible to know *whether or not they are agents.*

109   In contrast to bricks, tables and other objects for which it is not possible and meaningful to treat them as having any generic interests just in case they (unknowably) happen to be agents: Pattinson 2002a, 73, and Beyleveld & Pattinson 2010, esp 262–263. cf Holm & Coggon 2008.

The rationale and method 21

What if Anna is faced with a conflict between respecting one of Otto's will-rights and respecting Maram's equivalent interest-right, *and no other relevant factor arises?* Anna is required to try her best, in the light of the ineluctably imperfect nature of her knowledge, to give effect to the PGC. She must seek to handle conflicts between Otto and Maram in accordance with the 'criterion of avoidance of more probable harm'.[110] It has already been established that Anna must consider agency-like characteristics and behaviour as evidence of agency, and Otto can be treated as an agent and therefore displays more of those characteristics than Maram. Thus, in a single-variable conflict of the type under consideration, Anna's duties to Otto take precedence over her duties to Maram. To put this in more general terms, Anna has duties to others[111] in proportion to the degree to which they approach being ostensible agents. It follows that, in single variable disputes, an embryo counts for less than a fetus; a fetus counts for less than a neonate; a neonate counts for less than a child who has reached the stage of being capable of being treated like an agent, and so on.[112] In multi-variable conflicts, where other relevant factors arise, matters are not so simple and, as will be explained below, it is then necessary to apply the PGC indirectly.

1.3.4 Indirect applications of the PGC

According to Gewirth, there are some matters that must be addressed indirectly by the PGC in the form of procedures that are to be applied and obeyed.[113] Beyleveld and Brownsword argue that even in a mythical Gewirthia, where the PGC is accepted and applied as the fundamental and overriding constitutional principle, there are three reasons why applications of the PGC leave room for 'rational and not unreasonable disagreement'.[114]

The first arises where the application of the PGC involves 'a decision between two or more answers that the PGC leaves optional, but between which a choice must be made'.[115] They cite a rules-of-the-road example: the PGC requires a common rule on whether we drive on the left or right hand side of the road, but 'does not (without more) have a preference' for one option over the other.[116]

The second arises because application of the PGC to cases where the generic rights of different individuals are in conflict will generally involve assessing (a) the importance of the generic conditions affected and (b) the probability of

---

110 Beyleveld & Pattinson 2000a, 44. The 'criterion of degrees of needfulness of action' is, when used to rank generic rights claims, an instance of this principle.
111 Any entity in the empirical world that it is possible and meaningful to treat as having generic interests.
112 The word 'fetus' is often spelt 'foetus', but I prefer the etymologically correct spelling for its simplicity: see also Williams 1994, 71 (n 1), and Grace 1999, 57.
113 See Gewirth 1978, 272–365.
114 Beyleveld & Brownsword 2006, 147.
115 Beyleveld & Brownsword 2006, 147.
116 Beyleveld & Brownsword 2006, 147. See also Dworkin 1986, 145.

22 The rationale and method

their actions having effects on the generic conditions.[117] The problem is, they argue, that it is not easy to see how the scales of probability and scales of importance for different agents are commensurable.

The third arises where, 'unlike in the previous two examples, [there is] a dialectically necessary answer to an application of the PGC', but the application is so complex that rational doubt arises about the correct answer.[118] By way of example, they refer to the possibility of rational disagreement over the scientific judgments about human biology and psychology required to apply the criterion of needfulness for action.

Beyleveld and Brownsword argue that where it is not possible for disputants to co-exist without settlement or regulatory intervention in the three above situations, then the PGC requires a procedural turn. Where the decision-making procedure represents a competent and good faith attempt to give effect to the PGC, any rule or decision thereby made must be treated as authoritative. Otherwise, the interests that the PGC protects are either not defended (such as where there is no common side of the road) or are undermined by individuals taking matters into their own hands when they have disputes. A procedural turn is, in effect, required by the criterion of avoidance of more probable harm: greater harm occurs, relative to the values of the PGC, if disputes that cannot be uncontroversially resolved directly are not resolved indirectly. The nature of the procedural turn will depend on the complexity and controversiality of the situation.

Where the choice is between otherwise optional answers, it would seem acceptable to use a procedure relying on chance, such as the flipping of a coin. In a complex society, however, it is likely that there will also be dispute over whether two or more answers are actually morally optional. In the rules-of-the-road example, the 'without more' proviso could be invoked by disputants. The practices of any existing road users (within the territory or in nearby territories) would be relevant to driver response times, at least initially. There may also be relevant geographical (such as land features), mechanical (such as existing vehicles), social or biological features relevant to response times or implementation costs within that territory. Thus, there could be reasonable disagreement over whether to prefer one choice over the other. Such disputes would be likely to involve both value and scientific controversy and therefore require a procedure robust enough to deal with this.

Value controversy arises not only because of different probabilities of different levels of generic harm, but also because practical situations will often involve beings with different degrees of agency-like behaviour. Imagine, for example, seeking to weigh the likely loss of a leg for a dog against the unlikely chance that Otto will suffer some diminution in his ability to develop his capacity for purpose-fulfilment. This requires a judgment between a high probability of a basic harm to a being that does not display sufficient agency-like behaviour to be treated as an agent and a low probability of an additive harm to a being that can be treated as an agent. But the earlier discussion of the direct applications of the PGC provided

---

117 See Beyleveld & Brownsword 2006, 148.
118 Beyleveld & Brownsword 2006, 148.

The rationale and method 23

no simple algorithm for multi-variable disputes. Where all PGC-relevant values have not been rendered commensurable within an algorithm directly supported by the PGC, the best that we can do is rely on a procedural turn, operating to protect the unequivocally most important values of the PGC.

The most straightforward procedure would be one operating to ensure proper application of the PGC to which everyone has consented, but in a complex society unanimous agreement (even on matters of procedure) is unlikely to be obtainable. The justification for proceduralism also requires that Gewirthia avoid 'an infinite regress of one layer of proceduralism on another'.[119] What should Anna make of the processes of representative government adopted by large modern democracies? Anna will probably not have consented to the process by which delegated authority happens to be exercised by the state in which she lives and she might not have voted for those who are elected at any given time. She must, however, recognise that her own judgment is not infallible and a free, fair and transparent democratic process is simply the 'optimal compromise' by which committed Gewirthians can mutually co-exist in a complex society governed by the PGC.[120] Gewirth refers to this as the 'method of consent'.[121] Because, in principle, individual rights of sufficient weight trump decisions yielded by majoritarian politics or processes, some form of independent judicial oversight is also required.

This is not the place to develop a full account of the limitations placed on democracy and adjudication by the PGC. There may be some differences between Gewirthian societies, because many variant procedural details are capable of representing good faith attempts to apply the PGC in the light of the imperfect nature of knowledge and the fallibility of human agents. Within Gewirthian societies, the products of the democratic process will have considerable weight. It would therefore not be appropriate for unelected judges to usurp the legitimate functions of those who represent the people or are directly accountable to those who represent the people. But the common law method need not involve judicial legislation and can therefore be interpreted and applied in a way that is consistent with a good faith attempt to apply the PGC.

1.4 Modified law as integrity

Beyleveld and Brownsword's account of law as a moral judgment can support a modified version of Dworkin's law as integrity. A judge would act consistently with the PGC if she interpreted both 'fit' (coherence to existing rules and rulings) and 'justifiability' (moral soundness) in accordance with its terms. A judge adopting such a method could act in good faith to give effect to the PGC. If, however, she is to be a model for an actual judge, we must not imbue her with the super

---

119 Beyleveld & Brownsword 2006, 150.
120 Beyleveld & Brownsword 2006, 152.
121 See Gewirth 1978, 304–312.

24   *The rationale and method*

powers granted by Dworkin. So interpreted, I can do no better than express law as integrity in the words of Toddington and Olsen:

> We might say that the aspiration of 'fit' is an aspiration to make the decision coherent with the mediated attempts (*via* legislation, previous decisions etc.) to install a moral order; whereas the aspiration of 'justification' represents the aspiration to interpret these mediated attempts in accordance with what moral soundness requires. For this perspective, the dimensions of 'fit' and 'justification', rather than being two parallel lines, are seen to have a common point of departure. The reason a case presents itself as a hard case is that the existing legal material presents itself as less than morally rational, because previous authorities (legislators, Judges etc.) have acted with less insight or resources (morally or empirically) than are available in the case at hand.[122]

It will not have escaped your notice that we do not live in a polity in which previous rules and rulings were presented as good faith attempts to apply the PGC. Is it legitimate for a judge to treat the rules and rulings of any polity outside a mythical Gewirthia *as if* they did represent mediated attempts to install moral order? I think so. Where the rules and rulings of the polity in which the judge operates could be interpreted in a way that is consistent with the PGC, then no violation of the PGC occurs if she treats those materials as if they did represent mediated attempts to install moral order. In fact, to do otherwise in such a polity would prevent her from being able to adjudicate morally (and therefore legally) or would involve usurpation of a legislative role. Such usurpation would occur were a judge to substitute an existing democratically enacted rule that is plausibly consistent with the requirements of the PGC with her own choice of rule that has no greater claim to consistency with the PGC. Substitutions of that type are properly left to official bodies with the democratic mandate lacked by judges.

There are, of course, societies in which a judge could not plausibly view the existing rules and rulings in a way that is consistent with the PGC. Dworkin envisages Judge Siegfried, who acts within a wicked, Nazi-like 'legal' system.[123] A Gewirthian Siegfried would not be able to treat official materials within such a polity as if they were mediated attempts to apply the PGC. He would therefore not be able to treat it as a valid *legal* system. His options would be to resign, undermine those rules from within or act outside a legitimate judicial role by giving effect to those immoral rules to protect his own skin. The second of these would seem to be more likely to protect the generic rights of others.

If I am to convert Dworkin's Hercules into a Gewirthian Athena, must she nail her colours to the mast? A judge operating within a liberal democratic society will often be faced with rules, rulings and declared principles that are either compatible with the PGC or capable of being so interpreted without rejecting the legal

---

122 Olsen & Toddington 1999, 143–144.
123 See Dworkin 1986, 105.

conventions of that society. Athena would then seem to face a choice over whether to explicitly refer to the PGC. On the one hand, it is better for judicial reasoning to illuminate all the argumentative steps so that the decision can be as transparent and coherent as possible. On the other hand, a judge who appeals to a supreme moral principle over the hegemonic dictates of the pluralist society in which she operates will very rapidly lose the respect and support of her fellow judges and society at large. I confess that much of my own academic writing has been influenced by this counter consideration and I have presented arguments consistent with the requirements of the PGC without appealing to it.[124] Many theorists similarly present arguments within applied ethics without explicitly appealing to their underlying moral theory.[125] Fortunately, the judgments of a Gewirthian judge who does not directly refer to the PGC are likely to be indistinguishable in their expression from the judgments of a Dworkinian Hercules or, in many cases, those of a judge who is not cognisant of his or her theoretical assumptions. Taking advantage of this, *the idealised judgments in this book will not explicitly appeal to the PGC*. Readers will, however, be guided on the compatibility of the reasoning with (a plausible attempt to give effect to) the PGC by this chapter and the analysis in the chapter in which the idealised judgment is presented.

Perhaps Athena could gradually build understanding and support for the PGC, and thereby move towards more explicit judgments over time. Initial judgments would thereby not explicitly appeal to the PGC, but as the established jurisprudence builds protection for the generic rights, more direct appeal could be made to specific features of the underlying PGC-based reasoning.[126] This is what is attempted in this book, as Athena's first move is away from Devlin J's duty-based approach in *Adams* towards an implicitly rights-based approach and then, in subsequent cases, towards an explicitly rights-based approach.

1.5 Crafting judgments

All the idealised judgments in this book are written as majority judgments of an appeal court by an imagined judge, Athena. In her idealised judgment in *Adams*, she appears as Athena J sitting in the Criminal Division of the Court of Appeal. This takes place 27 years before the next case, by which point she appears as Lady Athena, initially as a Lord of Appeal in Ordinary and then as the Master of the Rolls. This requires Lady Athena to be regarded as having a judicial career of around 40 years, which is only two years longer than Lord Denning's 38 years.[127]

---

124 See eg Beyleveld & Pattinson 2002 and Pattinson 2015a, which argue for PCG-compliant interpretations of the Human Rights Act 1998 solely on the basis of internal coherence.

125 See eg Harris 1998, 5–6, as discussed in Pattinson 2017b, 572–573.

126 See Olsen's insightful discussion of the need for international courts to gradually expand their jurisdiction to give effect to the PGC in Olsen 2017, esp 205.

127 Lord Denning retired at 83. He was exempt from the mandatory retirement age of 75 imposed by s 2 of the Judicial Pensions Act 1959, because (as per s 3) he was appointed before the commencement of that Act. For the current law, see s 26 of the Judicial Pensions and Retirement Act 1993.

26 The rationale and method

If we ignore the gender issue (to which I will return), additional plausibility to this fiction can be obtained from the *Guinness Book of Records*, which records the oldest recorded active judge as Judge Albert R Alexander (1859–1966) of Plattsburg, Missouri, USA, who retired at 105 years, 8 months.[128] In England and Wales, Sir William Francis Kyffin Taylor (later Lord Maenan) is recorded as having retired as presiding judge of the Liverpool Court of Passage at age 94, having served for 45 years in that role. What is, alas, less historically plausible is the gender of my idealised judge. The first female High Court judge, Elizabeth Lane, was appointed in 1965 and no woman has held the office of Master of the Rolls (or been the senior judge in the House of Lords or, until September 2017, the UK Supreme Court). Indeed, no woman reached the highest court of this jurisdiction until Lady Hale in 2004, which is after my four focal cases, and she wasn't joined by a second for another 13 years. I have adopted a female counterpart to Dworkin's Hercules to avoid reinforcing the view that an ideal judge must be a male judge, and to draw attention to the need for the English legal system to address such gender issues. Athena thereby embodies a vision of gender equality, but there are far-reaching gender and equality issues that are not examined in this book.

Athena does not have the superhuman powers of a Dworkinian Hercules; rather she represents an attempt to interpret the law in accordance with the theory of law articulated above. My task is not to jump out of an imaginary time machine and replace each appellate judgment with an academic treatise, fully referenced with anachronistic citations to future works and developments. Rather, my task is to suggest an approach – resting on alternative justificatory principles or extensions of invoked principles – that could plausibly have constituted the ratio decidendi of the court. Athena therefore presents herself within the institutional contingencies of the English judicial system. She adopts the approximate style, tone and form of contemporary judicial language, with its concomitant limitations. Also, where possible, Athena adopts the statement of facts from the original lead judgment. Rackley has pointed out that 'though not engaged in making findings of disputed facts, an appellate judge can nonetheless retell the facts of a case, as presented and found, to reinforce their decisions on the points of law'.[129] I have done my best to avoid reconstructing the facts as presented by the appeal courts to focus on applying modified law as integrity to the facts as presented. In so doing, I in no way deny the problems inherent in judicial construction and presentation of the facts.

Appellate courts are typically regarded as confined to the issues and arguments raised by the parties in the appeal, and appellate judges confined to the legal authorities raised in argument by the parties or the judges themselves.[130] Paterson refers to the expectation that 'a Law Lord in deciding a hard case' will:

---

128 http://www.guinnessworldrecords.com/world-records/longest-serving-judge.
129 Rackley 2010, 46.
130 See Hunter et al 2010b, 14.

- produce a decision between the parties to the appeal that does not go beyond the issues raised in the case and
- justify that decision by reasoned argument framed as a judgment between competing claims of right made by opposed parties.[131]

There is scope for some relaxation of these expectations in this book. A fictitious appeal creates a degree of freedom as to which issues are raised, what claims are made, and which materials are cited. The idealised judgment in *Adams* takes the form of a fictional Attorney General's reference to the Court of Appeal. It is regrettable that the process by which a reference may be made to the Court of Appeal on a point of law, following an acquittal on indictment, was introduced by s 36 of the Criminal Justice Act 1972 and thereby post-dates *Adams*. I have allowed this anachronism because it was necessary to escape the confines of a direction to a jury to provide developed judicial reasoning and formally treat the idealised judgment as a precedent. This seems to me to be appropriate in the light of later appeal courts elevating *Adams* to a status akin to a precedent (on which see Chapter 2), which has also happened to McNair J's direction to the jury in *Bolam*.[132] Additional scope for relaxation of the expectation that appellate judges will confine themselves to legal materials on which the parties have had the opportunity to comment follows from the nature of this enterprise. Clearly, had Athena been sitting in the court at the time, she would have raised arguments and materials for comment from counsel.[133]

---

131 Paterson 1982, 127. Paterson refers to these as the 'decide the case' and 'provide justification' expectations and goes on to refer to three other expectations: 'don't legislate', 'be consistent' and 'be fair'.
132 *Bolam v Friern Hospital Management Committee* [1957] 1 WLR 582, 587.
133 cf Hunter et al 2010b, 15.

2 *Adams*

Life-shortening pain relief

2.1 Introduction

Dr John Bodkin Adams administered large doses of heroin and morphine to Mrs Morrell. This 81-year-old patient was incurably, but not terminally, ill. Dr Adams was charged with her murder. Devlin J's direction to the jury in *R v Adams* gave rise to a new legal principle. The crucial words were that a doctor 'is entitled to do all that is proper and necessary to relieve pain and suffering, even if the measures he takes may incidentally shorten life'.[1] Many judges and legal scholars have interpreted those words as invoking the principle of double effect.[2] A widely held interpretation is that a doctor's intention (to relieve pain) is to be distinguished from what he or she foresees as a consequence of administering pain relief to the patient (hastening of the patient's death), so that a doctor who merely foresees death does not commit murder. The 'direct' intention (purpose) is thereby distinguished from what Bentham called the 'oblique' intention.[3] Bentham used 'oblique intent' to cover consequences foreseen as 'likely', but it will be used in this chapter to refer to consequences foreseen as 'virtually certain'.

Dr Adams was acquitted after what was then the longest murder trial ever in this jurisdiction.[4] The case was not officially reported, but there was a detailed contemporary case note[5] and the judge published a book following the death of the doctor nearly 30 years later.[6] Devlin J's direction to the jury is quoted at length in a case note on a later case.[7]

---

1 [1957] Crim LR 365, 375. Also quoted in Devlin 1985, 171.
2 See eg Kennedy & Grubb 1994, 1205; Lord Steyn in *R (Pretty) v DPP* [2001] UKHL 61, [55]; and Williams 2007, 34–37.
3 See Bentham 1780 (Burns & Hart 1970, 86). As Williams (1987, 420) points out, 'oblique intent' is better than 'indirect intent', because '[i]f you intend to do *x* in order to achieve *y* you "indirectly" intend *y*, in a sense, but it is not oblique intent'.
4 See Neuberger 2015.
5 *R v Adams* [1957] Crim LR 365, which can also be referenced as Palmer 1957.
6 See Devlin 1985. This book is the source of the factual information cited from the case below.
7 See Arlidge 2000, 34–35.

Despite the jury taking only 46 minutes to find Dr Adams not guilty, he is widely believed to have got away with killing at least 132 patients.[8] His behaviour with regard to Mrs Morrell was particularly suspicious. Dr Adams prescribed large quantities of heroin and morphine to this old lady, who was suffering the effects of a stroke but does not appear to have been in pain. In fact, the prosecution claimed, he continued this regime when she was in a coma during the last days of her life. At the same time as prescribing substantial quantities of opioids, Dr Adams displayed notable concern for the contents of Mrs Morrell's will. He went so far as to tell her solicitor that she intended to leave him the Rolls-Royce and a case of her jewellery, and asked him to prepare a codicil that could be destroyed later if it did not meet with her son's approval. Yet, when later filling out her cremation certificate, Dr Adams stated that he was not a beneficiary under her will. And, when charged with her murder, his response was not to plead his innocence, but to ask: 'Murder? Can you prove it?'[9]

Dr Adams had accumulated considerable wealth from patient bequests. He received legacies of over £21,600 in an 11-year period prior to the trial, which was more than he earned as a partner in a lucrative medical practice during that period.[10] Those who are convinced that he was a mass murderer will take little solace from the fact that he was later convicted of numerous counts of forging prescriptions, making a false statement on cremation forms (not including Mrs Morrell's cremation form), obstructing a police search and failing to keep a dangerous drugs register.[11] He did not receive a custodial sentence. The sentencing judge indicated that he would have imposed a custodial sentence for one of those convictions had Dr Adams not already spent time in jail for the murder charge for which he was found not guilty. Instead, Dr Adams was fined and the General Medical Council struck him off the medical register. His registration was reinstated on his third application four years later.

The judge's view was that Dr Adams was probably a greedy mercy killer, rather than a 'monster':

> He might have murdered – it must be remembered that euthanasia is murder – either as a mercy-killer or perhaps just to finish off a troublesome patient who was dying anyway and for whom he could do no more.[12]

Lord Devlin (as he was by the time of writing his book) was critical of both the police and the Attorney General, not for bringing the case but for its conduct. He was particularly dismissive of the Attorney General, 'Reggie', whom he describes as having received a crucial political promotion when the supply of 'first-class barristers'

---

8 See Kaplan 2009, esp 118 and 125, and Devlin 1985, 18 and 179.
9 Quoted from the judge's summing up: Devlin 1985, 173. Also quoted as 'Murder. Murder. Can you prove it was murder?': ibid, 7.
10 Devlin 1985, 9–10.
11 Devlin 1985, 192–195.
12 Devlin 1985, 199.

30 Adams: *life-shortening pain relief*

was so thin as to be 'a year of famine'.[13] The prosecution was brought six years after the death of Mrs Morrell and was then wrong footed when the defence was able to challenge the nurses' recollections by producing their contemporaneous notes. This chapter is not, however, concerned with whether or not Dr Adams should have been convicted of murder, but with the principle advanced by Devlin J.

This chapter is divided into six further sections. The *first* will put the principle advanced by Devlin J into its present day legal context. Despite the principle's subsequent affirmation, it is not easy to reconcile it with what is now the leading authority on murder, namely, *R v Woollin*.[14] The *second* section will examine the principle of double effect. Particular consideration will be given to the views of Keown, a leading supporter of the operation of the principle of double effect in English law. The *third* section will consider whether Devlin J's principle is properly considered an instance of the principle of double effect by examining his Lordship's words and subsequent judicial statements in this and other common law jurisdictions. The *fourth* section will analyse the issue of pain relief capable of accelerating death using the moral principle outlined and defended in the first chapter – namely, the Principle of Generic Consistency (PGC). The *fifth* section will provide an explanatory link from the fourth section to the idealised judgment in the *sixth* section. That idealised judgment will support the proper administration of life-shortening pain relief, but reject appeal to the principle of double effect and adopt an approach that is compatible with the later case of *R v Woollin*.

2.2 Legal developments

Devlin J's crucial direction was that a doctor 'is entitled to do all that is proper and necessary to relieve pain and suffering, even if the measures he takes may incidentally shorten life'.[15] This direction, or something very similar to it, has been affirmed in numerous subsequent decisions. The case of *R v Cox* involved a doctor who administered a lethal dose of potassium chloride, which is a drug that stops the heart but has no therapeutic or pain-relieving value.[16] Ognall J's direction to the jury made repeated reference to 'the line to be drawn between a primary purpose [to] alleviate pain, which may, or even will, incidentally cause death, and, on the other hand, a purpose to kill which may – for however short a time – incidentally alleviate suffering'. This principle acquired further support in obiter statements in the Court of Appeal and House of Lords.[17] The most notable was by Lord Goff in *Bland*, who re-affirmed:

---

13 Devlin 1985, 41.

14 [1999] 1 AC 82, 96.

15 [1957] Crim LR 365, 375. Also quoted in Devlin 1985, 171. I will consider Devlin J's use of the language of causation in the fourth part of this chapter.

16 *R v Cox* (1992) 12 BMLR 38.

17 *Re J* [1991] Fam 33, 46 (Lord Donaldson), and *Airedale NHS Trust v Bland* [1993] AC 789, 867 (Lord Goff) and 892 (Lord Mustill).

Adams: *life-shortening pain relief* 31

the established rule that a doctor may, when caring for a patient who is, for example, dying of cancer, lawfully administer painkilling drugs despite the fact that he knows that an incidental effect of that application will be to abbreviate the patient's life.[18]

A couple of years later, Annie Lindsell, a woman suffering from motor neurone disease, withdrew a case after it became clear that the drug she wanted her doctor to administer was one that would shorten her life only as a side-effect of easing her pain.[19] The judge indicated that he 'thoroughly approved and endorsed the discontinuance'.[20] Four years later, in 1999, Dr Moor was charged with the murder of George Liddell following his admission in the media to having administered large doses of diamorphine to help patients die a pain-free death.[21] The judge directed the jury that they could only convict Dr Moor if he intended to kill Mr Liddell, which would require that he gave the relevant injection 'for the purpose of killing'.[22] Hooper J went on to say:

> If Dr Moor thought or may have thought that it was only highly probable that death would follow the injection, then the prosecution would not have proved that he intended to kill and he would be not guilty.

Do these cases put it beyond doubt that Devlin J's statement represents English law? Two issues arise. First, none of these cases is formally a precedent, because the approval is either obiter or a statement given by a judge at first instance. They merely assert a conclusion without supportive reasoning. Secondly, in *R v Woollin*, the House of Lords outlined the requirements of murder in such a way that they fit uneasily with the *Adams* principle.[23]

Woollin was not a medical law case, but one in which a father in a fit of temper threw his three-month-old son on to a hard surface. The infant died and the father was convicted of murder. Lord Steyn, when giving the leading judgment, approved a model direction to a jury given in an earlier case to the effect that jury members who are satisfied that:

> the defendant recognised that death or serious harm would be virtually certain (barring some unforeseen intervention) to result from his voluntary act . . . may find it easy to infer that he intended to kill or do serious bodily harm, even though he may not have had any desire to achieve that result.[24]

---

18 *Airedale NHS Trust v Bland* [1993] AC 789, 867.
19 See BBC 2000 and Keown 2002, 22–24.
20 Quoted in Keown 2002, 24.
21 See Arlidge 2000.
22 Quoted in Arlidge 2000, 39.
23 [1999] 1 AC 82, 96.
24 *R v Woollin* [1999] 1 AC 82, 96, citing Lord Lane CJ in *R v Nedrick* [1986] 1 WLR 1025, 1028, but substituting the word 'find' for 'infer'.

32 Adams: *life-shortening pain relief*

Yet, this same judge made no reference to *Woollin* in the later *Pretty* case on assisted suicide when he opined:

> Under the double effect principle medical treatment may be administered to a terminally ill person to alleviate pain although it may hasten death: *Airedale NHS Trust v Bland* [1993] AC 789, 867d, per Lord Goff of Chieveley. This principle entails a distinction between foreseeing an outcome and intending it . . .[25]

Thus, Lord Steyn expressly permits a jury to infer direct intention from oblique intention in *Woollin* and then in *Pretty* approves of a sharp distinction between direct and oblique intention when a doctor administers life-shortening palliative care. Similarly, two Supreme Court Justices in *Nicklinson* cited Lord Goff's words with approval without referring to *Woollin*.[26] The conclusion we must reach is that the principle first articulated by Devlin J is still regarded as good law, but the difficulty is explaining how this is so. Four possibilities arise.[27]

The first possibility is that, in law, the principle only applies to proper medical care.[28] Such an approach would enable *Woollin* to be distinguished, but would then present a problem with regard to the justification for sharply separating intention and foresight in the context of life-shortening palliative care. We have seen that Devlin J's words have been equated with the principle of double effect, but (as will be explained below) that principle is not restricted to life-shortening pain relief.

The second possibility is that juries who consider the defendant to have foreseen death or really serious bodily harm have discretion as to whether to rely on the principle of double effect or infer intention. This approach is perfectly compatible with *Woollin*. As McEwan put it:

> Evidence that a defendant foresaw death or really serious bodily harm is evidence from which a jury *may*, not *must*, infer intention. It appears therefore that there is, before the jury, a 'get-out' clause whereby they may decide that although a defendant foresaw death as virtually certain, he or she did not intend it.[29]

The Court of Appeal has affirmed that the *Woollin* direction allows foresight of a virtual certainty to be used to infer intention 'as a rule of evidence', rather than as 'a rule of substantive law', though admitting that there is 'very little to choose' between these two approaches.[30] Indeed, even as a rule of evidence, a jury could infer intention from foresight of a virtually certain consequence in the context of

---

25 *R (Pretty) v DPP* [2001] UKHL 61, [55].
26 See *R (Nicklinson, AM and Lamb) v Ministry of Justice* [2014] UKSC 38, [18] (Lord Neuberger) and [252] (Lord Sumption).
27 See Pattinson 2017b, 507–509.
28 See eg Hoppe & Miola 2014, 260.
29 McEwan 2001, 257.
30 *R v Matthews, R v Alleyne* [2003] EWCA Crim 192, [43].

proper medical care, which would mean that doctors administering life-shortening palliative care must always operate under the threat of a murder conviction. Such an approach is not actually compatible with the direction given by Devlin J in *Adams* or its subsequent affirmation by Lord Goff and others. Devlin J did not say that the issue of whether to infer intention from foresight attributed to Dr Adams fell to the jury, but that a doctor was 'entitled' to administer proper pain relief, even if he foresaw that the measures may shorten life.

The third possibility is that *Woollin* was wrongly decided. Keown argues that the decision 'should be overruled as a matter of urgency'.[31] He considers *Woollin* to grossly misrepresent the state of mind of doctors engaged in proper palliative care, as they do not intend to kill.[32] He argues that the decision of the House of Lords unacceptably exposes the lawfulness of proper palliative care to doubt. But notice that the judge who gave the leading judgment in *Woollin* did not feel the need to even refer to that judgment when, in *Pretty*, he approved Lord Goff's dicta. Also, *Woollin* has stood for 20 years without legal challenge and approves the direction given by Lord Lane in *Nedrick* from over a decade before.[33] In *Re A*, the only judicial decision to address the difficulty of reconciling *Woollin* and the principle from *Adams*, the problem was simply left open.[34]

A fourth option would be to reject the sharp distinction between intention and foresight that many attribute to Devlin J's dicta. Any such response, however, seems to have been rejected by repeated judicial approvals of the distinction between direct and oblique intention in the context of medically administered pain relief. This fourth option would involve removing the issue from the mens rea requirement of murder and seeking another justification for considering it lawful for a doctor to administer potentially life-shortening palliative care. There are two legal hooks from which this conclusion may hang.

The first of these involves allowing the doctrine of necessity to be a defence to murder when a doctor properly administers pain relief that could shorten the patient's life. The majority of the Court of Appeal in *Re A*, faced with determining whether it would be lawful to separate conjoined twins so that one could survive when the separation would accelerate the death of the other, invoked the defence of necessity to support choosing the lesser of two evils.[35] It was recognised that the House of Lords had relied on necessity in other

---

31 Keown 2002, 29.
32 See Keown 2002, 28–29.
33 Lord Steyn changed only one word from the direction given by Lord Lane in *R v Nedrick* [1986] 1 WLR 1025, 1028.
34 *Re A* [2001] Fam 147, esp 198–199 (Ward LJ).
35 *Re A* [2001] Fam 147, 239–240 (Brooke LJ) and 255 (Robert Walker LJ). Ward LJ (at 204) appealed to 'quasi-self-defence', rather than the defence of necessity. Brooke LJ (at 236) said that in cases of 'pure necessity . . . [t]he claim is that his or her conduct was not harmful because on a choice of two evils the choice of avoiding the greater harm was justified'. Ward LJ also appealed to the principle of 'choosing the lesser of the two evils' (at 192) but only in the context of balancing the best interests of the twins.

areas of medical law.[36] In theory, the doctrine of necessity could encompass life-shortening palliative care, but the courts have recently shown reluctance to further develop this defence. In *Nicklinson*, the applicants wanted the doctrine of necessity to be developed to encompass voluntary lethal treatment, by which I mean the intentional and immediate ending of a patient's life with that individual's consent. Voluntary lethal treatment is, however, significantly more controversial than life-shortening palliative care. The Court of Appeal was not willing to accept that necessity could be used to fashion a defence to murder by voluntary lethal treatment when the 'unambiguous blanket ban on assisting suicide' imposed by the Suicide Act 1961 meant that it could not be a defence to the lesser offence of assisted suicide.[37]

The second alternative to relying on the principle of double effect to negate the mens rea of murder would be to deem proper medical care to fall outside the actus reus of murder, by deeming it not an *unlawful* act or omission causing death. This approach would prevent any reference to the doctor's mental state as part of the law's response to the problem of life-shortening palliative care. Crucially, to say that life-shortening palliative care is not unlawful immediately raises the question as to the underlying principle distinguishing the lawful from the unlawful.

Selecting one of the options outlined above is far from morally neutral. Crucial questions include whether Devlin J's principle is actually the principle of double effect and whether that principle is morally sound. Notice that the two alternatives just outlined (expanding the defence of necessity and regarding the administration of proper pain relief as not unlawful) could expand the circumstances in which a doctor may lawfully administer life-shortening palliative care. That is because both could be invoked by a doctor with a direct (rather than merely oblique) intention to kill the patient. A doctor's trial would then not turn on what she intended, but on whether she satisfied the conditions for lawful administration of palliative care.

2.3 The principle of double effect

Devlin J's principle is widely equated with the doctrine or principle of double effect. His Lordship was brought up a Roman Catholic and educated at a Catholic boarding school.[38] It is therefore perhaps not a stretch to assume that he wished to draw the distinction between intended effects and merely foreseen effects that has been drawn, subject to conditions, by Catholic scholars since at least the time of Aquinas.

In *Summa Theologica*, Aquinas addressed killing in self-defence by distinguishing between what is intended and what is 'beside the intention'.[39] This

---

36 See *Re F* [1990] 2 AC 1, esp 74–78, and *R v Bournewood Community and Mental Health Trust, ex p L* [1999] 1 AC 458, 490.
37 [2013] EWCA Civ 961, [39] and [66]. Necessity was not raised when the case came before the Supreme Court. On the defence of necessity in assisted dying, see also Lewis 2013.
38 Morton 1992.
39 Aquinas 1225–1274, as translated 1947, second part of the second part, question 64, article 7.

distinction, according to Aquinas, is permissible when (a) the end or intention is not evil, (b) the object of the action is not evil, and (c) the circumstances of the action are fitting.[40] There is, however, more than one version of the principle of double effect.[41] Keown, a leading legal scholar whose work invokes this principle in the context of life-shortening palliative care, holds that it has four components:

(1) our conduct must not be wrong in itself,
(2) we must intend only the good effect, not the bad effect,
(3) the bad effect must not be the means to the good effect, and
(4) there must be a proportionate reason for allowing the bad effect to occur.[42]

Each is a necessary condition, and together they form sufficient conditions, for the operation of the principle of double effect. Others have presented alternative conditions and alternative formulations of these four conditions.[43]

The principle evolved from a particular 'sanctity of life' tradition, according to which it is always wrong to intentionally kill an innocent human being.[44] This tradition regards it as morally wrong for *patients* to refuse life-sustaining treatment or otherwise accelerate their deaths with the intention of ending their own lives, and for *healthcare professionals* to administer life-shortening treatment or otherwise accelerate a patient's death with the intention of ending that patient's life.[45]

It arises for consideration in the context of palliative care only if we assume that effective pain management at least sometimes requires life-shortening doses.[46] Sykes and Thorns have cited studies questioning whether the dosages of opioids and sedatives typically used to control the symptoms of patients with advanced, terminal cancer actually shorten the patient's life.[47] In one study, they found that:

> in 238 patients in a specialist palliative-care unit (89% received strong opiates and 48% received sedation) there was no evidence that the doctrine [ie the principle of double effect] needed to be invoked in relation to any morphine therapy. In fact, the doctrine was only possibly relevant to two patients who were treated with sedatives.[48]

---

40 See ibid and Foster et al 2011, 57.
41 Foster et al 2011, esp 56.
42 Keown 2012, 106 (to which I have added numbers). See Keown 2002, 20, for an earlier summary of these four conditions, with the order of (2) and (3) reversed.
43 See eg Price 1997, 325; Sykes & Thorns 2003, 312; Boyle 2004, 53; and Beauchamp & Childress 2013, 164–168.
44 The 'innocent' in this sense are those who are not engaged in unjust aggression.
45 See eg Keown 2000. In a response to Price 2001, Keown has argued that the principle permits doctors to respect 'all refusals of treatment (perhaps even those that were clearly suicidal) provided the doctor's intention was not to facilitate suicide' (Keown 2006, 117). But Price (2007, 562) objects that knowingly assisting another's suicide would still implicate the assister.
46 See Wilkinson 2000, 301.
47 Sykes & Thorns 2003.
48 Sykes & Thorns 2003, 317, citing Thorns & Sykes 2000.

36 Adams: *life-shortening pain relief*

They conclude that the principle of double effect is 'for the most part, irrelevant to symptom control at the end of life'.[49] That is compatible with the view that medically indicated symptom control at the end of life may *sometimes* properly be predicted to be life-shortening.[50] And many doctors and judges do believe that effective dosages of opioids will sometimes have the effect of shortening the patient's life.

Keown considers the administration of potentially life-shortening pain relief to be capable of satisfying his four conditions. The first condition is directed at *the nature of the act* itself, which must not be considered morally wrong in itself. This is easily satisfied for the act of pain relief. The second condition draws a *distinction between intention and foresight*. This requires that the intention be to bring about the good effect (ease pain), rather than to bring about the foreseen bad effect (shorten life). The third condition is a *distinction between means and effects*, requiring that the bad effect (earlier death) not be the means by which the good effect (pain relief) is brought about. This is regarded as capable of being satisfied by the administration of appropriate opioids, but not by the administration of potassium chloride, which operates as pain relief only because a dead person feels no pain (as in *R v Cox*). The fourth condition requires a *proportionate reason for permitting the bad effect*. According to Keown, easing the pain of a patient who is near death is a sufficiently proportionate reason for allowing the hastening of death, as long the doctor does not seek to ease the pain *by* shortening life.[51] It would be different 'if the doctor administered life-shortening drugs to a health patient for a hangover', because, Keown tells us, easing a hangover is not a sufficient reason for foreseeably shortening life.[52]

The principle has a long history of being applied to other moral dilemmas. It has, in particular, traditionally been used to distinguish two situations in which a fetus is terminated in the process of saving the life of a pregnant woman.[53] In the first, a pregnant woman has a cancerous uterus and will die unless she has hysterectomy. In the second, the pregnant woman has a serious heart condition and will die if she attempts to carry to term.

The traditional view espoused by some theologians is that fetal death in the first scenario may sometimes satisfy the four conditions of the principle of double effect, whereas fetal death in the second scenario cannot meet those conditions. According to this view, a doctor acts permissibly when performing a hysterectomy to save the pregnant woman's life from uterine cancer with the foreseen (but unintended) effect of fetal death, because the death of the fetus is not the means to this good effect and there is a proportionate reason for allowing fetal death to occur. In contrast, the termination of fetal life is the means of saving the pregnant woman's life in the second scenario. The doctor is therefore said to intend the fetal death (as the *means* of saving the woman) in the second scenario,

---

49 Sykes & Thorns 2003, 317.
50 cf Finlay 2009, who simply denies that there is any evidence to this effect.
51 See Keown 2012, 107.
52 Keown 2012, 107.
53 See the discussion in Price 1997, 326; Beauchamp & Childress 2013, 165–166; and McGee 2013.

but might not have intended the fetal death (as a mere *side effect*) in the first scenario. Notice that in this application, intention is only determined by reference to the subjective mental state of the doctor where the other conditions are satisfied. Where those other conditions are not satisfied – such as where the bad effect is considered to be the means of the good effect – an intention to bring about the bad effect is imputed. As McGee puts the point, the principle of double effect 'recognises but forbids the possibility that a good effect could be sincerely intended, yet produced by means of the bad effect'.[54]

Much attention has focussed on the intention-foresight distinction (Keown's second condition), which is common among proponents of the principle of double effect. In a recent article, Foster and his co-authors quote the following passage from the second edition of my medical law textbook:

> This principle holds that an act with two predicted consequences, one good and one bad, can be morally permissible where the intention is to achieve the good and the bad is as undesired as it is unavoidable.[55]

They then immediately state that I am

> not alone in seeing the doctrine as simply emphasizing the distinction between intended and foreseen consequences. This is not the whole doctrine, although it is an important part of it . . . . Keown's fourth criterion (or something like it) is essential if the doctrine is not to be open to abuse.[56]

There are many parts of my analysis that I would now express differently, but, with respect, this selective citation and commentary is far from a charitable reading of my text. The footnote to the sentence that they quote from Chapter 1 of my book refers the reader to the detailed discussion in a specific section of Chapter 16, which starts by quoting and summarising the very passage from Keown they cite for his four conditions.

The distinction between intended effects and unintended side-effects was the focus of my previous book because it is the most controversial of Keown's four conditions. There are undoubtedly different possible states of mind with regard to the predicted effects of our willed actions. If I drink vodka because I want the pleasure of drunkenness, I may foresee but not want or desire the subsequent hangover. Beauchamp and Childress suggest that we avoid the language of 'wanting' and talk about those effects that are foreseen but not desired as 'tolerated'.[57] This is apt, because my hangover is not so undesirable that I choose

---

54 McGee 2004, 47.
55 Pattinson 2009, 18.
56 Foster et al 2011, 66.
57 Beauchamp & Childress 2013, 167, citing Castañeda 1979.

38 Adams: *life-shortening pain relief*

not to get drunk to avoid it. According to proponents of the principle of double effect, the unintended side-effect need not even be unwanted. Finnis discusses a war-time commander who orders the bombing of a factory without intending the civilian deaths, but welcoming the 'bonus' side-effect that civilian deaths will have on enemy morale.[58] Finnis declares that this side-effect is unintended if the war-time commander 'has in no way calibrated or adjusted his plans so as to achieve civilian deaths – not even as a secondary objective – and if he stops the bomb-ing as soon as the factory is destroyed'.[59] Since a welcomed side-effect is neither unwanted nor merely tolerated, it may be better to talk of 'accepted side-effects'.

In both the hangover and bombing examples, the actor has knowingly and vol-untarily brought about the accepted side-effects. This is just one of the reasons why the distinction between intended and unintended effects is controversial. It has been argued that this distinction often depends on how an action is described.[60] It can also be difficult to determine whether a particular consequence was intended, both from a 'first person' perspective (individuals can be unsure what they intend or do not intend) and from a 'third person' perspective (we cannot directly enter another's mind).[61] Others reject these concerns, arguing that the distinction is of moral sig-nificance, can be drawn without arbitrariness, is apparent from within a first person perspective, and the evidential difficulties from a third person perspective are no more complex than those facing juries every day.[62]

My present concern is whether Devlin J's principle or its subsequent re-articulation actually captures the conditions of the principle of double effect.

2.4 Devlin J's principle and the principle of double effect

Devlin J's direction did not explicitly refer to the principle of double effect. He declared that a doctor was 'entitled' to do all that is 'proper and necessary' to relieve a patient's pain and suffering, even if such measures could 'incidentally' hasten the patient's death.[63] He went on to say that no one, not even a doctor, 'has the right to deliberately cut the thread of life'. This distinction between what is done 'deliberately' and what is done 'incidentally' seems to have been meant to capture the distinction between intended effects and merely foreseen effects. The word 'deliberately' is not well chosen in this regard, because an unintended effect that is brought about voluntarily and knowingly is still deliberate, but Devlin J had started his direction by declaring that murder is 'an act or series of acts . . . which were *intended* to kill and did in fact kill'.[64] The words 'proper and necessary' are

---

58 See Finnis 1995c, 63–64.
59 Finnis 1995c, 64.
60 See Harris 1985, 46; Singer 1993, 209–210; and Beauchamp & Childress 2013, 166–168.
61 See Wilkinson 2000, 301.
62 See eg Finnis 1995a and (on the last point) House of Lords Select Committee 1994, para 243.
63 Quoted in Arlidge 2000, 34.
64 Arlidge 2000, 34 (emphasis added).

being asked to do a lot of work if they are to capture the other requirements of the principle of double effect. We saw earlier that Keown identifies those other requirements in terms of (a) the nature of the act, (b) a distinction between means and effects, and (c) a proportionate reason for allowing the bad effect. There was no need for Devlin J to direct the jury to consider the acceptability of the nature of the act, because the law clearly regards the administration of pain relief as a legitimate act. But do the words 'proper and necessary' provide enough direction for a jury to apply conditions (b) and (c)? Perhaps not;[65] even Keown's conditions need elaboration beyond their mere assertion if they are to provide advice to the jury on how to identify and weigh the relevant variables.

My selective quotation has simplified Devlin J's direction. As will be seen by reading the extract quoted in the rewritten judgment in 2.7 below, he told the jury that if the patient's death had been accelerated by proper medical treatment, 'the cause of her death was the illness or the injury' and not the drugs. This approach, which can easily descend into an unnecessary legal fiction, will be examined below.

Many subsequent judicial mentions of life-shortening pain relief take us further away from the principle of double effect. Lord Goff's restatement of Devlin J's principle has been cited with approval by other Law Lords and Supreme Court Justices.[66] That restatement, which does not actually cite *Adams*, bears revisiting in context. The sentence immediately prior to the oft-quoted sentence adds to his Lordship's reasoning:

> As I see it, the doctor's decision whether or not to take any such step [that is, to prolong a patient's life] must (subject to his patient's ability to give or withhold his consent) be made in the best interests of the patient. *It is this principle* too which, in my opinion, underlies the established rule that a doctor may, when caring for a patient who is, for example, dying of cancer, lawfully administer painkilling drugs despite the fact that he knows that an incidental effect of that application will be to abbreviate the patient's life.[67]

Notice that Lord Goff's reason for upholding the lawfulness of life-shortening pain relief was *the principle that, subject to his patient's ability to make his own decision, a doctor must act in the best interests of the patient*. This principle, a version of which I will later show to be defensible under the PGC, will sometimes justify conclusions that are contrary to those apparently required by the principle of double effect. That is because the principle of double effect prohibits acting with the intention of shortening a patient's life, even if the doctor is administering painkilling drugs in accordance with the patient's wishes and best interests. To deny this by claiming that a patient's

---

65 See also Foster et al 2011, 62.
66 See *R (Pretty) v DPP* [2001] UKHL 61, [55] and *R (Nicklinson, AM and Lamb) v Ministry of Justice* [2014] UKSC 38, [18] and [252].
67 *Airedale NHS Trust v Bland* [1993] AC 789, 867 (emphasis added).

40   Adams: *life-shortening pain relief*

best interests must be identified by reference to the doctor's subjective intentions would be to confuse the patient's interests with the purposes of the doctor.

Lord Steyn in his judgment in *Pretty* expressly refers to Lord Goff's statement as 'the double effect principle'.[68] He then says that this 'principle entails a distinction between foreseeing an outcome and intending it: see also [Arlidge 2000]'. The inclusion of this reference is instructive. It is to a short case note on the *Moor* case in which the author concludes that the judge in that case had been

> prepared, in the very limited situation of a patient who was in pain and in the last stages of life, to allow a substantive defence to a doctor who whilst trying to relieve suffering knew that his actions were virtually certain to cause death in a short time span.[69]

That is, Arlidge was arguing that English law had fashioned a 'substantive defence' that only applies to doctors. Lord Steyn, who you will remember gave the leading judgment in *Woollin*, therefore seems to be supporting departure from *Woollin* only in the context of life-shortening pain relief. That means that what Lord Steyn took to be the principle of double effect is not the principle espoused by Keown and others, which they claim applies to murder in all contexts. Also, as we saw with the self-defence and abortion examples above, proponents of the principle of double effect would also go further than the legal use by applying the principle where the harm and benefit are not to the same person.[70]

2.4.1 Other jurisdictions

In 1997, the Supreme Court of the United States considered two cases on the same day in which support was given to (a version of) the principle of double effect.[71] Both were challenges to the constitutionality of state-level statutes prohibiting assisted suicide. The Supreme Court did not attempt to apply the principle of double effect to assisted suicide, which involves intentional killing and breaches all four of Keown's conditions for the principle of double effect. But it did seem to accept that the principle of double effect explains the permissibility of hastening death in the context of palliative care. Chief Justice Rehnquist, delivering the opinion of the US Supreme Court in *Vacco v Quill*, declared that 'in some cases, painkilling drugs may hasten a patient's death, but the physician's purpose and intent is, or may be, only to ease his patient's pain'.[72] He did not restrict the distinction between direct and oblique intent to palliative care, but regarded the law as having long distinguished 'actions taken "because of" a

---

68 *R (Pretty) v DPP* [2001] UKHL 61, [55].
69 Arlidge 2000, 40.
70 See Foster et al 2011, 60.
71 *Vacco v Quill*, 521 US 793, and *Washington v Glucksberg*, 510 US 702.
72 *Vacco v Quill*, 521 US 793, 802.

Adams: *life-shortening pain relief* 41

given end from actions taken "in spite of" their unintended but foreseen consequences'.[73] Like the English jurisprudence, no mention was made of the other conditions for the application of the principle of double effect.

Courts in other common law countries have also been willing to assume that the principle of double effect renders life-shortening palliative care legal. Devlin J's principle was directly quoted in a 1992 decision of the High Court of New Zealand,[74] But the judge in this first instance decision was addressing the withdrawal of ventilation and merely citing *Adams* to support the claim that the law generally permits a doctor to act in good faith in accordance with good medical practice. A year later, the Supreme Court of Canada in *Rodriguez v British Columbia (Attorney General)* approved of life-shortening pain relief by distinguishing it from assisted suicide.[75] This distinction was drawn on the basis of intention: 'in the case of palliative care the intention is to ease pain, which has the effect of hastening death, while in the case of assisted suicide, the intention is undeniably to cause death'.[76] Aside from the obvious objection that the intention in palliative care need not be purely to ease pain, again no other condition was mentioned beyond intention. In the 2015 case of *Carter v Canada (Attorney General)*, the Supreme Court again contrasted the lawfulness of 'palliative sedation' with the federal prohibition of physician-assisted dying.[77] There was no mention of the basis of this conclusion and, in contrast to *Rodriguez*, the Court held that the federal criminal laws were inapplicable to competent adults who clearly consent to physician-assisted dying and are enduring intolerable suffering from a grievous and irremediable medical condition.

Overall, it seems that Devlin J's direction has been eagerly accepted by judges in common law systems as a means of supporting the conclusion that proper palliative care does not render the doctor a murderer. But the issue has not directly arisen for consideration by any appellate court. No appellate court has therefore had the opportunity to authoritatively consider and rule on the legal status of the principle of double effect.

2.5 Application of the PGC

We have seen that Keown presents three conditions for intended effects to be properly distinguished from merely foreseen effects: (a) the nature of the act, (b) a distinction between means and effects, and (c) a sufficient balance between the good and bad effect. Its reliance on terms like 'good' and 'bad' requires the principle of double effect to be applied by reference to a position defining those terms. Keown,

---

73 *Vacco v Quill*, 521 US 793, 802–803.
74 *Auckland Area Health Board v Attorney-General* [1993] 1 NZLR 235, 252 (decided in August 1992).
75 [1993] 3 SCR 519, [25] and [57] (Sopinka J with whom La Forest, Gonthier, Iacobucci and Major JJ concurred).
76 [1993] 3 SCR 519, [57].
77 [2015] 1 SCR 331.

42 Adams: *life-shortening pain relief*

and others in that tradition, adhere to the 'sanctity (or inviolability) of life' (SoL), according to which it is always wrong to intentionally kill an innocent human being. But the SoL is not consistent with the PGC.

The rights granted to all agents by the PGC are will-rights, so an agent may waive the benefit of her generic rights, including her right to life. Contrary to the SoL, intentionally taking one's own life only violates the PGC where it thereby violates the generic rights of others, such as where the suicidal person is piloting a passenger plane or wishes to jump in front of a train. A doctor who shortens a patient's life *with that patient's proper consent* therefore does not perform an act that is intrinsically immoral, even if the doctor's declared intention is to hasten the patient's death.

The plausibility of the principle of double effect stems from its recognition of the limited human capacity to avoid bad effects from permitted choices.[78] Our freely chosen purposes are those that we consider ourselves to have the power not to pursue, but we are not thereby empowered to select every effect that will follow from pursuit of our purposes. Our choice is only between pursuing or not pursuing a particular purpose with whatever risk of generic harm to others we are able to predict will follow from that choice. We are not required to avoid all foreseen generic harms to others. Not all generic harms are unavoidable or accorded equal weight by the criterion of needfulness for action. But such an assessment does not map on to the four conditions of the principle of double effect. Further, even if a sincere and competent attempt to comply with the requirements of the PGC may sometimes evoke a distinction between direct and oblique intention, or something close to it,[79] the PGC's rejection of the SoL remains crucial. Without such a constraint a patient is not absolutely prohibited from suicide and a doctor is not absolutely prohibited from acting for the purpose of assisting that suicide.

The most straightforward case is one in which the patient is properly considered to have made a voluntary, informed and competent decision to request or permit the administration of life-shortening drugs. Under the PGC, if the doctor has come to a competent judgment in good faith that the medical options present a choice between a longer, more painful life and a shorter, less painful life, then the decision is properly for the patient. That is not merely because all the generic rights have waivable benefits, but because the suffering of debilitating pain interferes with a basic generic condition and an agent therefore has a positive basic right to relief from pain, as per the direct application of the PGC discussed in Chapter 1 (1.3.3). Sufficient safeguards must, of course, be in place to ensure that the doctor's judgment is both sincere and competent and the patient's decision is sufficiently free and informed.[80] The precise nature of those safeguards, being context specific and requiring assessment of complex variables, is to be determined

---

78 cf Boyle 2004, 56.

79 Waldron 1984, 15–16, has argued that Gewirth's 'principle of intervening action' – invoked in Gewirth 1981 to support his claim that the right of a mother not to be tortured to death by her son is an absolute right – depends on 'the sort of distinction invoked by the Doctrine of Double Effect'.

80 See further ch 3 (3.4).

as an indirect application of the PGC. One reason why particular attention needs to be given to the safeguards is that the case for consensual life-shortening pain relief shares many features with the case for consensually putting an *immediate* end to the patient's life. Making the case for permitting consensual administration of immediately lethal treatment is not, of course, my purpose here and any such case must not make the mistake of either treating death itself as if it were a generic condition or overlooking any greater risks presented by this further step.

Where the patient lacks the cognitive-functional ability to make a decision (on which see Chapters 3 and 5), then the doctor must still act consistently with the patient's rights: will-rights (if the patient is an ostensible agent) or interest-rights (if the patient is not an ostensible agent). An incompetent patient's rights also include the positive basic right to pain relief, because debilitating pain can hinder the incompetent patient's ability to act for any purpose at all and the patient will require assistance to address this basic generic need. Subject to the patient's competently expressed prior wishes,[81] this right supports a doctor who administers pain relief to a patient apparently suffering from otherwise unbearable pain, even if the lowest effective dosage is foreseen to be life-shortening. Where a doctor acts for multiple purposes, the fact that one of those purposes is to hasten the patient's death as a means of relieving the patient from pain and suffering, is not inconsistent with acting in accordance with the patient's rights. Distinguishing between intending to kill and intending to relieve pain in the way required by the principle of double effect creates too much scope for a doctor to be required to act contrary to the wishes of the patient or contrary to the generic interests of a patient who is unable to make decisions. A patient should not be required to spend her dying moments in pain merely because one of the doctor's purposes (underpinned by a sincere and competent assessment of the patient's needs) is to shorten her life as a means of addressing her pain.

2.6 Options available to Athena J

My decision to revisit *Adams* raises some difficulties, because it necessitates that I assume the contemporary existence of a reference procedure to the Court of Appeal following an acquittal, bestow on the Attorney General grounds for utilising that procedure in this case and assume opposition to that reference from counsel acting on behalf of Dr Adams. These three leaps of imagination extend beyond what is required when revisiting the other selected cases. A reference procedure of this type was not actually introduced until the Criminal Justice Act 1972.[82] At no point did the Attorney General display any concern about the direction given to the jury on the issue on which my appeal will focus and, contrary to what I assume below, when Dr Adams was acquitted the Attorney

---

81 On which see Pattinson 2017a.

82 Criminal Justice Act 1972, s 36 provides for a procedure for reference to the Court of Appeal of a point of law following an acquittal on indictment.

44 Adams: *life-shortening pain relief*

General famously told the court that he would not be pursuing a further trial on a second indictment for the murder of a Mrs Hullett. In fact, Devlin J's summing up to the jury suggests that counsel acting on behalf of Dr Adams did not support the submissions attributed to him in the judgment below.[83]

These three imaginary features are necessary because the principle first judicially articulated by Devlin J in *Adams* has gained acceptance as good law without it giving rise to a subsequent ruling potentially subject to plausible appeal. The principle could not assist Dr Cox (because he administered a life-shortening drug without pain relieving effects), it did not apply on the facts in the appeal cases in which we find supportive dicta, the Annie Lindsell case never made it to trial and, by the time of the *Moore* case, the principle had become legal orthodoxy and the alternatives harder to support using the case law. Yet, to ignore the effect of this principle being considered to be good law would be to sidestep an important issue of legal coherence and overlook its importance to the contemporary euthanasia debate. Devlin J's direction on the mens rea requirement of murder is difficult to reconcile with *Woollin*, as discussed above; it is simply not adhered to in the law of murder outside the administration of life-shortening pain relief. Also, as we saw in the previous section, its operation potentially threatens protection of patients' rights.

Once we grant the required imaginary features to our appeal, we can apply the method of modified law as integrity, as explained in Chapter 1. It is important to remember that this method does not permit Athena J to approach a case as if given a blank slate onto which she may write principles that most directly give effect to what she in good faith considers to be the requirements of the PGC. In Dworkin's approach, Hercules must seek a principle that 'both *fits* and *justifies* some complex part of legal practice' and thereby provides 'the consistency of principle' required by integrity.[84] Even as revised so that the PGC operates in the determination of both fit and justification, Athena is constrained by previously decided cases and the key features of the common law method. As Lord Mustill declared in one appeal: 'The common law must build for the future with materials from the past'.[85] The law in 1957 was far from settled on the relationship between direct and oblique intention,[86] but it was settled on most other features of the law of murder, and on the criminality of suicide ('self-murder') until the Suicide Act 1961.[87] Athena J cannot simply ignore that context.

---

83 Consider, for example, the contrast between views that I attribute to Mr Lawrence and the fact that Devlin J's summing up declared that a doctor does not have the right to 'deliberately cut the thread of life' and it was not 'contended by the defence that Dr Adams had any right to make that determination': Devlin 1985, 172.

84 Dworkin 1986, 228 (emphasis added).

85 *Attorney-General's Reference (No 3 of 1994)* [1998] AC 245, 255.

86 In *DPP v Smith* [1960] 3 WLR 546, esp 327, the House of Lords actually held that a person intends what an ordinary responsible man would have contemplated to be the natural and probable result of his act.

87 See Williams 1958, 245–256 (on attempted suicide) and 264–267 (on secondary parties in a suicide).

The approach in *Adams* is not devoid of merit. It does provide a legal basis for the conclusion that a doctor who attends a patient approaching the close of her life in pain may administer the drugs necessary to ease that pain, even if this is likely to shorten her life. This is significant in a context of legal prohibitions on suicide and intentional killing. The specific approach adopted by Devlin J was to manipulate both the actus reus and mens rea requirements for murder. He directed the jury that if the patient's death were accelerated, the cause of death in law would be the illness and not the drugs. It was in this context that Devlin J told the jury that a doctor was entitled to do all that was 'proper and necessary' to relieve pain and suffering, even if doing so incidentally shortens that patient's life. As Williams pointed out on the causation issue, if the evidence does show that the death was caused by the administration of drugs, then the jury is being asked to perform 'the gymnastic'.[88] In essence, the direction adopted both a legal fiction for causation *and* (a version of) the principle of double effect. The further claim made to the jury that 'there is no special defence for medical men' must be regarded as another fiction; otherwise we cannot reconcile Devlin J's principle with the general law of murder.[89] Legal fictions are to be avoided unless their use is required to render the law coherent or compliant with the PGC.[90]

Devlin J's reference to doing all that is 'proper and necessary to relieve pain' is not incompatible with an alternative legal response. In 1958, only a year after the *Adams* case, Williams provided a different solution to the legal problem facing Devlin J. He declared that:

> a physician may give any amount of drug necessary to deaden pain, even though he knows that that amount will bring about speedy or indeed immediate death. His legal excuse does not rest upon the Roman Church's doctrine of 'double effect', for it would be both human and right for him in these circumstances to welcome his patient's death as a merciful release. The excuse rests upon the doctrine of necessity, there being at this juncture no way of relieving pain without ending life.[91]

As Williams went on to explain in another book published three years later:

> It would seem clearer [than Devlin J's approach to causation] to base the defence frankly upon the doctrine of necessity: the value of saving the dying patient from pain is preferred to the value of postponing death.[92]

Williams' reference to a 'speedy or indeed immediate death' expresses his view that the defence of necessity does not support a sharp line between shortening life

---

88 Williams 1958, 290.
89 As acknowledged by the Law Commission 2005, [4.72]–[4.91], esp [4.90].
90 See further ch 4 (4.2.1).
91 Williams 1958, 288.
92 Williams 1961, 727–728.

46 Adams: *life-shortening pain relief*

and accelerating death. He argued that to invoke a principle based on the 'lesser of two evils' to support a doctor knowingly, for a sufficient reason, shortening a patient's life is to support a doctor knowingly, for a sufficient reason, putting an end to the patient's life immediately.[93] Yet, directly making this last move would, Williams bemoaned, run up against the precedents.[94] From the perspective of the PGC, the prohibition of immediate mercy killing would need to be supported – and my concern here is not with whether it is in fact supported – by reference to the need to protect against the risk of ending patients' lives without their consent or otherwise contrary to their rights. The idealised judgment below does not imply the legality of immediate mercy killing, because the legal context requires Athena J to give a restrictive interpretation to the principle of the lesser of two evils. A pressing concern for Athena J is guarding against imbuing this legal principle with Williams' utilitarianism.[95] The lesser of two evils principle must be interpreted and applied by reference to the underlying rights and, in contrast to utilitarianism, the rights of different individuals cannot be aggregated. It is such aggregation, rather than consequentialism as such, that we need to avoid. As Gewirth put it, the PGC is 'deontological consequentialist'.[96] For this reason, Athena J prefers alternative phrasing to that advocated by Williams.

No mention will be made of Williams in the idealised judgment below, despite some of his work being contemporary and anticipating the general thrust of the judgment.[97] This is, in part, due to the 'quaint convention forbidding explicit reliance in argument or judgment on the writings of the living to which English courts were still adhering in the 1960s'.[98] Similarly, and for more obvious reasons, no references are provided to later materials from which ideas and inspiration have been drawn.[99]

The idealised judgment does not, again for obvious reasons, address issues that were only later to be raised in the literature. One of these is the issue of 'terminal sedation', by which I mean the practice of sedating a patient into a deep and continuous coma and then *not* providing food or hydration, so that the inevitable result will be her death.[100] A study published in 2009 reported

---

93 See Williams 1958, 288.

94 Williams 1958, 284.

95 Williams sometimes directly invoked a 'secular, utilitarian' calculus (see eg Williams 1977, 97–98), and has been called 'the illegitimate child of Jeremy Bentham' (Radzinowicz quoted in Spencer 1997).

96 Gewirth 1978, 216. See also Gewirth 1999, 210: 'my distributive or deontological consequentialism is . . . different from aggregative consequentialism'.

97 The discussion of *R v Bourne* [1939] 1 KB 687 in the idealised judgment should, according to proper academic standards, cite Williams 1958, 151–152.

98 Glazebrook 2013, 16.

99 The discussion of *R v Dudley and Stephens* (1884–85) LR 14 QBD 273 should reference the judgment of Brooke LJ in *Re A* [2001] Fam 147, 220–231, and the quotation from Gury's work in the mid-nineteenth century is cited from Boyle 2004, 53, with spellings put into British English.

100 See Williams 2001, Seale 2009, esp 199, and Jackson 2012, 16–17.

that 'continuous deep sedation' preceded 16.5 per cent of deaths in the UK.[101] The purpose of this practice is often described as relieving the patient's pain and distress by sedation, with medically assisted nutrition and hydration later being withheld because 'given that the patient will not regain consciousness, it has become futile'.[102] Such an explanation treats these as two connected medical choices, rather than a single choice for which the hastening of death is a purpose. By contrast with the principle of double effect, the defence of necessity permits the decision to opt for terminal sedation to be considered, as some doctors surely do, as a single medical choice.

Another issue subsequently raised in the literature is the distinction between the defence of necessity as a 'justification' and as an 'excuse'. Dresser, who argues that Williams overlooked this distinction in his commentary on *Dudley and Stephens*,[103] claims that:

> a justified act is an act that is right, tolerable, or, at a minimum, not wrong. In contrast, we excuse a person when her conduct was unjustifiable, but when we also believe that she is not morally to blame for her wrongdoing.[104]

The distinction between a 'justification' and an 'excuse' for a *prima facie* wrongful act is compatible with the PGC. A *justified wrong* could be understood as one where the rights infringement is itself justified (by, for example, the criterion of degrees of needfulness for action). An *excused wrong* could be understood as one where the rights-infringement is not strictly justified, but criminal sanction is either not required or not justified. But the idealised judgment below need not draw this distinction. Athena J invokes the defence of necessity in a situation where committing (what would otherwise be) a legal wrong is justified, not merely excused. She thereby relies on justificatory necessity, rather than excusatory necessity.

The Court of Appeal (Criminal Division) judgment below is given by Athena, who sits as Athena J at that time. I have designated her as Justice of the High Court, rather than Lord Justice, to keep her career longevity within plausible limits.[105] High Court Justices do sit on Attorney General reference cases,[106] though the judgment would usually be read by the senior judge.

The punctuation and style of the judgment below complies with the standard in contemporary law reports and therefore differs from that adopted in the main text.

---

101 Seale 2009, 198 and 201.
102 Jackson 2012, 17.
103 Williams 1977 commenting on *R v Dudley and Stephens* (1884–85) LR 14 QBD 273.
104 Dresser 2013, 135.
105 It is noticeable just how long it has taken the English courts to accept the title Ms Justice, rather than Mrs Justice. The first High Court judge to be formally addressed as 'Ms Justice' was Ms Justice Russell in 2014: see Bowcott 2014.
106 See eg the first case under s 36 of the Criminal Justice Act 1972: *Attorney-General's Reference (No 1 of 1974)* [1974] QB 744 (Lord Widgery CJ, Ashworth and Mocatta JJ).

48 Adams: *life-shortening pain relief*

2.7 Idealised judgment: *Attorney-General's Reference (No 1 of 1958) (CA, Crim)*

To be cited in later judgments as:
Attorney-General's Reference (No. 1 of 1958) [1958] R.L.C. 1

Athena J. read the following opinion of the court.

This matter comes before the court on a reference from Her Majesty's Attorney-General. By this reference the opinion of the court is sought upon a point of law arising out of an acquittal before the Central Criminal Court of Dr. John Bodkin Adams upon a charge of murder. Mr. Geoffrey Lawrence, appearing on behalf of Dr. Adams, has exercised the acquitted man's right to take part in the proceedings before this court.

The point of law upon which the court is asked to give its opinion is as follows:

"Whether a doctor commits murder by administering large dosages of narcotics to relieve his patient from pain and suffering, where the intention and effect is to shorten the patient's life."

The facts of the case for the purposes of this reference may be stated briefly because the court's opinion is sought upon a very narrow point of law. Dr. Adams prescribed large quantities of heroin and morphine to Mrs. Morrell who was suffering the effects of a stroke. There was a large discrepancy between the quantity prescribed and the quantity recorded as administered. The judge, in his summing-up, told the jury that there was no evidence from which they could infer that any drugs were administered to Mrs. Morrell over and above the injections recorded in the nurses' notes. The judge went on to say that it was a most curious situation that the act of murder had to be proved by expert evidence and the jury could only conclude that the act of murder had taken place if they wholly accepted the evidence of Dr. Douthwaite, who had given evidence for the prosecution.

The matter before this court stems from the judge's direction on the circumstances in which the administration of medicines that shorten life amounts to murder. The judge directed the jury in these terms:

"Murder is an act or series of acts done by the prisoner which were intended to kill and did in fact kill the dead woman. It does not matter for this purpose that her death was inevitable and her days were numbered. If her life was cut short by weeks or months; it is just as much murder as if it were cut short by years.

We have heard a good deal of discussion in the course of the evidence in this case about the circumstances in which doctors might be justified in administering drugs which would shorten life. Cases of severe pain have been suggested and generally approved by the witnesses in the box; and also there have been suggested cases of helpless misery. It is my duty to tell you that the law knows of no special defence of this character. But that does not mean that a doctor who is aiding the sick and the dying has to calculate in minutes, or even in hours, and perhaps not in days or weeks, the effect upon a patient's life of the medicines which he administers or else be in peril of a charge of murder. If the first purpose of medicine, the restoration of health can no longer be achieved there is still much for a doctor to do and he is entitled to do all that is proper and necessary to relieve pain and suffering, even if the measures he takes may incidentally shorten life. That is not because there is any special defence for medical men; it is not because doctors are put into any different category from other citizens for this purpose. The law is the same for all and what I have said rests simply upon this, which is part of the definition of murder that I gave you: no act is murder which does not cause death. 'Cause' means nothing philosophical or technical or scientific. It means what you twelve men and women sitting as a jury would regard in a commonsense way as the cause. Manifestly there must be cases in hospitals that are going on day after day in which what a doctor does by way of giving certain treatment prolongs or shortens life by hours or even longer. The doctor who decides to administer or not to administer a drug is not, of course thinking in terms of hours or minutes of life. He could not do his job properly if he were. If, for example, because a doctor has done something or has omitted to do something death occurs at eleven o'clock instead of twelve o'clock, or even on Monday instead of Tuesday, no people of common sense would say 'oh, the doctor caused her death.' They would say the cause of death was the illness or the injury, or whatever it was, which brought her into hospital and the proper medical treatment that is administered and that has an incidental effect on determining the exact moment of death is not the cause of death in any sensible use of the term. But it remains the fact, members of the jury, and it remains the law, that no doctor, nor any man no more in the case of the dying than the healthy, has the right to deliberately cut the thread of life."

There are four key statements:

(1) Murder is an act or series of acts which were intended to kill and did in fact kill.
(2) If the restoration of health can no longer be achieved, the doctor is entitled to do all that is proper and necessary to relieve pain and suffering, even if the measures he takes may incidentally shorten life.
(3) Medical men have no special defence to murder.
(4) If a patient were to die following the administration of proper medical treatment, the legal cause of death would be the illness or injury which brought the patient into hospital.

The Attorney-General has referred the judge's direction to us in unusual circumstances. He does not argue that it contains a misdirection. He is concerned to

50 Adams: *life-shortening pain relief*

confirm all four statements because there is to be a further trial on a second indictment for the murder of a Mrs. Hullett with the same judge and Mr. Lawrence has again been retained as counsel for the defence. Mr. Lawrence has made it clear that had Dr. Adams been convicted he would have sought to appeal on grounds of misdirection. This issue therefore remains relevant to the second indictment.

The Attorney-General submits that (2) is supported by the doctrine of double effect, according to which a doctor may only seek to relieve a patient's pain and suffering if his intention is not to shorten the patient's life. Mr. Lawrence submits that the legal ground for administering painkilling drugs, in circumstances where there is no way of relieving pain without hastening death, rests not upon the doctrine of double effect but the doctrine of necessity. He therefore submits that (2) and (3) are misdirections and, if that is so, then he would see no reason to defend (4).

The Attorney-General elaborated the distinction drawn by proponents of the doctrine of double effect between an intended effect (the purpose) and an incidental side-effect (the double effect). He referred us to the classic formulation by J.B. Gury in the mid-nineteenth century:

> "It is licit to posit a cause which is either good or indifferent from which there follows a twofold effect, one good the other evil, if a proportionately grave reason is present, and if the end of the agent is honourable – that is, if he does not intend the evil."

We recognise that a distinction may properly be drawn between what is intended and what is merely foreseen. Despite this, we are not persuaded that the doctrine of double effect with its attendant conditions is a principle of English law requiring the question put before this court to be given an unqualified answer in the affirmative. In our view, English law recognises the lawfulness of proper and necessary pain relief, even where one of its effects is to hasten death, under the doctrine of necessity.

We consider the doctrine of necessity to have been the proper basis for the defence to abortion recognised in *R. v. Bourne* [1939] 1 K.B. 687. Mcnaghten J., in a direction to the jury, read into the offence in section 58 of the Offences Against the Person Act 1861 an exception to preserve the life of the mother. The result was Mr. Bourne's acquittal. The judge's direction did draw an analogy with the Infant Life Preservation Act 1929, which contains an express exemption for the preservation of the life of the mother, but the only legal principle on which such an exception could be based was the defence of necessity. The direction did, in part, proceed on the ground that the 1861 Act's use of the word "unlawfully" implies that some abortions are lawful, but that word does not indicate which abortions are lawful, and again the principle providing this detail is the defence of necessity. The defence of necessity accepts an action as justified where it is necessary to avoid the greater of two evils. The judge's direction implies that where an unavoidable choice arises between the life of the mother and the life of the child, it is proper and lawful for the doctor to act to save the life of the mother. Mcnaghten J. explained that "the unborn child in the womb must not be destroyed unless the destruction of that child is for the purpose of preserving the yet more precious life of the mother": [1938] 3 All E.R. 615 at p. 620, which provides almost a page omitted from the Law Reports version. It seems to us correct that the mother's right to life outweighs the right to life of the unborn child. The Crown was therefore required to prove beyond reasonable doubt that Mr. Bourne did not procure the miscarriage of the girl in good faith for the purpose of preserving her life. Mcnaghten J. went on to hold that the doctor is thereby provided with a defence to the charge of unlawfully procuring a miscarriage where he acts, on reasonable grounds and with adequate knowledge, in the honest belief that "the probable consequence of the continuance of the pregnancy will be to make the woman a physical or mental wreck".

If the defence of necessity can provide an exception to a statutory offence, there can be no objection to it providing an exception to a common law offence, even one as serious as murder. Against this conclusion, the Attorney-General has submitted that *R. v. Dudley and Stephens* (1884–85) L.R. 14 Q.B.D. 273 is authority for the proposition that necessity can never provide a legal justification for murder. This was a case in which two sailors had killed and (with a third) eaten a seventeen-year-old cabin boy on the yacht *Mignonette* after twenty days on the open sea without sufficient food or water. A jury found the facts of the case in a special verdict and the case was then argued before a court of five judges. Giving the judgment of the Queen's Bench Divisional Court, Lord Coleridge C.J. concluded that the facts stated in the jury's verdict provided no legal justification for murder. The key passages can be found at pp. 286–288:

> "Now it is admitted that the deliberate killing of this unoffending and unresisting boy was clearly murder, unless the killing can be justified by some well recognised excuse admitted by the law. It is further admitted that there was in this case no such excuse, unless the killing was justified by what has been called 'necessity'. But the temptation to the act which existed here was not what the law has ever called necessity. Nor is this to be regretted. . . .
>
> It is not needful to point out the awful danger of admitting the principle which has been contended for. Who is to be the judge of this sort of necessity? By what measure is the comparative value of lives to be measured? Is it to be strength, or intellect, or what? It is plain that the principle leaves to him who is to profit by it to determine the necessity which will justify him in deliberately taking another's life to save his own. In this case the weakest, the youngest, the most unresisting, was chosen. Was it more necessary to kill him than one of the grown men? The answer must be 'No'."

We cannot support Mr. Lawrence's submission that this supports the claim that the defence of necessity can *never* be available to a charge of murder. The defence of necessity could not provide legal justification for the action of the defendants, Dudley and Stephens, because this was not a situation in which the defendants had selected the lesser of two evils. The force of Lord Coleridge's rhetorical question as

52 Adams: *life-shortening pain relief*

to why the cabin boy was selected over the others rests with the unstated premise that his right to life was just as important as the right to life held by any of the others; it was no more necessary to kill the boy to protect the right to life of Dudley or Stephens than it would have been to kill either one of them to save his life.

In our view, the defence of necessity does apply where the only means by which a doctor may relieve a dying patient from pain will hasten the patient's death. The easing of pain and suffering is to be preferred, subject to the patient's ability to give or withhold his consent, to preserving maximal life expectancy. It is true that the theological doctrine of double effect also permits a harmful effect (hastening of death) when bringing about a proportionately weightier good effect (alleviation of unbearable pain and suffering), but the legal doctrine of necessity delivers this more directly and enables proper focus on the patient. The logic of the doctrine of double effect is that a doctor who acts for multiple purposes commits murder if one of those purposes involves the hastening of death, but not if he were to provide exactly the same treatment in exactly the same situation without such a purpose. In our view, the lawfulness of providing proper pain relief does not require a jury to conclude that the doctor had, in purely subjective *mens rea* terms, no purpose to hasten the patient's death. It requires, instead, that the jury conclude that the doctor acted, on reasonable grounds with adequate knowledge, on the honest belief that the administration of painkilling drugs was a proper and proportionate, and thereby necessary, means of addressing the dying patient's right to relief from pain. It is only a proper and proportionate response where the doctor reasonably believes four things. First, he either has the consent of the patient or the patient lacks the ability to consent. Secondly, the patient is suffering from an incurable and fatal illness. Thirdly, no alternative pain relief exists that is equally efficacious but does not shorten life. Fourthly, the chosen dosage is the minimum required to alleviate the patient's pain. These conditions follow from the principle of the lesser of two evils.

We conclude that the doctrine of necessity provides a defence to a doctor where it has not been shown, beyond reasonable doubt, that he did not reasonably believe that the administration of painkilling drugs to a dying patient was a proper and necessary means of addressing that patient's pain and suffering. This defence has two further advantages over the judge's particular reliance on *mens rea* (intention) and *actus reus* (causation): it does not import the conditions of the doctrine of double effect into all legal uses of the notion of intention and it does not require the law to treat life-shortening pain relief as if it has no causal effect on the timing of the patient's death in circumstances where the evidence suggests otherwise.

The judge directed the jury that:

> "If the first purpose of medicine, the restoration of health can no longer be achieved there is still much for a doctor to do and he is entitled to do all that is proper and necessary to relieve pain and suffering, even if the measures he takes may incidentally shorten life."

It is only the word "incidentally" that transfers the legal ground from the doctrine of necessity to the doctrine of double effect. But the use of that word, which was repeated later, does amount to a misdirection. The defence of necessity is not a special defence for doctors, but the statement that there is no "special defence for medical men" encouraged the jury to overlook the special role that the defence of necessity has to play with regard to the administration of proper pain relief to a dying patient. For the same reason, it would have been better had the judge not told the jury that "There is no legal justification and there is no moral justification that you have to consider in this case".

3 *Gillick*
Consent from a child

3.1 Introduction

Victoria Gillick challenged guidance issued by the Department of Health and Social Security, which advised that in exceptional circumstances a doctor may prescribe contraception to a girl under 16 without her parents' knowledge or consent. Mrs Gillick was the mother of five girls under the age of 16, a committed Roman Catholic and opposed to what she has called 'secret schoolgirl contraception'.[1] She sought a declaration that the guidance was unlawful on the basis that (a) a child under 16 could not consent to medical treatment, (b) parental rights included the right to veto any medical treatment and (c) a doctor following the guidance would be aiding the offence of sexual intercourse with a girl under 16, contrary to the Sexual Offences Act 1956.

Mrs Gillick lost in the High Court, won a unanimous decision in the Court of Appeal and then lost in the House of Lords by a majority of three to two.[2] She therefore had the support of five of the nine judges who heard her case, but lost because only two of those judges sat in the House of Lords.[3] The three in the majority did not speak with one voice, and differences within and between the leading judgments have supported alternative interpretations. In subsequent years, Lord Donaldson led a 'retreat from *Gillick*' when dealing with *refusals* of medical treatment[4] and Mrs Axon lost a 'very similar' case to that mounted by Mrs Gillick 20 years earlier.[5] *Gillick* is a case where different underlying moral views could easily support reliance on different legal principles.

Before proceeding, I first want to address a preliminary terminological issue with regard to the use of 'competence' and 'capacity' in this book.[6] An individual will be described as *competent* when judged to possess sufficient

---

1 Gillick 1989, 7 and 91.
2 [1984] QB 581 (Woolf LJ); [1986] AC 112 (CA, Eveleigh, Fox and Parker LJJ; HL, Lords Fraser, Scarman, Bridge, Brandon and Templeman). AC report hereafter cited as *Gillick*.
3 A point made by many: Eekelaar 1986, 180; Lee 1988, 36; and Fortin 2011, 201–202.
4 Douglas 1992, *Re R* [1991] 4 All ER 177, and *Re W* [1993] Fam 64.
5 Fortin 2011, 222, and *R (Axon) v Secretary of State for Health* [2006] EWHC 37.
6 See further Pattinson 2017b, ch 5.

cognitive-functional faculties to be able to make a decision with respect to a given situation. An individual will be said to have *capacity* when judged to possess the attributes required to have authority to make a legally valid decision. This terminology enables easier expression of a crucial distinction and evades the inconsistencies of terminology that beleaguer the case law and literature.[7] So defined, capacity need not track competence. In fact, as we shall see, the consequence of Lord Donaldson's retreat from *Gillick* is that a child who is considered cognitively-functionally able to make a particular treatment decision (competent) may be denied the legal authority (capacity) to refuse treatment in the face of judicial or parental consent. Both competence and capacity operate as binary decisions (competence/incompetent; capacitated/incapacitated), but that does not imply that those below the relevant threshold fall off a cliff-edge 'into the clinging embrace of paternalism'.[8] First, temporary factors affecting competence or capacity may change or be alleviated. Secondly, the patient's incompetent or incapacitated wishes and feelings could still be given significant weight and the patient could be assisted to participate in any decision-making within the limits of their abilities. Thirdly, the patient's wishes and values when previously competent could be given effect.[9]

The chapter below is divided into five sections. The *first* will outline the decision of their Lordships in *Gillick*. The *second* will examine three issues that were not fully addressed in *Gillick* and have subsequently been subject to controversial judicial interpretation – namely, a competent child's refusal of life-sustaining treatment, the specific requirements of the *Gillick* test, and the relationship between the *Gillick* test and the adult capacity test. It will be argued that some of the difficulties presented by *Gillick* stemmed from the (then) lack of precedent on the test for capacity applicable to adults, and there is now a pressing need to reconcile the child test with the adult test. The *third* section will analyse the treatment decisions of mature children using the Principle of Generic Consistency (PGC). The *fourth* section will provide an explanatory link from the third section to the idealised judgment in the *fifth* section. That idealised judgment will support the conclusion that a child under 16 with sufficient cognitive-functional abilities may consent to *or refuse* treatment.

3.2 The decision in *Gillick*

There were, as Lord Fraser put it, three questions raised in the appeal to the House of Lords in *Gillick*. These were:

---

7 The word 'capacity' was, however, used in this sense in *Gillick* itself, such as 186: 'There are some indications in statutory provisions . . . that a girl under 16 years of age in England and Wales does not have the capacity to give valid consent to contraceptive advice and treatment'.
8 Keene 2015.
9 See further the discussion on substituted judgment in ch 5 (5.2.5 and the idealised judgment at 5.6)

56 Gillick: consent from a child

(1) Whether a girl under the age of 16 has the legal capacity to give valid consent to contraceptive advice and treatment including medical examination.

(2) Whether giving such advice and treatment to a girl under 16 without her parents' consent infringes the parents' rights.

(3) Whether a doctor who gives such advice or treatment to a girl under 16 without her parents' consent incurs criminal liability.[10]

That is, the (1) capacity question, (2) parental question and the (3) criminality question.

Lord Fraser and Lord Scarman rejected Mrs Gillick's answers to all three questions, but did so in different terms with regard to the first two, and Lord Bridge agreed with both. Lord Brandon only considered the third question and held that contraceptive facilities could not lawfully be provided by a doctor to a girl under the age of 16. Lord Templeman held that contraception could be lawfully provided, but not by reliance solely on the consent of the under-aged girl. These divisions and differences make it difficult to discern the ratio.

Commentators have paid particular attention to the differences between the two leading judgments.[11] Lord Fraser and Lord Scarman both rejected the absolute control of parents over their minor children and accepted the capacity of mature minors to make treatment decisions for themselves.[12] Lord Fraser apparently confined himself to medical treatment and reasoned by reference to the child's welfare,[13] whereas Lord Scarman reasoned in more general terms by reference to the 'right' of a child with sufficient understanding and intelligence to make his or her own decisions.[14] Thus, Lord Scarman's avowed agreement with Lord Fraser's opinion indicates joint rejection of Mrs Gillick's application, rather than concurrence on the details of his colleague's approach to adolescent autonomy.[15] On this point, I agree with Victoria Gillick's assessment that '[t]he two judgments just did not marry up'.[16]

3.2.1 The capacity test

The House of Lords agreed that a child under 16 could have capacity to consent to some forms of medical treatment, but were divided on both the capacity test and its application to contraceptive advice and treatment.

---

10 *Gillick*, 166.

11 See eg Parkinson 1986 and Fortin 2011.

12 *Gillick*, esp 171 (Lord Fraser) and 186–189 (Lord Scarman).

13 *Gillick*, 173: 'Once the rule of the parents' absolute authority over minor children is abandoned, the solution . . . depends upon a judgment of what is best for the *welfare of the particular child*' (emphasis added).

14 *Gillick*, 186: 'parental right yields to the *child's right to make his own decisions* when he reaches a sufficient understanding and intelligence to be capable of making up his own mind on the matter requiring decision' (emphasis added).

15 See Fortin 2011, 206.

16 Gillick 1989, 273.

Unlike children under 16, there is a statutory provision applying to 16- and 17-year-olds. Section 8(1) of the Family Law Reform Act 1969 states that a child who is at least 16 may provide consent to 'any surgical, medical or dental treatment' that is 'as effective as it would be if he were of full age' with regard to what would otherwise constitute a trespass to the person. When such consent is obtained 'it shall not be necessary to obtain any consent for it from his parent or guardian'. Section 8(3) elaborates by stating that the section does not make 'ineffective any consent which would have been effective if this section had not been enacted'. The majority considered s 8(3) to preserve the validity of consent at common law for those under the age of 16.[17]

Lord Fraser considered that a child under 16 who 'is capable of understanding what is proposed, and of expressing his or her own wishes' has capacity to consent to medical treatment.[18] Lord Scarman agreed with Lord Fraser but went on to require much more. After declaring that the relevant principle was the attainment of 'sufficient discretion to enable him or her to exercise a wise choice in his or her own interests',[19] his Lordship went on to state:

> It is not enough that she should understand the nature of the advice . . .: she must also have a sufficient maturity to understand what is involved. There are moral and family questions, especially her relationship with her parents; long-term problems associated with the emotional impact of pregnancy and its termination; and there are the risks to health of sexual intercourse at her age, risks which contraception may diminish but cannot eliminate. It follows that a doctor will have to satisfy himself that she is able to appraise these factors before he can safely proceed upon the basis that she has at law capacity to consent to contraceptive treatment.[20]

Thus, according to Lord Scarman, an under 16-year-old would need to be able to understand 'moral and family questions' to have capacity to consent to contraceptive treatment.

Their Lordships agreed that the threshold for child capacity did vary according to the complexity of the decision. Lord Fraser specifically stated that a child of 15 would ordinarily be able to consent to the treatment of 'trivial injuries' or even the setting of a broken arm,[21] and went on to hold that some would have the understanding required to consent to contraception. Lord Templeman declared that the effect of consent 'depends on the nature of the treatment and the age and understanding' of the child, so that an 'intelligent boy or girl of 15' could consent to a tonsillectomy and appendectomy.[22] His Lordship did not, in contrast to

17 *Gillick*, 166–167.
18 *Gillick*, 169.
19 *Gillick*, 188.
20 *Gillick*, 189.
21 *Gillick*, 169.
22 *Gillick*, 201.

58   Gillick: consent from a child

the majority, think that an under-age girl would have the requisite understanding to be able to consent to contraception, which requires 'not only knowledge of the facts of life and of the dangers of pregnancy and disease but also an understanding of the emotional and other consequences to her family, her male partner and to herself'.[23] While Lord Templeman's blanket response to contraception was at times dressed up as a decision as to the cognitive-functional abilities of an under 16-year-old, it is clear that his disagreement with Lord Scarman is over more than whether such a child can ever actually understand the 'moral and family questions' presented by contraception. Lord Templeman's decision was, in effect, that capacity to consent to contraceptive treatment should not track competence alone.

3.2.2 Parental rights

Lords Fraser and Scarman both expressly approved Lord Denning MR's description in *Hewer v Bryant* of the parental right as a 'dwindling right'[24] and considered parental rights to derive from their duties and thereby exist only for the benefit of the child.[25]

The headings of Lord Fraser's judgment only address medical treatment and, in the process of declaring that a child under 16 with sufficient understanding could provide a legally valid consent, his Lordship stated that '[o]f course the consent of the parents should normally be asked'.[26] This might suggest that he thought that only in exceptional circumstances should doctors proceed with just the consent of a sufficiently mature child. Indeed, his Lordship gave particular emphasis to the need to promote a child's welfare and later declared that in the 'overwhelming majority of cases' the child's parents would be the best judges of her welfare.[27] In what have become known as the 'Fraser guidelines', he provided specific advice on the provision of conceptive advice and treatment to young girls without parental knowledge.[28] The doctor, Lord Fraser opined, must be satisfied that (1) the girl understands his advice, (2) she cannot be persuaded to inform her parents of the matter, (3) she is likely to go ahead with sexual intercourse with or without contraception, (4) her physical or mental health is likely to suffer without contraceptive advice and treatment, and (5) her best interests require her to receive treatment without her parents' consent.[29] These requirements place a great deal of power in the hands of doctors. As Parkinson notes, Lord Fraser accepts that a doctor may lawfully interfere with parental rights, and act without their consent,

---

23 *Gillick*, 201.
24 *Hewer v Bryant* [1970] 1 QB 357, 369, cited and approved in *Gillick*, 172 (Lord Fraser).
25 *Gillick*, 170 (Lord Fraser) and 184 (Lord Scarman).
26 *Gillick*, 168.
27 *Gillick*, 173.
28 See eg discussion in Wheeler 2006.
29 *Gillick*, 174.

Gillick: *consent from a child* 59

'because it is in the minor's best interests that he do so and he cannot persuade the girl to involve the parents. It is a discretion vested in the doctor'.[30] This leads him to object that Lord Fraser's approach takes 'power away from parents and give[s] it to doctors without any real means of reviewing a doctor's discretion'.[31] Kennedy has similarly protested that Lord Fraser simply replaced 'parental power with doctor power'.[32] Teff goes further by arguing that *Gillick* as a whole 'symbolized the primacy of the "doctor's right" to exercise judgment and discretion over the alleged "parental right" to prior consultation'.[33] This is debatable in light of Lord Scarman's judgment.

Lord Scarman was more general and less deferential to parental rights. His Lordship opined:

> The underlying principle of the law . . . is that the parental right yields to the child's right to make his own decision when he reaches a sufficient understanding and intelligence to be capable of making up his own mind on the matter requiring decision.[34]

His Lordship later repeated that principle in the context of medical treatment, stating that the parental right to determine 'whether or not' a minor below the age of 16 will have medical treatment 'terminates' when the child 'achieves a sufficient intelligence to enable him or her to understand fully what is proposed'.[35] Thus, parts of Lord Scarman's speech appealed to a general 'underlying principle' to the effect that the parental right to make decisions for a child under the age of 16 '*yields* to the child's right' and '*terminates*' when a child has sufficient understanding and intelligence to make her own decisions.

Lord Scarman's approach does not glue the protection of child autonomy to the child's best interests in the way expounded by Lord Fraser. But Parkinson objects that this alternative approach leaves the doctor with little practical guidance:

> Lord Scarman's approach leaves the doctor to make his own assessment of a girl's maturity with the possibility of a civil action in which a judge may second guess his opinion. Doctors [would] benefit from a clear-cut rule . . . . Nor does a doctor necessarily have the facts to make a reasonable decision. In a family planning clinic, he may know nothing about the girl or her family. As Lord Templeman said, he only knows what she chooses to tell him.[36]

30 Parkinson 1986, 13.
31 Parkinson 1986, 14.
32 Kennedy 1988, 94.
33 Teff 1994, 39.
34 *Gillick*, 186.
35 *Gillick*, 188–189.
36 Parkinson 1986, 14.

60   Gillick: consent from a child

Parkinson's first criticism is one that is relevant whenever a doctor treats a patient, because a judgment is required as to whether the presumption of capacity or incapacity has been rebutted. The Mental Capacity Act 2005 deals with this issue by providing that the lawfulness of relying on s 5 to treat an incapacitated patient in her best interests is triggered by the doctor's 'reasonable belief' that the patient lacks capacity. Prior to the 2005 Act, there had been no case addressing the situation where a doctor acts in the face of a refusal as a result of falsely believing that the patient lacks capacity, but Grubb has suggested that the judges would have been likely to fashion a defence of reasonable mistake to what would otherwise be a trespass.[37] No such defence would be needed where a doctor mistakenly treats an incapacitated adult's consent as valid (because no trespass occurs at common law where an incapacitated adult is treated in her best interests)[38] or mistakenly treats an incapacitated patient's refusal as valid (because no negligence occurs where the doctor has acted as a reasonable doctor).[39] Lady Athena will expound a reasonable belief defence for a doctor who may otherwise fear being second guessed on a patient's capacity or incapacity. This would also provide a response to Parkinson's second criticism: what matters is not whether the doctor knows the girl's full social circumstances, but whether a reasonable doctor would have made further inquiries.

From the above it is apparent that Lord Bridge's endorsement of both leading judgments leaves plenty of material to construct alternative interpretations of the ratio of *Gillick*. Readers will, however, no doubt have already noted that Lord Scarman's rights-based approach to the exercise of children's autonomy chimes more closely with the PGC than Lord Fraser's duty-based approach.

3.2.3 Criminality

Counsel on behalf of Mrs Gillick argued that following the guidance could lead a doctor to commit an offence under ss 28 or 6 of the Sexual Offences Act 1956.[40] Section 28 made it an offence for a person to cause or encourage the commission of unlawful sexual intercourse with a girl under 16 for whom he is responsible. Section 6 made it an offence for a man to have unlawful sexual intercourse with a girl under the age of 16, and Mrs Gillick argued that a doctor who acted on the guidance could be an accessory to this crime.

Lord Fraser opined that whether a doctor who follows the guidance would commit an offence would depend on the doctor's intentions.[41] In his Lordship's

---

37 Grubb 2004, 161, citing Butler-Sloss LJ in *Re MB* [1997] 2 FLR 426, 438: 'The only situation in which it is lawful for the doctors to intervene is if it is *believed* that the adult patient lacks the capacity to decide' (emphasis added). See also Kennedy & Grubb 2000, 764–765.
38 *Re F* [1990] 2 AC 1.
39 Grubb 2004, 160.
40 These provisions were later repealed and replaced by the Sexual Offences Act 2003. s 73 of the 2003 Act states that a doctor who provides contraceptive treatment and advice is not guilty of aiding, abetting or counselling the commission of a sexual offence against the child.
41 *Gillick*, 175.

view, it was 'unlikely' that doctors who 'honestly intend' to act in the best interests of a girl when providing contraceptive advice or treatment would commit an offence under s 28. Lord Scarman agreed and distinguished between intending to facilitate the patient having unlawful sexual intercourse and intending to maintain or restore her health. He added:

> The bona fide exercise by a doctor of his clinical judgment must be a complete negation of the guilty mind which is an essential ingredient of the criminal offence of aiding and abetting the commission of unlawful sexual intercourse.[42]

This view, whereby doctors who act on bona fide clinical judgments are considered not to have intended all the foreseen consequences of their actions, seems to cohere with Devlin J's direction in *Adams*, as analysed in Chapter 2. It is, however, difficult to reconcile with the general principles of criminal law on intention and on complicity in another's crime.[43] In a contemporary case note, Smith suggests that:

> we have here encountered a concealed defence of necessity. The doctor is acting lawfully if he is doing what he honestly believes to be necessary. All the normal conditions for liability for an aider and abettor may be satisfied, yet the doctor is to be excused.[44]

In the latest edition of *Smith and Hogan's Criminal Law*, it is argued that the approach of Woolf J at first instance and the majority of the House of Lords 'puts an undue strain on the concept of intention because it means that to be liable as an accessory [the doctor] must not only intend to provide the assistance, but intend the principal offence be committed'.[45] They argue that *Gillick* is therefore better regarded as based on necessity, whereby 'a minor encouragement of sexual intercourse was a lesser evil than an unwanted pregnancy in the young girl'.[46] Since Lady Athena relied on necessity in *Adams*, this is the route she adopts in the idealised judgment below, albeit again giving a deontological construction to necessity.

3.3 Gaps and legal developments

Gillick left many issues unresolved and has frequently being invoked when addressing matters far beyond its specific facts, thereby creating much scope for judicial interpretation. This section will address three particular issues: (1) subsequent

---

42 *Gillick*, 190.
43 On intention see ch 2; on complicity in another's crime see *NCB v Gamble* [1959] 1 QB 11, 23; *Lynch v DPP for Northern Ireland* [1975] AC 653, 678; Smith 1989, 64–68; and Ormerod & Laird 2015, 127ff.
44 Smith 1986, 117. cf Williams 1985.
45 Ormerod & Laird 2015, 227.
46 Ormerod & Laird 2015, 122; see also 227.

62 Gillick: consent from a child

judicial limits on the capacity of competent children to refuse treatment aimed at preventing death or severe permanent injury, (2) the manipulation of the *Gillick* capacity test to provide a higher threshold test for children than for adults, and (3) the relevance of *Gillick* to 16- and 17-year-olds.

3.3.1 Refusal of medical treatment

None of their Lordships in *Gillick* addressed capacity to refuse, but their dicta suggest symmetry between capacity to consent and refuse. We saw earlier that Lord Scarman's language, at least, stands in opposition to parental consent depriving a child of capacity to refuse, because he said parental decision-making 'yields' to the child's rights and 'terminates' when a child satisfies the *Gillick* test.[47]

Yet, Lord Donaldson soon led what is described by Douglas as a 'retreat from *Gillick*' and by Kennedy as driving 'a coach and horses through *Gillick*'.[48] In *Re R*, the Court of Appeal ruled that while the 15-year-old girl with a fluctuating mental state failed to satisfy the *Gillick* test, even if she had satisfied the test the court's wardship powers could be used to override her refusal.[49] Lord Donaldson added that parental consent could also override the refusal of a child who satisfied the *Gillick* test, because consent unlocks the door to lawful action and parents were also 'keyholders'.[50] Despite criticism of Lord Donaldson's interpretation of *Gillick* as a 'retrograde step' and an 'ebb in the tide of judicial enlightenment',[51] his Lordship displayed no desire to backtrack.

A year later, in *Re W*, the Court of Appeal affirmed Thorpe J's view that the refusal of a 16-year-old girl who had 'sufficient understanding to make an informed decision' could be overruled using the court's inherent jurisdiction.[52] The Court of Appeal held that s 8 of the Family Law Reform Act 1969, which states that a 16- or 17-year-old's 'consent' to medical treatment is as effective as that of an adult, did not apply to *refusal* of medical treatment. Judicial or parental consent could override the refusal of a competent child. Lord Donaldson, recognising that keys can also lock, now preferred to think of consent as a 'flak jacket' protecting the doctor from liability.[53] The Court reaffirmed the view that consent from the court or someone with parental responsibility could override the refusal of a competent child. A refusal would be a 'very important consideration', increasing in importance with the child's age and maturity, but it would not be determinate.[54] Balcombe and Nolan LJJ suggested that the power to override a competent child's refusal was

---

47 *Gillick*, 184–185.
48 Douglas 1992 and Kennedy 1992, 60.
49 *Re R* [1991] 4 All ER 177.
50 [1991] 4 All ER 177, 183 and 187.
51 Thornton 1992, 37, and Murphy 1992, 542, respectively. cf Rae 1992, 1583: 'To permit the child . . . to be the final arbiter may well be the equivalent to signing the child's death warrant'.
52 *Re W* [1993] Fam 64, 76.
53 [1993] Fam 64, 78.
54 [1993] Fam 64, 84 and 88.

limited to situations where the treatment is necessary to prevent death or serious permanent harm.[55] Nolan LJ limited this power to the courts where the refusal to be overridden was of major surgery or procedures such as abortion.[56]

Two and a half decades later, no English court has permitted a mature child to reject life-saving treatment. In *Re M*, for example, a 15-year-old's refusal of a heart transplant was overridden without the judge ruling on whether she satisfied the *Gillick* test.[57] Some cases have, however, been resolved without the involvement of the court. Hannah Jones, at the age of 13 in 2007, had her decision respected by hospital staff when she initially refused a life-saving heart transplant.[58] Her reasons for refusal were similar to those of the patient in *Re M*: 'more operations and taking drugs for life and she preferred to die with dignity'. But Jones changed her mind when she was close to death and underwent surgery in 2009. In 2010, 15-year-old Joshua McAuley died following refusal of a blood transfusion, on grounds of religious belief, with the support of his parents.[59] In a case that was taken to court, *An NHS Foundation Hospital v P*, Baker J authorised life-saving treatment contrary to the refusal of a 17-year-old girl who, he held, satisfied the capacity test in the Mental Capacity Act 2005 (on which see below).[60] His Lordship followed *Re W* and exercised the court's inherent jurisdiction to 'override the child's wishes in her best interests and give its consent to her treatment'.[61]

Gilmore and Herring have recently sought to provide a partial defence of *Re W* by distinguishing cases in which a child is only refusing one particular treatment ('refusal of consent') from those where a child is refusing all treatment ('refusal of treatment').[62] This distinction, they argue, provides a basis not only for defending Lord Donaldson's view that parental power survives a child's '(mere) acquisition of such power', but also for distinguishing *Re W* once a child displays the abilities required to refuse all treatment. They thereby support a different threshold for capacity according to whether a child is consenting to or refusing a particular treatment, or refusing all treatment. A child has the power to consent if she understands in broad terms the nature and purpose of that particular treatment, without her having to understand the consequences of a failure to treat, because that is sufficient to protect the doctor from battery.[63] Yet, a child's refusal of all treatment

---

55 [1993] Fam 64, 88 and 94.
56 [1993] Fam 64, 94.
57 *Re M* [1999] 2 FLR 1097. See also *Re P* [2003] EWHC 2327 (refusal of blood transfusion overridden in best interests of child of nearly 17 without application of the *Gillick* test).
58 See Barkham 2008 and BBC 2013.
59 See BBC 2010.
60 *An NHS Foundation Hospital v P* [2014] EWHC 1650.
61 [2014] EWHC 1650, [12].
62 Gilmore & Herring 2011a, esp 7, and 2011b.
63 Accordingly, for a child to validly consent to treatment, *Gillick* required 'merely an understanding of that which is proposed by way of treatment': Gilmore & Herring 2011a, 10. An under-aged girl can therefore consent to contraception if she understands the proposed treatment and its wider implications without her having to understand the consequences of her not receiving contraceptive treatment, such as the nature of pregnancy, childbirth and rearing a child.

64   Gillick: consent from a child

only has force against parental consent if she fully understands the consequences of receiving no treatment. So, a child who reaches the threshold to consent will sometimes be unable to satisfy the higher threshold to refuse all treatment.

Cave and Wallbank offer a different approach to ambiguities in *Gillick* as to what a child must be able to understand.[64] They suggest focussing on the decision itself in preference to Gilmore and Herring's distinction between one particular treatment and all treatment. A decision-based approach, they argue, is embraced by the adult capacity test: s 3 of the Mental Capacity Act requires understanding of 'the information relevant to the decision', which 'includes information about the reasonably foreseeable consequences of – (a) deciding one way or another, or (b) failing to make the decision'.[65] They argue that *Gillick* requires a child to 'fully understand the implications of *her* decision, which might involve more than one treatment'[66] and might also include refusal of all treatment. They argue:

> In practice, clinicians must assess capacity in relation to the decision rather than each potential treatment, in which case his or her assessment . . . may cover more than one treatment and potentially also a refusal of all treatment.[67]

It is, they aver, 'artificial and unworkable' to require clinicians to adopt Gilmore and Herring's treatment-based approach.[68] They point out that treatments requiring different levels of understanding can be intrinsically connected (their example: a heart transplant requires post-operative drug therapy to prevent rejection) or there could be treatment options so the choice is not purely between treatment and non-treatment, especially where one option is less efficacious. They recognise that their interpretation places significant discretion in the hands of doctors as to what information must be understood by a child patient. In response, they suggest adopting the approach taken by Bodey J in *Re A* on the application of s 3 of the 2005 Act: the patient needs to be unable to understand the 'proximate medical issues'.[69] A doctor must make a judgment about whether the 'proximate medical issues' include one or all of the following:

- A specific treatment and not having that treatment;
- A range of alternative treatments and their respective risks and benefits;
- The risks and benefits of having no treatment at all.[70]

Bodey J's judgment does indeed place limits on the range of factors of which the doctor may require understanding. His Lordship held that capacity to consent to

---

64 Cave & Wallbank 2012.
65 See Gilmore & Herring 2011a, 12; and Cave & Wallbank 2012, 436.
66 Cave & Wallbank 2012, 448.
67 Cave & Wallbank 2012, 438.
68 Cave & Wallbank 2012, 440.
69 Cave & Wallbank 2012, 441, citing *Re A* [2010] EWHC 1549.
70 Cave & Wallbank 2012, 443.

contraceptive treatment required only that the patient be considered able to understand 'the immediate medical issues surrounding contraceptive treatment' (such as the reason for contraception and what it does, and the alternatives, effectiveness and side effects), rather than the 'social consequences' (such as what would be involved in caring for and committing to a child).[71] Bodey J's view on s 3 differs from some statements made by Lord Scarman in *Gillick* on what a child must be able to understand to have capacity (see 3.2.1, above). Lord Scarman's insistence that a child must be able to understand 'moral and family questions' covers the 'social consequences' excluded by Body J's interpretation of s 3.

Gilmore and Herring respond by arguing that references to 'decision' by Lords Scarman and Fraser in *Gillick* were references to the particular treatment proposed.[72] To avoid committing a battery, they argue, a child patient need not have 'full understanding' and any such requirement would deprive many more children of capacity. Accordingly, a 9-year-old can consent to a nurse putting a plaster on a scratch on her knee without her fully understanding that if no plaster were used she would face risk of infection; and a sexually active 14-year-old girl can consent to contraception if she understands that that will stop her having an unwanted pregnancy, even if she does not understand the experience and possible complications of bearing, delivering and looking after a child.[73] Spending more time assisting such children to understand, they argue, might not be enough for those with developing abilities and would overstretch overworked practitioners. They conclude:

> We cannot see that there is any legal authority for the proposition that the minor should need to be able to choose between treatments A and B in order to consent to treatment, or why as a matter of principle or practice it should be necessary to impose such a requirement. Take the following general examples. If I am offered two holidays in France, one sky-diving and the other rock climbing, do I have to understand all the risks incurred in sky-diving to consent to rock climbing? If I have a risk of deep vein thrombosis and I am offered two ways of travelling to France, one by air (which would increase my risk) and one by train (which would not), do I need to understand my risk of travelling by air before I can consent to train travel? We think not, and neither, we submit, does the law so require.[74]

The opportunities available to Lady Athena in *Gillick* include the option of siding with Cave and Wallbank or Gilmore and Herring. Notice that Gilmore and Herring's examples assume that competence requires *actual understanding*, rather than merely possession of the *ability to understand*. While assessment of a

---

71 [2010] EWHC 1549, [64] and [56], respectively.
72 Gilmore & Herring 2012.
73 Gilmore & Herring 2012, 977.
74 Gilmore & Herring 2012, 978.

66 Gillick: consent from a child

patient's ability to understand will require assessment of what she actually understands, the two should not be conflated because non-disclosure of information may deprive a patient of the latter but not the former. For this reason, Lady Athena's approach will not be expressed in such terms, though it will accept Gilmore and Herring's view than the abilities required to consent are often not coterminous with those required to refuse.

3.3.2 Gillick v the MCA test

The common law *Gillick* test is not the only capacity test operating in English law. The Mental Capacity Act 2005 (the 2005 Act) provides a protective scheme that is triggered by reasonable belief that a person over 16 is unable to satisfy a two-stage test (the MCA test). This test is to be applied by reference to the s 1 principles: capacity is to be assumed (s 1(2)), a person is not to be treated as unable to make a decision unless 'all practicable steps to help him to do so have been taken without success' (s 1(3)), and a person is not unable to make a decision merely because he makes an unwise decision (s 1(4)). Under stage one of the MCA test – the diagnostic stage – a person will only lack capacity if 'he is unable to make a decision for himself in relation to the matter because of an impairment of, or a disturbance in the functioning of, the mind or brain' (s 2(1)). Under stage two, a person is only to be considered unable to make a decision if he cannot understand, retain or use the relevant information or communicate his decision (s 3(1)).

At first sight, the two capacity tests seem to be very similar. Both are connected to competence and therefore track decisional complexity, so that an individual can have capacity to make a particular decision but not to make a more cognitively demanding decision. They differ in three ways. First, the *Gillick* test has no equivalent to the s 2(1) diagnostic requirement. A child may be deprived of capacity under the *Gillick* test, but not under the MCA test, where, by reason *other than* an impairment or disturbance in the function of the mind or brain, she is overwhelmed by the consequences of a decision or lacks maturity.[75] Secondly, the MCA operates with a presumption to the effect that it has been satisfied (s 1(2)), whereas the presumption is reversed in *Gillick*. Thirdly, the courts have applied the *Gillick* test in a way that sets the threshold higher than it would be set for an adult and they have not adhered to principles equivalent to those in s 1 of the 2005 Act.

This third point has been made elsewhere by myself and others.[76] As already noted (in 3.3.1), Bodey J's ruling in *Re A* – that capacity to consent to contraceptive treatment only requires an adult patient to be able to understand 'the immediate medical issues surrounding contraceptive treatment', rather than the

---

75 On the *Gillick* test, see *Re M* [1999] 2 FLR 1097 and *Gillick* itself. On the adult test, see the discussion in Department for Constitutional Affairs 2007, [12.13] (on which see below); Cave 2014, 105; and Gilmore & Herring 2011a, 13.

76 Pattinson 2017b, 162–166; eg Cave 2009 (who at p 316 describes the *Gillick* test as 'vague and easily manipulated') and Archard 2015, 119.

'social consequences'[77] – stands in contrast to Lord Scarman's opinion that the child must be able to understand 'moral and family questions'.[78] However, Lord Fraser's phrasing (which was followed in a recent case involving a 13-year-old's consent to abortion) is consistent with Bodey J's approach.[79] Fluctuating competence presents another issue that has been treated differently under the *Gillick* test than it would be under the MCA test. Section 3(3) of the 2005 Act states that an ability to retain the information relevant to a decision for only a short period does not prevent the patient from having capacity for the duration of lucidity. Yet, in *Re R* it was held that a child who on a good day met the *Gillick* criteria, but on other days did not, could not be regarded as '*Gillick* competent'.[80]

In cases in which a child has refused a life-saving blood transfusion on grounds of adherence to the Jehovah's Witness faith, it is notable that the child has been judged against a test of *full* understanding *without all practical steps being taken to assist* the patient to gain that level of understanding. In *Re E*, a child of just under 16 was found to have insufficient understanding of the implications of refusing a blood transfusion.[81] The patient did consent to an alternative form of treatment with a 40–50 per cent chance of success, as opposed to the 80–90 per cent chance of success with a blood transfusion. Ward J declared:

> Impressed though I was by his obvious intelligence, by his calm discussion of the implications, by his assertion even that he would refuse well knowing that he may die as a result, in my judgment A does not have a full understanding of the whole implication of what the refusal of that treatment involves.[82]

His Lordship reasoned that A was insufficiently aware that he will become increasingly breathless, *about which he had not been informed*, and lacked sufficient comprehension of the pain that he would suffer. Freeman has argued that were Ward J's reasoning 'applied to an adult, it is dubious whether refusal to be treated would ever be allowed'.[83] The stroke of midnight on A's eighteenth birthday changed his legal position and he died after then validly refusing blood transfusions.[84] In the later case of *Re L*, a 14-year-old girl was found to lack capacity to refuse the life-sustaining blood transfusions required after being severely scalded from falling into a hot bath during an epileptic attack.[85] Sir Stephen Brown found that L was 'certainly not "*Gillick* competent"' in the context of all the necessary details which

---

77 [2010] EWHC 1549, [64] and [56], respectively.
78 *Gillick*, 189.
79 *Gillick*, 169–170, as applied in *An NHS Trust v ABC* and *A Local Authority* [2014] EWHC 1445, [8], [12] and [15].
80 [1991] 4 All ER 177, 186 (Lord Donaldson) and 191 (Farquharson LJ).
81 *Re E* [1993] 1 FLR 386.
82 [1993] 1 FLR 386, 391.
83 Freeman 2005, 208.
84 As stated by Johnson J in *Re P* [2003] EWHC 2327, [8].
85 *Re L* [1998] 2 FLR 810.

68 Gillick: consent from a child

it would be appropriate for her to be able to form a view about'.[86] Once again, the judge happily found that she did not understand the consequences of her refusal in a situation in which she had not been told what would happen without treatment. Despite considering L to be 'for her age mature', the judge drew negative inferences from her 'sheltered life' and 'limited experience of life'.[87]

3.3.3 16- and 17-year-olds

Debate has arisen with regard to the application of the *Gillick* test to those aged 16 and 17. *Gillick* was concerned with whether children under 16 should be able to access contraceptive treatment without parental involvement and did not consider the position of children at or above that age. The *Gillick* test has the potential to operate as the common law test for the capacity of minors as such, but the capacity of 16/17-year-olds to consent to medical treatment is also subject to specific statutory provision.[88] Section 8(1) of the Family Law Reform Act 1969 was mentioned earlier. In full it states:

> The consent of a minor who has attained the age of sixteen years to any surgical, medical or dental treatment which, in the absence of consent, would constitute a trespass to his person, shall be as effective as it would be if he were of full age; and where a minor has by virtue of this section given an effective consent to any treatment it shall not be necessary to obtain any consent for it from his parent or guardian.

Thus, a 16 or 17-year-old child's consent to 'any surgical, medical or dental treatment' is 'as effective as it would be if he were of full age' with regard to what would otherwise constitute a trespass to the person. It seems to me that a child's consent is only 'as effective as' that of an adult if the child has the capacity to consent in those situations in which an adult would have capacity to consent.[89] From this it would follow that (a) a 16/17-year-old's capacity to consent to medical treatment can only be rebutted where that child fails to satisfy the adult capacity test and (b) the *Gillick* test can only apply to matters falling outside the ambit of s 8, such as consent to organ donation and clinical research.

The 2005 Act's protective scheme also applies where a person is 16 or older and is unable to make a decision. Under s 5, 16/17-year-olds who are reasonably believed to fail the MCA test may be treated in what is reasonably believed to be their best interests. The 2005 Act is silent on the law applying to those who satisfy

---

86 [1998] 2 FLR 810, 813.

87 [1998] 2 FLR 810, 812 and 813.

88 Other examples of statutory provisions that distinguish between a child of 16 or 17 and other minors (such as the Children Act 1989, s 9(6)) are listed by Munby LJ in *Re D* [2017] EWCA Civ 1695, [64].

89 See Pattinson 2006, 159, and Pattinson 2017b, 162. See also Munby 2010, 519.

Gillick: consent from a child 69

the MCA test. At common law, an adult who satisfies the MCA test has capacity to consent to, or refuse, medical treatment.[90] The relationship between the *Gillick* test and the MCA test was considered in the last section, where it was argued that the MCA test sets a lower threshold of understanding. It follows that it is more difficult to show that a 16/17-year-old does not satisfy the adult capacity (MCA) test than it would be to show that the child does not satisfy the *Gillick* test.

An alternative interpretation of the effect of s 8(1) of the 1969 Act is suggested by Cave, who has argued that there is an overlap between the schemes provided by the 1969 and 2005 Acts,

> but there are also points of departure. For example, a 16-year-old who cannot make a decision because he lacks maturity is likely to have MCA capacity but lack competence [ie capacity in my terminology] under the Family Law Reform Act.[91]

Since Cave expressly recognises that both Acts operate a presumption of capacity, this implies that she considers the presumption operated by the 1969 Act in relation to consent to medical treatment to be easier to rebut that the presumption operated by the 2005 Act. In other words, the claim being made is that the capacity test for consent to medical treatment under the 1969 Act is the *Gillick* test. This is also the implication of Cave's more recent article in which, when addressing 'medical treatment decisions made by minors aged 16/17', she points out that:

> the MCA Code of Practice recognizes that while some 16/17 year olds might lack capacity due to an impairment of the mind or brain (so as to satisfy the test for incapacity in section 2), others 'will be unable to make a decision for some other reason' in which case they 'should be assessed under common law principles'.[92]

This issue has received some judicial attention. In *Re W*, Lord Donaldson declared that where s 8 applies,

> [n]o question of '*Gillick* competence' in common law terms arises. The 16- or 17-year-old is conclusively presumed to be '*Gillick* competent' or, alternatively, the test of '*Gillick* competence' is bypassed and has no relevance.[93]

---

90 See eg *Re MB* [1997] 2 FLR 426 and *Re B* [2002] EWHC 429, which applied the common law predecessor to ss 2–3 MCA (*Re C* [1994] 1 WLR 290). There are two provisos to this claim: the compulsory treatment powers under the Mental Health Act 1983 and the court's inherent jurisdiction to protect vulnerable adults (considered below).

91 Cave 2014, 105.

92 Cave 2015, 90, quoting Department for Constitutional Affairs 2007, [12.13].

93 [1993] Fam 64, 77.

70 Gillick: consent from a child

There are also pre-MCA cases in which the adult capacity test is applied to 16/17-year-olds[94] and the President of the Family Division and Court of Protection (Sir James Munby) has provided extrajudicial support for this interpretation of the 1969 Act.[95]

In a recent case concerning a 17-year-old who was refusing life-saving treatment, Baker J stated that a child 'with capacity under 18 who is "*Gillick* competent" . . . is deemed to have legal capacity to consent to treatment'.[96] But closer examination indicates that little reliance can be placed on this dicta, because Baker J stressed that the case was decided as a matter of 'extreme urgency' without 'lengthy submissions or analysis' and, crucially, his judgment makes no mention of s 8(1) of the 1969 Act.[97] More recently, Sir James Munby, giving the leading judgment of the Court of Appeal, declared:

> Given that there is no longer any 'magic' in the age of 16, given the principle that '*Gillick* capacity' is 'child-specific', the reality is that, in any particular context, one child may have '*Gillick* capacity' at the age of 15, while another may not have acquired '*Gillick* capacity' at the age of 16 and another may not have acquired '*Gillick* capacity' even by the time he or she reaches the age of 18.[98]

His Lordship's conclusion in the case before him was that where a 16- or 17-year-old lacked '*Gillick*-capacity', a parent could consent to arrangements made for that child that would otherwise amount to a deprivation of liberty under the 2005 Act. Munby P reasoned that 'the exercise of parental responsibility comes to an end not on the attaining of some fixed age but on attaining "*Gillick* capacity"'.[99] These references to *Gillick* capacity make no concessions for s 8(1) of the Family Law Reform Act, but it would be odd if they did given that Munby P was referring to the limits of parental consent, rather than the limits of a child's consent. His Lordship's reasoning is neutral on the question of whether the consent of a 16- or 17-year-old child to medical treatment (which need not involve a deprivation of liberty) is valid where that child has MCA capacity but lacks *Gillick* capacity.

It is also worth quoting the section of the MCA Code of Practice cited by Cave at greater length:

---

94 *A Metropolitan Borough Council v AB* [1997] 1 FLR 767, 773, and *Re C (Detention: Medical Treatment)* [1997] 2 FLR 180, 195–196, applied the common law adult capacity test laid down in *Re C* [1994] 1 WLR 290 to a 17 and 16-year-old, respectively.
95 Munby 2010, 519.
96 *An NHS Foundation Hospital v P* [2014] EWHC 1650, [12].
97 [2014] EWHC 1650, [2].
98 *Re D* [2017] EWCA Civ 1695, [84].
99 [2017] EWCA Civ 1695, [125].

Even where a young person is presumed to have legal capacity to consent to treatment, they may not necessarily be able to make the relevant decision. As with adults, decision-makers should assess the young person's capacity to consent to the proposed care or treatment . . . . If a young person lacks capacity to consent within section 2(1) of the Act because of an impairment of, or disturbance in the functioning of, the mind or brain then the Mental Capacity Act will apply in the same way as it does to those who are 18 and over. If however they are unable to make the decision for some other reason, for example *because they are overwhelmed by the implications of the decision*, the Act will not apply to them and the legality of any treatment should be assessed under common law principles.[100]

On the face of it, this paragraph supports the view that the capacity test for a 16/17-year-old to consent does not align with the adult capacity test. Such an interpretation invites the response that the Code of Practice cannot override the clear wording of the 1969 Act. The Code of Practice has legal status in relation to the 2005 Act,[101] but not in relation to the 1969 Act or the common law applying to matters not covered by the Act.

The view expressed in the quoted paragraph does, however, align with the wording of the 1969 Act if an adult would be equally unable to consent in those circumstances. In 2012, the Court of Appeal confirmed that the court's inherent jurisdiction could be used to protect vulnerable adults who just satisfy the MCA test, but are nonetheless unable to make a decision by reason of 'constraint, coercion, undue influence or other vitiating factor'.[102] In a subsequent case, Baker J held that the inherent jurisdiction could even be used in a medical context to protect an adult who also lacked capacity under the MCA test.[103] These developments are controversial[104] and create some uncertainty as to when an adult may lack capacity outside the 2005 Act. It may be that a vulnerable adult who does not have an impairment or disturbance in the mind or brain but is nonetheless 'overwhelmed by the implications of the decision' could be protected by the court's inherent jurisdiction. If so, then a child's consent may lack legal force in those circumstances while remaining 'as effective as' that of an adult.

The approach to adult capacity just mooted would ensure that capacity tracks competence, because a vulnerable adult who is overwhelmed by the implications

---

100 Department for Constitutional Affairs 2007, [12.13] (emphasis added). Para 12.22 also refers to a child who lacks 'capacity within section 2(1) or for some other reason'.

101 Those seeking to rely on the 2005 Act have a legal duty to have regard to its provisions (s 42(4)) and failure to do so will be taken into account in any subsequent legal proceedings (s 42(5)).

102 *Re L* [2012] EWCA Civ 253, [10] and [31]–[32].

103 *A NHS Trust v A* [2013] EWHC 2442. His Lordship held that force-feeding A was permissible under the court's inherent jurisdiction, even though it was not permissible on the facts under either the Mental Health Act 1983 (ibid, [78]–[80]) or the 2005 Act (ibid, [66]).

104 See eg Hewson 2013.

72 Gillick: consent from a child

of the decision would not have competence on the definition used in this chapter. This is because a cognitive-functional definition of competence requires that the patient be considered (1) to have the cognitive ability to understand and (2) able to exercise that ability in the context under consideration. Thus, a patient who is, say, completely overcome with emotion every time she thinks about her cancer is incompetent to make decisions concerning her cancer, even if she is considered cognitively able to make other decisions at an equivalent level of complexity. It follows that if, contrary to the view suggested above, an adult who was unequivocally overwhelmed was still regarded as having made a capacitated decision, then that adult's consent would be fictionalised.

It seems to me that debates on the import of the 1969 Act could easily have been foreclosed if their Lordships in *Gillick* had placed the capacity test for children under 16 in its wider legal context. Setting down a child capacity test before articulating the adult capacity test is a recipe for gaps and inconsistency.

3.3.4 Other jurisdictions and international instruments

Other jurisdictions were also much quicker to recognise the autonomy of adults than children.[105] Nonetheless, by the time of *Gillick*, there had been judicial recognition of the capacity of mature minors to consent to medical treatment. In *Johnston v Wellesley Hospital*, the Ontario High Court rejected the argument that the 20-year-old plaintiff could not consent to medical treatment on the basis that he was then below the age of majority (21).[106] Addy J expressly approved the opinion of the author of a textbook that 'an infant who is capable of appreciating fully the nature and consequences of a particular operation or of particular treatment can give an effective consent thereto'.[107] Just over a decade later, the US Supreme Court confirmed that a state ordinance could not make a blanket determination that all minors under the age of 15 were too immature to make abortion decisions.[108] The US Supreme Court has yet to consider treatment refusals by mature minors.[109]

The approach in *Gillick* itself was quickly approved in other common law jurisdictions. Only a year later, the Alberta Court of Appeal applied Lord Scarman's principle and ruled that a pregnant 16-year-old had 'sufficient intelligence and understanding to make up her own mind' on abortion.[110] She could thus consent

---

105 For early recognition that treatment of an adult without consent is a battery, see the US case of *Schloendorff v Society of New York Hospital* (1914) 211 NY 125, 129.
106 (1970) 17 DLR (3d) 139.
107 (1970) 17 DLR (3d) 139, 143.
108 *City of Akron v Akron Center for Reproductive Health, Inc*, 462 US 416 (1983), 417.
109 A point also made by Lennings 2015, 461.
110 *C (JS) v Wren* (1986) 76 AR 115.

Gillick: *consent from a child* 73

to an abortion against her parents' wishes. In 1992, Australia's highest court similarly declared that *Gillick* 'reflect[s] the common law in Australia'.[111]

The retreat from *Gillick* in *Re W* has been cited with approval in many recent cases. In *AC v Manitoba*, the Supreme Court of Canada held that provincial legislation, which provided for children under the age of 16 to be treated against their will, was not in conflict with the Canadian Charter of Rights and Freedoms.[112] Abella J, giving the principal judgment, examined *Re W* and noted that Canadian and international jurisprudence 'have not generally seen the "mature minor" doctrine as dictating guaranteed outcomes, particularly where the consequences for the young person are catastrophic'.[113] In *X*, the New South Wales Court of Appeal similarly cited *Re W* with approval and upheld a trial judge's overruling of the refusal of blood products by a child of the Jehovah's Witnesses faith.[114] This was despite that child being only four months away from his eighteenth birthday and the trial judge considering him 'a mature child of high intelligence'.[115] The Court of Appeal reasoned that *Gillick* 'does not diminish the scope of the *parens patriae* jurisdiction'.[116] In *Jamie*, the Full Court of the Family Court of Australia took a contrasting approach to the relationship between *Gillick* and the *parens patriae* jurisdiction.[117] The Family Court held that an 11-year-old child could consent to treatment for gender identity disorder on the basis that the court has no role to play 'if the child is *Gillick* competent'.[118] It is difficult to reconcile these two decisions of intermediate appeal courts.[119] There is, at its core, legal debate about whether the *parens patriae* powers are triggered by minority or incompetent minority.

National developments now operate in a context of international instruments providing legal recognition for the rights of children, particularly the United Nations Convention on the Rights of the Child (UNCRC) 1989.[120] Article 12 of the UNCRC requires that those with the ability to form their own views are recognised as having the right to express those views freely in all matters affecting them, with 'the views of the child being given due weight in accordance with the

---

111 *Secretary, Department of Health and Community Services (NT) v JWB and SMB* (Marion's Case) (1992) 175 CLR 218, [24]. The High Court of Australia went on to rule that non-therapeutic sterilisation was beyond parental capacity and required juridical approval.
112 [2009] 2 SCR 181.
113 [2009] 2 SCR 181, [69].
114 *X v The Sydney Children's Hospitals Network* [2013] NSWCA 320.
115 *The Sydney Children's Hospital Network v X* [2013] NSWSC 368, [50]. See also [2013] NSWCA 320, [47].
116 [2013] NSWCA 320, [46].
117 *Re Jamie (No 2)* (2013) 278 FLR 155.
118 (2013) 278 FLR 155, [129].
119 See Lennings 2015, esp 463–466.
120 See further Freeman 2000.

74 Gillick: consent from a child

age and maturity of the child'. This, however, seems to be compatible with *Re W*, because a child can be involved in decision-making relevant to matters affecting her without being granted the final say (capacity).

3.4 Application of the PGC

3.4.1 Relational autonomy

It is increasingly common for contemporary scholarship, particularly feminist scholarship, to commend a relational view of individual decision-making. The term 'relational autonomy' is used to refer to a range of views on self-determination or self-governance that share the assumption that 'persons are socially embedded and that agents' identities are formed within the context of social relationships and shaped by a complex of intersecting social determinants, such as race, class, gender, and ethnicity'.[121] Such views deny that we are 'atomistic individuals'[122] in the sense of 'self-made or self-sufficient beings who exist in complete isolation from others'.[123] They combine a social conception of self with an individual conception of autonomy.[124] These claims need to be carefully unpacked.

Four preliminary points from Chapter 1 are worth restating here in alternative form. *First*, the locus of any dialectical argument or practical precept (a rule, norm or principle) must be an agent, understood as a being that acts for freely chosen purposes. Conceptually, such a being need not be human, be gendered, exist in a community or interact with others; but a particular agent could be all of these things. This is because a particular agent is not *merely* an agent.[125] I cannot be an agent without being the particular agent that I am, just as I cannot be the particular (socially embedded) agent that I am without being an agent.[126] *Secondly*, to act for freely chosen purposes in this sense is not to suppose free will over determinism. Anna need only possess a phenomenological awareness of herself as having her own chosen purposes for her to be able to reason dialectically with regard to practical precepts. *Thirdly*, the PGC can be defended as a dialectically necessary or dialectically contingent commitment. The dialectically necessary argument derives the PGC as a strict implication of agential self-understanding, whereas dialectically contingent arguments rely on additional premises that can be denied without implicitly denying that one is an agent.[127] The former, if sound, requires all agents to accept the PGC (that all agents have will-rights to the generic conditions of agency) and reject the contrary claims of communitarian, virtue and

---

121 Mackenzie & Stoljar 2000, 4. See also Nedelsky 1989, Christman 2004 and Kalbian 2005, 94.
122 Nedelsky 1989, 8.
123 Bauman 2008, 445.
124 Christman 2004, 146.
125 See Brown 2016, esp 82–84.
126 Beyleveld 2017b.
127 See 1.3.1 and 1.3.2.

relativistic ethics. *Fourthly*, to avoid denying that the PGC is categorical, Anna (any agent) must interpret her experiences and the beings with whom she interacts according to the principle of precaution. This means that she must treat all those whom she can meaningfully treat as agents (*ostensible agents*)[128] as agents, even if she thinks that any such being is acting on incoherent or irrational beliefs or is morally unworthy of being treated as an agent with generic rights.

These four points are consistent with a variant of relational autonomy, or at least with some claims typically made in favour of a 'relational' over an 'individualist' model of autonomy.[129] They require that the human subjects of English law be regarded as 'individuals' with rights, but not as isolated and separate from their context and relations with others.[130] This is because the contingent context and relations of an individual in her community are relevant to the identification of what needs to be done to protect her possession of the generic conditions and enable her to exercise her generic rights. The attempt to recognise and give effect to the generic rights of any ostensible agent will, in other words, require that contextual pressures, power imbalances and decision-making needs are taken into account as part of the process of determining whether she has exercised her rights.[131]

According to Christman, what makes 'a conception of autonomy *uniquely* "relational" or "social" is that among its defining conditions are requirements concerning the interpersonal or social environment of the agent'.[132] Relational autonomy theories can be divided into 'procedural' and 'substantive' accounts.[133] 'Procedural' accounts focus on the decision-making process and remain neutral on the content of individual decisions. In contrast, 'substantive' accounts demand that particular values or commitments be part of the agent's decision and claim that expressed preferences that do not comply with this demand or are made in contexts that are not conductive to compliance with this demand cannot be autonomous.

Stoljar defends a substantive account of relational autonomy by appeal to what she calls '*the feminist intuition*, which claims that preferences influenced by oppressive norms of femininity cannot be autonomous'.[134] She argues that procedural theories of autonomy are incompatible with this intuition, because they do not regard decisions as non-autonomous when the decision-maker has internalised 'false norms' ('such as that women should not actively desire sex or prepare for sex in advance, that pregnancy is an expression of "real" womanhood . . .') and

---

128 See the discussion in ch 1 (1.3.3).
129 McLean similarly seeks a midpoint between these two models of autonomy and concludes that '[h]uman rights are both individualistic and relational': 2010, 32.
130 See also Gewirth 1988, esp 141, and Gewirth 1996, esp 117.
131 Reasoning of this type will be attributed to Lady Athena in the final chapter of this book to support the principled development of the common law doctrine of undue influence in *U v Centre for Reproductive Medicine* [2002] EWCA Civ 565 (see 6.4.2).
132 Christman 2004, 31 (emphasis in original).
133 See Mackenzie & Stoljar 2000, 19–21, Christman 2004 and Donnelly 2010, 31.
134 Stoljar 2000, 95 (emphasis in original).

76 Gillick: *consent from a child*

is thereby unable to recognise them as false.[135] Stoljar would, it seems, regard as non-autonomous an infertile woman's request for medical assistance to reproduce where that request is underpinned by a belief that 'pregnancy and motherhood increase her worthiness' as a woman.[136] But Stoljar's view rests on no more than a 'feminist intuition'. She offers no other reason why Anna (any agent) must accept that she has not exercised her will merely because others consider her decision to be the product of her internalising an 'oppressive norm of femininity'.

Under the PGC, the role for agential self-governance is centred on the exercise of an individual's generic rights[137] and these rights are subject to the generic rights of others. The 'oppressive norms of femininity' identified by Stoljar are unethical *as other-regarding maxims* as they restrict the ability of women to maintain and acquire the generic conditions of agency against their will. It does not, however, follow that an agent would cease to be an agent or even fail to exercise her own generic rights by acting on such oppressive norms. Anna could have freely chosen to act on a particular maxim, in the sense presupposed by agency, even if that maxim is unethical when applied to others or is otherwise irrational. The restrictive norms cited by Stoljar also do not involve the complete subservience of Anna's will to an other.[138]

Before considering what is required to regard a preference expressed by the patient as representing her will on the exercise of her rights, we should consider the extent to which healthcare decisions engage the rights of others. It would be a mistake to think that – aside from issues of resource allocation, conscientious objection and diseases/conditions presenting a danger to others – healthcare decisions are of relevance to the patient alone. Many healthcare decisions also have consequences for the generic needs of others, including those others for whom the patient cares or who care for her. For example, someone who cares for another can be profoundly affected by her decision to have an abortion or refuse a life-saving blood transfusion, and a patient who is responsible for the care of a young child or an elderly parent can profoundly affect them by accepting or refusing treatment directed to her own needs.

Under the PGC, however, the crucial issue is not merely whether the generic interests of others are affected, but whether they could plausibly take precedence over the patient's generic rights. The patient's positive duties to others are subject to the comparative cost proviso[139] and her treatment decisions will almost invariably

---

135 Stoljar 2000, 109.

136 Stoljar (2000, 109) identifies this belief as a 'false' norm.

137 For an agent to exercise her generic rights is for her to freely choose to either defend her possession of the generic capacities or accept damage to her possession of the generic capacities.

138 Complete subservience of one's will to another involves not just waiving the benefit of one's generic rights, but denying that one has the generic rights. Voluntary slavery must therefore be rejected as a function of the rationally necessary commitment to the PGC: see Beyleveld & Brownsword 2001, 190. cf the discussion of the voluntary slave, subservient housewife and religious devotee in Oshana 1998 and Christman 2004, esp 149ff.

139 See ch 1 (1.3.3).

affect her own generic needs equally or more significantly than those of family members with opposed values or beliefs, family members who benefit from her care and support, and other affected persons. The power to decide whether to protect, endanger or sacrifice one's own generic interests is the essence of what it means to be an agent with dignity and generic rights. This reasoning is reinforced by Beyleveld and Brownsword's argument that an agent (again, let's call her Anna) must be granted the right to use and exclude others from her body that precludes the need for her to offer a case-by-case justification.[140] She requires 'rule-preclusionary control' over what happens to her body, because her body (however it is metaphysically related to her) is necessary for her to act for any purpose at all, and even permitting inquiry as to why she needs control over her body for a particular purpose would threaten her agency.[141] In short, Anna has a basic, rule-preclusionary right to decide for herself whether or not to accept interference with her bodily integrity. But others can only meaningfully recognise her exercise of this or any generic right when she appears to possess the requisite decision-making abilities.

3.4.2 Competence

The discussion of competence just presented requires further unpacking as to what it means for an agent to exercise her will and what is required to assess whether another has exercised her will.

Only those who display the attributes of agency (ostensible agents) can meaningfully be treated as acting for the purpose of exercising a right, and the specific cognitive-functional abilities required will depend on the particular right and context. In other words, what is required to make a decision on a specific purpose is not simply agency, but (specific task) *competence:* the cognitive-functional ability to act for that task in that context. This requires possession of the *cognitive ability* to understand and weigh the information relevant to performing that specific task and the *functional ability* to exercise that cognitive ability in the situation in question. Competence, so understood, is the point at which an individual is judged to possess sufficient cognitive-functional ability to understand and weigh the information relevant to her decision. Information is relevant to the exercise of a generic right if it concerns her possession of the generic conditions of agency or something that may lead her to choose to sacrifice or endanger a generic condition. Thus, for a patient to be competent she must be considered (cognitively and functionally) able to identify and weigh her desires in relation to the likely consequences of her decision on her possession of the generic conditions.

Since a patient will be socially embedded, her relationships with others (particularly, but not exclusively, those for whom she cares or care for her) will be

---

140 See Beyleveld & Brownsword 2001, ch 8, and the discussion in the final chapter of this book (6.4.5).
141 See Beyleveld & Brownsword 2001, 188.

78 Gillick: consent from a child

relevant to both her desires and her possession of the generic conditions. The focus, nonetheless, is on the patient's exercise of *her* generic rights. It follows that the appropriate account of her will is procedural, rather than substantive, in the sense that her will need not defer to the interests of others to be identified as such. The version of relational autonomy that is consistent with the PGC is therefore one that situates an individual in her social context, rather than limits what may be identified as her will.

Competence is the judgment that a patient has displayed sufficient ability to understand the relevant information and weigh her desires in relation to that information. The threshold of expected informational understanding and reflection displayed by the patient must accord with the nature of the particular decision. *Informational understanding* can range from the broad-brush to the detailed; from understanding only the general nature and effects of what is to be done to understanding the detailed nature and effects of the full range of available options. Similarly, the process of *weighing desires* can range from intuitive to considered evaluation. These reflective options are well captured by Gerald Dworkin's distinction between first- and second-order desires[142] and John Coggon's distinction between 'current desire autonomy' (decision-making according to impulsive desires or settled desires on which she has not reflected) and 'best desire autonomy'.[143]

The easy case for a designation of competence is where the patient – let's call her Patience – displays the ability to weigh the nature and consequences (for herself and others) of the treatment proposed, the available alternatives and non-treatment, and thereby determine her overall choice, even if it runs contrary to her immediate desires, with regard to her generic interests. This level of understanding and reflection requires a high level of cognitive-functional ability and, assuming no relevant defects in her voluntariness or informational resources, provides the strongest possible support for the conclusion that she has exercised her will in relation to her generic rights.[144] It involves Patience exercising her *reflective will*.

Patience, however, exercises her generic rights, using both her reflective and unreflective will. That is to say, she may exercise her will by considered evaluation with detailed informational understanding and by unevaluated intuition with only general informational understanding. She is indeed entitled to insist that others respect her unreflective will where the matter does not apparently endanger her own or others' generic interests or the process of requiring more from her would itself disproportionately endanger her generic interests. If every decision had to represent her reflective will, then her ability to pursue her purposes as such would be seriously restricted. Purpose-restricting burdens are placed on Patience

---

142 Dworkin 1988, 15–20.

143 Coggon 2007, 240.

144 What Coggon calls 'ideal desire autonomy', where the patient's decision-making is 'measured by reference to some purportedly universal or objective standard of values' (Coggon 2007, 240), can be dismissed here as not tracking the patient's will. See further below.

every time she is asked to exercise her reflective will or display evidence to others that she has done so. And, in many situations, treating Patience's expressed preference as her will does not require her to be regarded as choosing to sacrifice or endanger a generic condition. It is for this reason that others may not ordinarily ask for more than her unreflective will when she selects sparkling over still water or seeks to spend her leisure time reading, watching television, visiting a museum or any equivalent activity. Her unreflective will should similarly suffice when she seeks to permit physical contact that is not likely to endanger her generic interests. That is to say that for many purposes her expressed agreement, preference or selection may be treated as representing her will where it signals no more than a current desire with understanding of only its general nature and effects. This is not disconsonant with everyday practice for most social interactions. In practice, an adult's unreflective will is accepted for activities as important as voting in elections and deceased organ donation, and evidence suggests that patients frequently fail to exercise their reflective will.[145]

There are, however, circumstances where treating Patience's expressed preference as her will involves regarding her as choosing to sacrifice or endanger a generic condition for which mere whim and general understanding will not do. Competence as a moral judgment must be risk-relative in the sense that riskier outcomes require a greater indication of cognitive-functional ability. Nonetheless, even where giving effect to Patience's expressed preference almost inevitably involves her sacrificing her most basic generic needs, the identification of her will cannot require more than it be her reflective will. The demands placed upon her when identifying her signalled preference as her will must align with the waivability of the benefit of her rights and her basic right to make self-regarding decisions with regard to her bodily integrity.

Imagine Ned, a nurse, offers to clean and bandage Patience's open wound. He seeks to prevent infection and stem significant blood loss in what is otherwise an unexceptional situation. Patience's reflective will would be displayed if she has apparently made a decision following reflection on the nature and consequences (for herself and others) of cleaning and bandaging as opposed to leaving the wound untreated. But her signalled consent need not capture her reflective will for it to be regarded as her will. Giving effect to her signalled will accords with what is most likely to protect her generic interests and, even if she is incapable of considering and weighing all the probable consequences of leaving the wound untreated, since she is signalling consent she does not thereby fail to consider whether she is willing to accept generic harm. To exercise her right to bodily integrity in these circumstances, all she needs to understand is that she is permitting her wound to be bandaged to help it to get better. In contrast, if she were both refusing treatment and incapable of considering the consequences of leaving

---

145 Empirical studies suggest that 'patients frequently fail to understand the information they are told or are expected to read': Berg et al 2001, 65.

80 Gillick: consent from a child

the wound untreated, then giving effect to her wishes as signalled would involve treating her as accepting a risk to her generic interests that she has not actually accepted. Thus, Ned should ask that Patience's refusal indicates her reflective will before giving effect to it.

Insofar as medical treatment is likely to be supportive of a patient's generic needs and refusal is likely to be counter to her generic needs, the threshold for competence may vary for these two options. I say 'insofar as' because not all procedures and treatments are equivalent to the bandaging of an open wound. Some healthcare interventions are irreversible and carry additional long-term consequences for the patient, her familial-social relations or the generic needs of others. Notable examples are gender reassignment, sterilisation and experimental treatment. This also applies to interventions not directed at the patient's treatment needs, such as organ donation, participation in clinical research and ritual circumcision. Conversely, some non-interventions are unlikely to have long-term consequences for anyone. If basic generic harm is likely to result, or if divergent likely consequences need to be balanced, then the cognitive-functional abilities required for competence will be those required for the patient to display her reflective will.

Where the patient lacks the requisite abilities, then treating her as having capacity will fictionalise the decision ascribed to her. That does not mean that a patient's expressed preference lacks normative force if she is not quite competent. A patient with some level of decision-making ability can still participate in decision-making up to the limit of those abilities. And the involvement of those for whom she cares may well facilitate the exercise and development of her cognitive-functional abilities. The Mental Capacity Act's injunction that those who lack capacity under the Act be treated in their best interests requires in s 4(4) that the patient 'so far as reasonably practicable' be permitted and encouraged to participate, or improve her ability to participate, as fully as possible in any act done for her and any decision affecting her, and s 4(7) requires consultation with anyone engaged in caring for the patient or interested in her welfare. *Gillick* is less clear on the first of these points.

Many cases involving mature children involve the difficult situation where the patient is perceived to be an agent with behaviour that could reasonably lead to different views on whether the patient is competent against the relevant threshold. The mechanism for determining whether a patient displaying borderline abilities is competent to make a treatment decision will need to operate in accordance with moral precaution in two ways.

On the one hand, efforts to assist the patient to make a decision must be proportionate to the harm of *mistakenly treating a competent agent as incompetent*. All things being equal, a patient bordering on the threshold of being considered incompetent must be provided with assistance, because she has positive rights to possession of the generic conditions and the harm inflicted upon her by mistakenly designating her as incompetent will outweigh the harm inflicted by requiring that a reasonable level of help be provided by others, including by the healthcare professional treating her. This precautionary mechanism is consistent with procedural relational autonomy and is reflected in the Mental Capacity Act's principle that an individual is not to be treated as lacking capacity 'unless all practical steps to help . . . have been taken without success'.[146] No such precautionary assistance was advocated by their Lordships in *Gillick*.

On the other hand, the level of scrutiny given to the (assisted) patient's decision-making abilities must be proportionate to the harm of *mistakenly treating an incompetent patient as competent*. This means that the procedure for identifying an expressed preference as an autonomous decision – which goes beyond the threshold issue considered above – may properly be more demanding where giving effect to that preference threatens significant generic harm to the patient or others. For this reason, particular care needs to be taken before designating as autonomous a child's refusal of life-saving treatment. This approach, in which the assessment of competence in borderline cases operates under precaution, is to be contrasted with the approach of English law to a mature child's capacity to refuse treatment in *Re R* and *Re W*. The approach in those cases was to enable the refusal of a mature child to be overridden by a parent or the court *even if she is considered competent*. The PGC supports *weak risk-relativity*, whereby the threshold (reflective versus unreflective will) and procedural safeguards (such as the burden of proof) may vary in accordance with the risk of generic harm. The PGC does not support the *strong risk-relativity* adopted in *Re W* and by some theorists,[147] whereby a serious risk could support depriving a competent patient of capacity over her own treatment. There can be no place under the PGC for prioritising a child's future interests, including her long-term autonomy, over her reflective will.[148]

Grubb claims that 'consent or refusal of consent by a competent child must be opposites of the same coin'.[149] Such a claim is intuitively appealing, but I have just argued that the threshold for competence for consent to many forms of treatment may properly differ from the threshold for competence for refusal. Now, I am arguing that the procedure for determining whether the relevant threshold has been reached in borderline cases should also take account of the likely consequences for that patient's generic interests. The precautionary judgment as to whether a patient with borderline abilities *is or is not competent* may thus vary according to, for example, whether she is consenting to or refusing life-sustaining treatment. I therefore find myself agreeing with the conclusion of Gilmore and Herring that 'refusing medical treatment is not always the simple obverse of consenting to a particular treatment'.[150] Gilmore and Herring, however, do not seek to rest their conclusion directly on risk-relativity because they do not distinguish the weak version from the strong version.[151]

---

146 s 1(3) and Cave 2015, 96.
147 See eg Ross 1998, 7 and 12: 'competency is a necessary but not a sufficient condition to require respect for the child's autonomy'.
148 The PGC therefore rejects the 'moral argument' for restricting a competent child's 'short-term autonomy' in favour of the 'child's lifetime autonomy': Ross 1998, 61.
149 Grubb 1993a, 62.
150 Gilmore & Herring 2011a, 5.
151 See Gilmore & Herring 2011a, 20–21.

82 Gillick: *consent from a child*

Much of the above discussion has referred to patients as such, rather than children as patients. Calendar age is relevant to species developmental expectations, but it is not itself a measure of either ostensible agency or competence. A child's unreflective will is usually displayed (albeit inconsistently) from a very young age and displays of reflective will (in the absence of a serious impairment) start well below the legally relevant ages of 16 and 18. Freeman has pointed out that evidence going back over two decades demonstrates that some, albeit it not many, 'young child can be highly competent, technically, cognitively, socially and morally'.[152]

3.5 Options available to Lady Athena

This book's project is to provide an idealised judgment for each of the four focal cases and thereafter to treat that judgment as if it were the majority view. To enable Lady Athena's judgment to be the ratio of the House of Lords in *Gillick*, I will consider the panel to have seven members, which did sometimes happen in particularly important cases.[153] Readers are asked to imagine, first, that the two additional members simply agree with Lady Athena and, secondly, a slight amendment to the speech of Lord Bridge, Lord Scarman or both, so that they agree with the views expressed by Lady Athena. Indeed, since Lady Athena's speech could be viewed as giving effect to a particular interpretation of Lord Scarman's speech, his Lordship may well have agreed with her judgment. His use of the language of legal principle and rights certainly fits easily with modified law as integrity.

I have argued that what is required to conclude that a patient is competent varies in accordance with the consequences for her generic interests, because this determines the nature of the generic rights she is exercising and the procedural hurdles supported by weak risk-relativity. Since, however, the law of trespass requires unlawful contact and the law of negligence requires actionable harm, there will be circumstances in which the law does not track the protection and exercise of the patient's generic rights. One way of addressing this would be to reshape the underlying legal wrongs. I was therefore tempted to revisit the decision of the House of Lords in *Sidaway*,[154] which was decided earlier in the same year as *Gillick*, to broaden the legal wrongs committed by a failure to obtain adequate consent. This could be done by extending the law of negligence, establishing a fiduciary duty owed by doctors to their patients or, probably more profitably, recognising a new vindicatory tort that is actionable per se.[155] I decided against this approach because the law of negligence has subsequently

---

152 Freeman 2007, 13.
153 See eg *Murphy v Brentwood District Council* [1991] 1 AC 398, *Pepper v Hart* [1993] AC 593, and *Arthur JS Hall v Simons* [2002] 1 AC 615. There were in fact only 10, out of the then maximum of 11, Law Lords at the time of the *Gillick* case: Dickson 1999, 129.
154 *Sidaway v Board of Governors of the Bethlem Royal Hospital* [1985] AC 871.
155 On fiduciary duties see Brazier 1987, 190–191, Grubb 1994, Bartlett 1997, Brazier & Lobjoit 1999, and Brazier & Glover 2000, 379. cf Kennedy 1996, esp 137–140.

been extended in the appropriate direction.[156] Lady Athena's speech will instead focus attention on those matters of medical law that she can deal with using the case law as it was. There is, for example, scope for her to align the adult and child capacity test. Williams was critical of their Lordships' failure to do this, arguing that what their Lordships gave with one hand, by accepting that a person under 16 can consent to common assault, they took away with the other, by concluding 'that the consent is ineffective if the child cannot assess risks that many adults would be unable to assess'.[157] As already argued above, under the PGC what matters is possession of sufficient cognitive-functional abilities, rather than age.

When attempting to translate the conclusions derived from the PGC into legal principles, we need to bear in mind four further points.

First, assessments of an individual patient's abilities are likely to be subject to the biases and values of the assessor. It is well recognised that children, like women and members of ethnic minorities, are more likely to be judged incompetent by healthcare professionals.[158] There is, according to Archard, a tendency to 'infantilise' children in the sense of regarding them as 'cute, lovable creatures, but above all, weak, vulnerable and dependent'.[159] It has also been pointed out that a health professional's values, particularly with regard to end of life decisions, are similarly liable to influence findings of incompetence.[160] Critics of empowering children often bring these two tendencies together in the view that children lack the life experience required to make life-changing decisions on matters such as refusal of medical treatment.[161] While understanding may be assisted by experience, we must be wary of asserting that it requires it, because this overlooks the faculties of empathy and imagination. In any event, children living with chronic, recurrent and familial conditions will have direct experience,[162] which is more pertinent than lived years or 'professional, textbook knowledge'.[163] Lady Athena will therefore warn against these tendencies and emphasise that cognitive-functional ability is not determined by the stroke of midnight on a particular birthday or by other blanket assumptions.

Secondly, the law operates within a context of limited healthcare resources in which a doctor will have limited time to come to terms with legal requirements and assess a patient's competence against those requirements. Indeed, some have doubted that the existing *Gillick* test is one that a doctor could apply in practice. This is a further reason for supporting a decision made by a patient that is indicative of only her unreflective will, where the consequences of following the

---

156 See, in particular, *Chester v Afshar* [2004] UKHL 41 and *Montgomery v Lanarkshire Health Board* [2015] UKSC 11.
157 Williams 1985, 1180.
158 Stefan 1993 and Foster 1998.
159 Archard 2015, 243.
160 Martyn & Bourguignon 2000.
161 Ross 1998, 61–62.
162 Hagger 2009, 235–236.
163 Alderson & Goodwin 1993, 305.

84 Gillick: consent from a child

patient's expressed preference are unlikely to be serious for the patient. It is also a reason why the law will need to utilise rules of thumb and rebuttable presumptions, as indeed it does with s 8 of the Family Law Reform Act.

Thirdly, the socio-relational context is one of significant power imbalances. For a start, there is a power imbalance in the relationship between a healthcare professional and her patient in light of the latter's reliance on the former at a time of need, uncertainty and, often, ill health. This point has particular poignance if we accept the views of those who consider *Gillick*, especially Lord Fraser's speech, to have transferred decision-making authority from parents to doctors, rather than to adolescent patients.[164] As stated above, however, it is debatable whether Lord Scarman's approach transfers power to the doctor beyond what is necessary to enable the exercise of child autonomy. The parent-child relationship is also characterised by unequal power and influence, and the core of child empowerment requires a doctor to take seriously a child's claim that parental involvement is likely to force a particular outcome.

Fourthly, if a competent decision cannot be overridden in what the court considers to be a child's best interests, then judges may be tempted to make 'convenient findings' of incompetence.[165] As Lennings has pointed out, an artificial finding of incompetence denigrates children's 'decision-making integrity with the added insult of being labelled "incompetent" to decide their own fate'.[166] The courts notably did this in cases in which adult women refused caesarean sections in late pregnancy, before the Court of Appeal expressly declared such practices to be unacceptable (see Chapter 5). Lady Athena will therefore need to be explicit in her warning against over-eagerness to find incompetence.

The idealised judgment below draws on academic commentary, particularly commentary published after *Gillick*.[167] It lays the ground for the idealised judgment in *Re MB* in Chapter 5 (5.6).

---

164 See eg Teff 1994, 39 and the discussion above at 3.2.2.
165 Huxtable 2000.
166 Lennings 2015, 468.
167 See, in particular, Skegg 1973; Smith 1989, 64–68; Bainham 1999; and Freeman 2005, 206.

3.6 Idealised judgment: *Gillick v West Norfolk and Wisbech AHA* (HL)

To be cited in later judgments as:
Gillick v. West Norfolk and Wisbech A.H.A. [1985] R.L.C. 2
17 October 1985

Lady Athena

My Lords, Victoria Gillick challenges the lawfulness of a Memorandum of Guidance ("the guidance") issued by the Department of Health and Social Security. She argues that the guidance unlawfully supports the provision of contraceptive advice and treatment to girls under the age of 16, such as her five daughters, without parental knowledge or consent. The background to the case and the terms of the guidance are set out in full in the speeches of my noble and learned friends, Lord Fraser of Tullybelton and Lord Scarman, which I have had the advantage of reading in draft. I gratefully adopt the statements of fact as set out in their speeches. I too would allow the Department's appeal.

For linguistic convenience alone, I will refer to the patient as "she" and the doctor as "he". It should not need to be pointed out that the provision of treatment other than the contraceptive pill may well involve a male patient and the doctor, indeed any healthcare professional, may well be a woman.

Encouraging or aiding and abetting unlawful sexual intercourse with a girl under 16

My Lords, we have been invited to consider whether a doctor who provides contraceptive advice and treatment to a girl under 16 would be committing an offence under the Sexual Offences Act 1956. Counsel for Mrs. Gillick contends that the doctor could be aiding and abetting the commission of unlawful sexual intercourse contrary to section 6, or committing the section 28 offence of causing or encouraging the commission of unlawful sexual intercourse with a girl under 16.

My Lords, I share the view of my noble and learned friends, Lord Fraser of Tullybelton and Lord Scarman, that a doctor who follows the guidance does not ordinarily cause or encourage unlawful sexual intercourse with a girl under 16 or aid and abet the commission of unlawful sexual intercourse. With respect to my learned friends, I depart from their view that this is because a doctor who exercises a *bona fide* clinical judgment will lack the *mens rea* of intending to commit the unlawful act. It is established principle that I may intend or aid and abet an unlawful act even if my motive is laudable and its commission is not my principal purpose: see *National Coal Board v. Gamble* [1959] 1 Q.B. 11 at p. 23; *Lynch v. D.P.P. for Northern Ireland* [1975] A.C. 653 at p. 678. It has also long been recognised that the principle of double effect, which draws a sharp distinction between direct and oblique intention, is not a principle of English law: *Attorney-General's Reference (No. 1 of 1958)* [1958] R.L.C. 1. In my view, a doctor who exercises a *bona fide* clinical judgment to the effect that contraceptive treatment is

86 Gillick: consent from a child

necessary to maintain or restore the girl's health has the defence of necessity, even if he foresees that she is likely to begin or continue to engage in sexual intercourse.

In the *Bourne* case [1939] 1 K.B. 687 it was held that necessity was a defence to the statutory felony of procuring an abortion, where the act was done in good faith for the purpose of preserving the life of the mother. As I explained on behalf of the Court of Appeal in *Attorney-General's Reference (No. 1 of 1958)* [1958] R.L.C. 1, necessity was properly invoked in *Bourne* because "the mother's right to life outweighs the right to life of the unborn child". This is the principle of the lesser of two evils and it also permits a doctor to act in accordance with the patient's right to relief from pain by administering proper and proportionate palliation with life-shortening effects.

A girl has both the right to protection from unlawful sexual intercourse and the right to protection of her mental and physical health. A doctor may face a choice between risk to one right and greater risk to the other where his *bona fide* clinical judgment is that contraceptive treatment is necessary to protect a girl under 16 from the risks of an unwanted pregnancy. On the one hand, prescribing the contraceptive pill may provide some minor encouragement for the girl's boyfriend to begin or continue unlawful sexual intercourse with her. On the other hand, the doctor's *bona fide* clinical judgment is that not providing the pill poses a much greater likelihood of harm to the girl's health. In these circumstances, the least detrimental alternative is to prescribe the pill and the doctor will thereby have the defence of necessity.

Capacity to consent and refuse treatment

Mrs. Gillick relies on both statute and case law to support her claim that minors are to be regarded as lacking the (legal) capacity to consent to medical treatment. She maintains that a doctor is therefore required to obtain parental consent to avoid committing trespass and section 8 of the Family Law Reform Act 1969 provides only a limited exception to this proposition. Subsection (1) of this section provides that a minor who has attained the age of 16 may give consent to "any surgical medical or dental treatment" that is "as effective as it would be if he were of full age" with regard to what would otherwise constitute a trespass to his person. Subsection (3) elaborates that nothing in this section makes "ineffective any consent which would have been effective if this section had not been enacted". Like my noble and learned friends, Lord Fraser of Tullybelton and Lord Scarman, I read subsection (1) as simply putting beyond doubt the capacity of a child of 16 to consent to medical treatment and subsection (3) as preserving the common law with regard to the capacity of a child falling outside subsection (1). I do not accept the submission of Mrs. Gillick's counsel that until the passing of the 1969 Act, any treatment of a minor without parental consent was unlawful save where provided in an emergency or by order of a competent court. Since the 1969 Act also reduced the age of majority from 21 to 18, such a view would mean that parental consent was required to vaccinate a 20-year-old married woman with children of her own. That was not the law. Only a year before the 1969 Act was passed, the Court of Appeal in *S. v. S.*, *The Times*, 14 March 1968, cited the need for a young mother of 16 to be able to consent to any medical treatment required by her baby as a reason for granting custody to her rather than to the baby's violent father. That case seems to me to be correctly reasoned and it would be perverse if a minor could make treatment decisions for her child but not for herself.

The 1969 Act did not explicate the details of the common law position. I agree with my noble and learned friend, Lord Scarman, that we must search past cases for principles, stripped of missteps and irrelevances, capable of explaining and justifying the law on the capacity of minors. I will start with the law applying to adults, because any distinctions between the rights of adults and those of children must be restricted to those supported by principle. I will endeavour to show that the key principle applying to both those above and below the age of majority is that capacity tracks competence, which is to say the cognitive and functional ability to make the relevant decision. (I will hereafter use the phrase "cognitive-functional ability" to emphasise the interconnection between the cognitive and functional aspects of competence.) I will then endeavour to show that parental rights stem from their duties so that parental capacity dwindles in line with the child's developing decision-making abilities until the point at which the child is able to make that decision for herself. This means that a doctor may treat a competent child with that child's consent alone and a competent 15-year-old girl could, for example, refuse to be touched by her male doctor even if the doctor has parental consent.

The capacity of adults

The right to decide whether or not to consent to medical treatment is a basic human right firmly entrenched in the common law: *Schloendorff v. Society of New York Hospital* (1914) 211 N.Y. 125; *In re Conroy* (1985) 486 A.2d 1209; *S. (an Infant) v. S.* [1972] A.C. 24, 43. This point was powerfully expressed by Lord Scarman in *Sidaway v. Board of Governors of the Bethlem Royal Hospital and the Maudsley Hospital* [1985] A.C. 871, at p. 882:

> "A doctor who operates without the consent of his patient is, save in cases of emergency or mental disability, guilty of the civil wrong of trespass to the person: he is also guilty of the criminal offence of assault. The existence of the patient's right to make his own decision . . . may be seen as a basic human right protected by the common law . . ."

Even outside the context of medical treatment, adults are generally presumed to have capacity to make legally valid decisions and take legal responsibility for their actions. They are, for example, presumed to have the capacity to be held responsible for a crime: *M'Naghten's Case* (1843) 10 Cl. & F. 200, 201, as approved by this House in *R. v. Sullivan* [1984] A.C. 156, 170–171. Capacity is dependent on the particular task or decision at hand. This is well illustrated by *In the Estate of Park* [1954] P. 112. On a day shortly before his death, Mr. Park had married and a few hours later executed a new will to replace the one invalidated by his marriage. His wife, who stood to gain a greater share of his property if

88 Gillick: *consent from a child*

Mr. Park had died intestate, successfully challenged his capacity to enter into the new will. His family then challenged his capacity to get married only a few hours before he had executed the new will. They failed. The question, according to the Court of Appeal, was whether Mr. Park had been capable of understanding the nature of the act or transaction (p. 127 per Singleton L.J.; p. 129 per Birkett L.J). To understanding the nature of a "contract of marriage", Mr. Park had to have been "mentally capable of appreciating that it involves the responsibilities normally attaching to marriage" (p. 127). The Court was prepared to accept that the nature of the will in question required greater understanding than the nature of marriage, so that he could have capacity to marry but lack capacity to make that particular will (p. 122). In my view, the underlying principle is that capacity rests on competence in the sense of possession of the cognitive-functional ability to make that decision at that time. The presumption of capacity is therefore rebutted where the person in question lacks the cognitive-functional ability to understand and consider the nature and consequences of her decision.

The right to decide whether or not to consent to medical treatment is meaningful because it is not dependent upon others agreeing with the decision that is made. One consequence of the presumption of capacity is that an adult is not generally required to give a reason for her decision. As Lord Templeman put the point in *Sidaway*, at p. 904, "the patient is entitled to reject . . . [the doctor's] advice for reasons which are rational, or irrational, or for no reason". This principle should not be misunderstood. Neither the outcome nor the patient's core values need be considered wise or rational by others, but the presumption of capacity is rebuttable by a patient's demonstrable inability to understand what is proposed or consider its implications for herself and her values.

A patient's acceptance of treatment will amount to consent for the purposes of the law of trespass where she understands in broad terms the nature and purpose of that treatment: *Chatterton v. Gerson* [1981] Q.B. 432, 443. Nonetheless, a doctor may only rely on a patient's consent, or refusal, for the purposes of the law of negligence where he has disclosed the risks relating to the treatment options that a reasonable doctor would disclose, including any particularly significant risks: *Sidaway* [1985] A.C. 871, especially at p. 900, per Lord Bridge with whom Lord Keith agreed, and p. 903, per Lord Templeman. It follows that a patient needs to be able to understand and consider this information to have capacity to consent.

The most straightforward situation will be one where a patient seeks to consent to non-experimental medical treatment recommended by a healthcare professional on the basis that it is required to protect her medical interests. In such a situation a patient need only broadly understand the medical information and risks. A greater level of ability is required where the nature, purpose or implications of what is proposed are more complex. Two types of decision-making complexity come to mind. First are those situations in which the patient seeks to either consent to an intervention that is not required by her medical interests, such as non-therapeutic sterilisation, organ donation or participation in a clinical trial, or seeks to refuse treatment needed to protect her from permanent harm. The second are situations in which the treatment is experimental, there are multiple

Gillick: *consent from a child* 89

medically appropriate treatment options with differing potential consequences or multiple decisions are required in the context of a dynamic medical situation. The nature, purpose and consequences of the interventions are simply more complex where there are treatment options or the treatment proposed is experimental or has potentially serious deleterious consequences for the patient. Where the nature and purpose of an intervention is of such complexity, the presumption that she has capacity will be rebuttable if she is unable to understand and weigh the implications of effect being given to her expressed view by reference to her overall values and relationships. English law not only "goes to great lengths to protect a person of full age and capacity from interference with his personal liberty" (per Lord Reid in *S. v. S.*, ante, at p., 43), it also goes to great lengths to ensure that expressed views with potentially serious consequences for the patient are not too readily identified as determinate exercises of personal liberty.

The capacity of a child under 16

The central dispute in this case concerns the authority conferred over a minor by "custody" or, to use the more accurate terminology of section 85 of the Children Act 1975, "parental rights and duties". The Court of Appeal relied on *In re Agar-Ellis* (1883) 24 Ch.D. 317 in which the court upheld the restrictions placed by a father on his 17-year-old daughter's communication with her mother. This 19th century case treated a father's authority as absolute until the acquisition of majority at 21. It is inconsistent with the principle exposed by my noble and learned friend Lord Scarman from Blackstone's Commentaries and the case law: *Blackstone's Commentaries*, 17th ed. (1830), vol. 1, chs. 16 and 17, *Reg. v. Howard* [1966] 1 W.L.R. 13, *Reg. v. D.* [1984] A.C. 778, p. 806. As my noble and learned friend opines, this House in *Reg. v. D.* is to be understood as accepting the principle that, except where statute provides otherwise, a minor's capacity to make decisions depends upon that minor having attained sufficient understanding and intelligence to make that decision, rather than attainment of a fixed age. Lord Brandon of Oakbrook, with whom their other Lordships agreed, rejected the authority of *Agar-Ellis*, before reasoning, at p. 806:

> "I see no good reason why, in relation to the kidnapping of a child, it should not in all cases be the absence of the child's consent which is material, whatever its age may be. In the case of a very young child, it would not have the understanding or the intelligence to give its consent, so that absence of consent would be a necessary inference from its age. In the case of an older child, however, it must, I think, be a question of fact for a jury whether the child concerned has sufficient understanding and intelligence to give its consent; if, but only if, the jury considers that a child has these qualities, it must then go on to consider whether it has been proved that the child did not give its consent. While the matter will always be for the jury alone to decide, I should not expect a jury to find at all frequently that a child under 14 had sufficient understanding and intelligence to give its consent."

90 Gillick: *consent from a child*

In my view, the principle here is that a minor's capacity depends on possession of "sufficient understanding and intelligence to give its consent". If, as I contend, "intelligence" refers to reflective ability, then the threshold for capacity for children is the same as for adults. The common law distinction between minority and majority is therefore to be understood not as determining capacity, but as determining the evidential presumption as to whether or not a person has capacity. Once capacity has been obtained, by presumed or evidenced possession of sufficient cognitive-functional ability, consent and refusal are matters for that person. It follows that parental authority exists only until a child is able to make the relevant decision for herself and chooses to exercise that ability. Lord Denning M.R., after rejecting *Agar-Ellis* as representing the modern law, said in *Hewer v. Bryant* [1970] 1 Q.B. 357, at p. 369:

> "the legal right of a parent to the custody of a child ends at the 18th birthday: and even up till then, it is a dwindling right which the courts will hesitate to enforce against the wishes of the child, and the more so the older he is. It starts with a right of control and ends with little more than advice".

The principle that capacity is established by competence thus supports the corollary principle that parental authority to make treatment decisions on behalf of a minor survives only where the minor lacks competence or fails to make her own decision, such as where she asks that her parents make the decision for her. I do not here comment on proxy decision making for adults other than to recognise that attainment of majority also extinguishes parental authority.

Applied to the facts before this House, a minor is able to consent to contraceptive treatment if she is able to understand the immediate medical issues around contraception and its potential consequences for her. I do not accept that she needs to understand moral and family questions beyond what matters to her and her relationships. Nor do I accept that, at common law, what is required of a child to have capacity may surpass what is sufficient to protect an adult from rebuttal of the presumption of capacity.

Judgments on a patient's decision-making abilities

A doctor who reasonably believes that a minor (or indeed any patient) is able to consent should not fear a civil action in which his assessment of her decision-making abilities is second guessed by a judge and found wanting. The law has long recognised that no trespass is committed where a potential tortfeasor acts on a reasonable belief, irrespective of the underlying truth of the situation. In the US case of *O'Brien v. Cunard S.S. Co. Limited* (1891) 28 N.E. 266, the plaintiff alleged that she had been given a smallpox vaccination against her will by the medical officer to whom she presented her arm for inspection. She had presented her arm upon reaching the front of a queue of women waiting to be vaccinated. Knowlton, J. in the Supreme Judicial Court of Massachusetts, at p. 273, was satisfied that no trespass had occurred:

> "If the plaintiff's behavior was such as to indicate consent on her part, he was justified in his act, whatever her unexpressed feelings may have been."

It seems to me that what was important was not that the judge agreed with the defendant's belief, but that it was a reasonable belief in the circumstances. The underlying principle with regard to judgments on a patient's decision-making abilities must similarly be one in which the doctor is not held liable for acting on a reasonable belief. A reasonable, but mistaken belief of this type will therefore provide the doctor with the defence of reasonable mistake of fact to what would otherwise be a legal wrong. Applying this principle, a doctor who acts on the belief that a girl under 16 has consented to contraceptive treatment, or any other medical treatment, commits no trespass to her as long as his belief on her actual decision-making abilities is a reasonable one. Conversely, a doctor has a defence if he acts on the reasonable belief that the patient lacks the competence to refuse treatment. A mistake either way has consequences for the patients' rights and what is reasonable must be commensurate with those consequences. Over eagerness to conclude that a patient is competent risks the mistaken bestowal of capacity on an incapable patient, which may be particularly serious if the patient is refusing life-prolonging treatment. Conversely, over eagerness to conclude that a patient is incompetent risks mistakenly depriving the patient of the power to make her own decisions and thereby preventing the exercise of a basic human right. These risks are serious and particular care must therefore be taken to ensure that assessments do not rest on assumptions based on the assessor's values or the patient's age.

Where a patient's competence or incompetence is in the grey area of uncertainty, a reasonable belief will be one formed after taking all practicable steps to assess capacity and assist a patient with the process of decision making. These practical steps should not ignore the fact that patients live within a web of social relationships and will often benefit from dialogue and the support of a loved one. In the case of a minor, such practical steps will usually include involving her parent(s), but that will not be the case where there is reason to believe that parental involvement is likely to prevent her from making a competent decision or otherwise seriously endanger her interests.

For these reasons, I would allow the department's appeal and set aside the declaration that the guidance is unlawful. I would also overrule the second declaration granted by the Court of Appeal, which concerns only the area health authority and was based on the same reasoning as the first.

Lord Hercules

I have had the advantage of reading in advance the opinion of my noble and learned friend, Lady Athena. For the reasons she gives, with which I am in full agreement, I too would dismiss this appeal.

Lady Ares

My Lords, I too would dismiss the appeal for the reasons given by Lady Athena.

4 *Bland*

Patients in a vegetative state

4.1 Introduction

Airedale NHS Trust v Bland[1] seminally considered the lawfulness of withdrawing life-sustaining care from a severely compromised adult patient. Tony Bland was receiving what was referred to then as 'artificial feeding' and would now be called 'clinically assisted nutrition and hydration' (CANH).[2] Such patients receive both food and water through a tube that runs from the nose (a nasogastric tube) or through the abdomen (a gastrostomy tube). Tony had a nasogastric tube. He was in what was then called a 'persistent vegetative state' (PVS) and, because his condition persisted long enough to be considered clinically irreversible, would now be called a 'permanent vegetative state'.[3] Such patients sleep, wake and breathe unaided, but are considered to have irretrievably lost all awareness and are thereby left unable to see, hear, taste, smell or feel pain.[4] Tony had been in a vegetative state for over three years and could have been kept alive in that condition for decades.

No case involving the withdrawal of life-sustaining treatment from a severely cognitively impaired patient had previously reached the House of Lords and those decided by the lower courts had concerned newborn babies who (unlike Tony) seemed capable of experiencing pain.[5] In *Bland*, there were only minor differences of emphasis between Lord Goff, with whom Lords Keith and Lowry agreed, and Lords Browne-Wilkinson and Mustill. Their Lordships sought to avoid the conclusion that withdrawing life-sustaining CANH from Tony would

---

1 [1993] AC 789 (hereafter *Bland*).
2 'Artificial feeding' became 'artificial nutrition and hydration' (see *R (Burke) v GMC* [2004] EWHC 1879, [1]), before becoming 'clinically-assisted nutrition and hydration' (see GMC 2010, para 3; *Aintree University Hospitals NHS Foundation Trust v James* [2013] UKSC 67, [2]). The modern label avoids the value-laden connotations of the word 'artificial': see NCOB 2015.
3 Unless otherwise specified or apparent, PVS will be used in this chapter to refer to a clinical prognosis of a 'permanent' VS: see further Laudreys 2000, RCP 2013, 10–11, and the discussion below (4.2.2 and 4.5).
4 See Jennett & Plum 1972, Jennett 2002 and Wijdicks 2014, 113–116.
5 *Re B* [1990] 3 All ER 927 (CA, August 1981), *R v Arthur* (1981) 12 BMLR 1 (Crown Court, November 1981), *Re C* [1990] Fam 26 (CA, April 1989), *Re J* [1991] Fam 33 (CA, October 1990), and *Re J* [1993] Fam 15 (CA, June 1992). See further Pattinson 2017b, 530–533.

Bland: *patients in a vegetative state* 93

automatically satisfy the actus reus of murder by classifying CANH as medical treatment (as opposed to basic care) and its withdrawal by the treating doctor as a mere omission (as opposed to an act). Omitting to provide medical treatment, their Lordships reasoned, would only amount to murder where the doctor was under a legal duty to treat and no such duty could arise where the treatment was not in the best interests of the patient. Since, their Lordships opined, the continued provision of CANH to patients in PVS was futile, it was not in their best interests and could lawfully be withdrawn. Approval was given to four safeguards suggested by counsel[6] and their Lordships held that prior judicial approval should be obtained before the removal of CANH from patients in PVS, even though it was not strictly required as a matter of law.[7] The courts have held that its reasoning withstands the Human Rights Act 1998[8] and the Mental Capacity Act 2005.[9]

The chapter below is divided into four sections. The *first* will examine legal fictions, developments and gaps. It will focus on various distinctions explicitly or implicitly drawn in *Bland* (acts v omissions; medical treatment v basic care; best interests v overall interests), the five safeguards accepted by their Lordships and the approach in other jurisdictions. The *second* section will analyse the withdrawal of life-sustaining treatment from patients in PVS using the Principle of Generic Consistency (PGC). The *third* section will provide an explanatory link from the second section to the idealised judgment in the *fourth* section. That idealised judgment will support the conclusion that it is lawful to withdraw CANH from a patient in PVS using an alternative legal route in which it is explicitly accepted that those in PVS count for less than those who display some cognitive-functional ability.

4.2 Tensions and developments

4.2.1 Legal fictions

As already indicated, their Lordships considered the withdrawal of CANH to concern an omission to provide medical treatment, rather an act in relation to basic care. Keown, one of *Bland's* most prominent critics, has heavily criticised their Lordships' approach to both distinctions: the act-omission distinction for cutting across sanctity of life concerns and the characterisation of tubefeeding as medical treatment.[10] These distinctions or their application in *Bland* could be challenged as legal fictions. This section will argue that even if they are understood as legal fictions, they are not ipso

---

6 *Bland*, 870–871 (Lord Goff).

7 *Bland*, 885, 873, and 885.

8 See eg *NHS Trust A v M, NHS Trust B v H* [2001] Fam 348 and the discussion in Pattinson 2017b, ch 15.

9 *Aintree University Hospitals NHS Foundation Trust v James* [2013] UKSC 67, esp [19]–[21] and [38].

10 See, in particular, Keown 1997 and 2002.

94 Bland: *patients in a vegetative state*

facto subject to Bentham's denunciation of legal fictions as deceptive judicial usurpations of legislative authority.[11]

The House of Lords invoked the distinction between actively and passively taking a patient's life and held that both withholding *and withdrawing* life-sustaining treatment were omissions. Their Lordships reasoned that the actus reus of murder is not satisfied where death is caused by an omission unless there is a legal obligation to act *and* there could be no such obligation where the treatment is not in the incapacitated patient's best interests. There was clear authority for the first step to the effect that the actus reus of homicide – either murder or manslaughter, depending on the mens rea of the accused – was constituted by death caused by either the accused's act or omission to do what the accused was under a duty to do for the deceased. The cases cited by their Lordships[12] included Court of Appeal decisions upholding the murder conviction of a man and his girlfriend for failing to ensure that his six-year-old daughter received food when in their care[13] and upholding the conviction for manslaughter of a couple for failing to look after and get medical help for a 43-year-old woman who was in their care.[14] Their Lordships then added the gloss that the withdrawal of CANH was a mere omission. Lord Goff recognised that it could be described actively or passively, but insisted that:

> discontinuance of life support is, for present purposes, no different from not initiating life support in the first place. In each case, the doctor is simply allowing his patient to die in the sense that he is desisting from taking a step which might, in certain circumstances, prevent his patient from dying as a result of his pre-existing condition.[15]

Lord Browne-Wilkinson went so far as to declare that the tube that was feeding Tony 'itself, without the food being supplied through it, does nothing'.[16] Nonetheless, Lord Goff stated, its withdrawal would be viewed as an act if performed by a passer-by, because such person would be regarded as interfering with the patient's medical care.[17] Thus, the distinction adopted in *Bland* between an act and an omission does not purely turn on what occurs. I have, elsewhere, suggested that their Lordships were therefore adopting a legal fiction.[18] Hoppe and Miola have similarly concluded that their Lordship's approach to the act/omission

---

11 'A fiction of law may be defined—a wilful falsehood, having for its object the stealing [of] legislative power, by and for hands, which could not, or durst not, openly claim it—and, but for the delusion thus produced, could not exercise it': Bentham 1776 (Burns & Hart 1977, 509). cf Fuller 1967.

12 *Bland*, 858 (Lord Keith), 881 (Lord Browne-Wilkinson) and 893 (Lord Mustill).

13 *R v Gibbins* (1918) 13 Cr App R 134.

14 *R v Stone and Dobinson* [1977] QB 354.

15 *Bland*, 866.

16 *Bland*, 882.

17 *Bland*, 866.

18 See Pattinson 2006, 518, and, in the latest edition, 2017b, 546.

Bland: *patients in a vegetative state* 95

distinction was 'clearly a legal fiction' and involved them bending the law to 'very nearly breaking point'.[19]

Even after classifying the withdrawal of CANH as a mere omission, their Lordships had to explain why it could be withdrawn when the cited Court of Appeal cases on omissions constituting homicide had involved the failure to feed persons in the care of those accused of murder or manslaughter. Their Lordships considered CANH to be part of Tony's 'medical treatment and care'[20] and the withdrawal of the nasogastric tube as analogous to withdrawing a ventilator.[21] This implies a distinction between 'basic care' and 'medical treatment', whereby only the latter may be lawfully withheld from those for whom responsibility has been assumed.[22] But the principle underlying this distinction was not articulated by their Lordships.

On the face of it, CANH seems straightforwardly medical treatment, because the insertion and use of a nasogastric or gastrostomy tube is a clinical response to a feature of PVS, namely, the inability to self-feed. Further, other forms of assisted feeding are either not possible or carry risk that the patient will inhale food. Keown objects, however, that 'it is not at all clear' that the insertion of a nasogastric tube is a medical intervention; in any event, it had already been inserted into Tony and the 'pouring of food down the tube' is not treating anything and need not even be conducted by a healthcare professional.[23] He adds that whereas ventilation replaces the capacity to breathe, patients in PVS still have the capacity to digest and some can even swallow.

In practice, the distinction between basic care and medical treatment is now firmly ensconced in the law. While the Mental Capacity Act 2005 does not mention basic care,[24] the Act's Code of Practice states that an advance refusal of medical treatment cannot apply to 'basic or essential care', such as 'warmth, shelter, actions to keep a person clean and the offer of food and water by mouth'.[25]

Since ordinary language may express the withdrawal of CANH as an act and not refer to food and water as medical treatment, the House of Lords in *Bland* could be considered to have relied on legal fictions. Bentham said that legal fictions were to justice 'as swindling is to trade'.[26] Adcock and Beyleveld have argued that Bentham's vituperative comments are merited by one type of legal fiction, which they call 'a fiction about the law', but not by what they call 'a fiction for the purposes of the law'.[27] Accordingly,

---

19 Hoppe & Miola 2014, 284. See also Law & Choong 2018, 9, who state that removal from Bland 'clearly require[ed] a physical act'.
20 *Bland*, 858.
21 *Bland*, 870.
22 See Keown 2002, 219.
23 Keown 1997, 491.
24 Contrary to the Law Commission's recommendation: Law Commission 1995, para 5.34.
25 See Department for Constitutional Affairs 2007, para 9.28.
26 Bentham 1843, 287
27 Adcock & Beyleveld 2007, 306.

96 Bland: *patients in a vegetative state*

[t]his distinction is between cases where the fiction that the law employs is a fiction from the perspective of science, or common understanding, but is a construction necessary to achieve fundamental legal values [a fiction for the purposes of the law], and cases where the fiction is a fiction about the very thing that the law purports to value [a fiction about the law].[28]

This is a distinction that I adopt here for two reasons. First, it is supported by modified law as integrity, which identifies fundamental legal values as legal principles that explain extant rules and decisions, and are compatible with the PGC. A 'fiction for the purposes of the law' can therefore be understood as a legal construction that is necessary to give effect to such principles. The products of these legal constructions are properly considered 'legal facts' within that legal system. In contrast, a 'fiction about the law' can be understood as one that avoidably obscures or distorts such principles. Secondly, my work has similarly placed the two core examples cited by Adcock and Beyleveld on opposed sides of the divide between the legitimate and illegitimate.[29]

The key question is therefore whether classifying withdrawal of CANH as an omission and CANH as medical treatment is supported by or undermines proper legal principle.[30] Full consideration of these issues requires consideration of the PGC's requirements, so must be left until later (4.3 and below). It should, however, be clear that the second of these issues is not determined by asking, as Keown does, whether healthcare professionals need be involved in the continuation of CANH or what precisely CANH is treating. Grubb has argued that 'public policy' provides the rationale for prohibiting removal of 'nursing care', even in the face of a refusal from a competent patient.[31] He argues that basic hygiene, pain relief and other nursing care cannot be lawfully withdrawn, because (a) that would have the effect of requiring the doctor to abandon the patient and (b) the interests of healthcare professionals and others affected by the consequences of its withdrawal take priority in 'this singular situation'.[32] Since Grubb's focus is on what a patient may lawfully refuse, his first policy-based rationale either relies on a duty-based ethic or reduces to the second rationale. The second, invoking the interests of other affected persons, could explain why pain relief falls on one side of the line, because a patient's unaddressed cries of pain are likely to cause considerable distress to healthcare professionals, other patients and loved ones. It might also explain why removal of CANH from a permanently insensate patient

---

28 Adcock & Beyleveld 2007, 306.

29 See Beyleveld & Pattinson 2004, 185–202, and Pattinson 2005 on *R (Bruno Quintavalle) v Secretary of State for* Health [2003] UKHL 13. On imputed/deemed consent see Pattinson 2006, 191 and 429, and Pattinson 2017b, esp 211 and 468.

30 This question arises under modified law as integrity irrespective of whether these classifications are characterised as legal fictions by reference to language usage outside the law.

31 See Grubb 1993, 85 (commenting on *Re T* [1993] Fam 95), and Grubb 2004, 141.

32 Grubb 2004, 141.

Bland: patients in a vegetative state 97

like Tony falls on the other side of the line, because this is far less likely to cause distress to others beyond that caused by the patient's condition and his death. This second rationale could also be expressed in terms of rights and will be considered in such terms by Lady Athena.

4.2.2 The best interests of patients in PVS and MCS

The House of Lords in *Bland* insisted that their decision rested on what was in the patient's best interests, rather than those of the wider community.[33] This meant that their Lordships could not appeal to the burden on others – emotional and financial – of keeping Tony alive. Their Lordships similarly insisted that the relevant question was whether treatment, rather than death, was in the patient's best interests.[34] This is a somewhat fine distinction given that withdrawing the treatment in question, CANH, would inevitably result in the patient's death.[35] Indeed, their Lordships went on to dismiss Tony's interest in continued biological life. Lord Keith opined that 'to an individual with no cognitive capacity whatever, and no prospect of ever recovering such capacity in this world, it must be a matter of complete indifference whether he lives or dies'.[36] It followed, his Lordship concluded, that continued life in PVS was simply 'not a benefit to the patient'.[37] Lord Goff similarly declared that 'the condition of the patient, who is totally unconscious and in whose condition there is no prospect of any improvement, is such that life-prolonging treatment is properly regarded as being, in medical terms, useless'.[38] Lord Lowry agreed with Lord Goff and added that it was a fallacy to consider 'that feeding in order to sustain life is necessarily for the benefit of the patient'.[39] Lord Browne-Wilkinson considered it 'pointless to continue life support' and concluded that it should not be continued as his doctors did not consider it to be for Tony's benefit.[40] Lord Mustill directly asserted that '[t]he distressing truth which must not be shirked' is that a patient in PVS 'has no best interests of any kind'.[41] Thus, the application of the best interests test was considered straightforward on the basis that Tony received no benefit from the continuance of life-sustaining treatment because his life no longer had any meaning.

With respect, this reasoning is tortuous. We have been told that it would be homicide to kill Tony by an act, which includes a passer-by withdrawing food and water, or by withholding/withdrawing anything that our obligations to him require

---

33 As was expressly stated by Lord Mustill: *Bland*, 896.
34 *Bland*, 868 (Lord Goff, with whom Lords Keith and Lowry agreed) and 897 (Lord Mustill).
35 See Wicks 2017, 125–126.
36 *Bland*, 858.
37 *Bland*, 859.
38 *Bland*, 869.
39 *Bland*, 876.
40 *Bland*, 884–885.
41 *Bland*, 897.

98 Bland: patients in a vegetative state

us to provide. And we are now told that the interests of others or the community as a whole are irrelevant, *yet* he has no interest in his continued life (and indeed no 'interests of any kind'). This reasoning cannot be saved by presenting the critical points as legal fictions, unless we are prepared to accept 'fictions about the law', because this goes to the heart of what the law regards as fundamentally valuable: we are simultaneously told that Tony has an interest in continued life and does not have any interest in his continued life. Something must give. If Tony has an interest in his continued life, then CANH must continue unless that interest is outweighed by a countervailing interest. If he has no interests, then the justification for being protected by the law of homicide at all must be something other than his interests.

Since *Bland*, the courts have considered the lawfulness of withdrawing and withholding life-prolonging treatment from incapacitated adults who are severely compromised but not in a vegetative state. Patients in what is now described as a 'minimally conscious state' (MCS) will display some, albeit minimal or inconsistent, awareness by occasionally tracking movements with their eyes, smiling or otherwise performing actions suggesting some awareness and recognition.[42] The most authoritative case concerning a patient in a MCS is *Aintree University Hospitals v James*, which was also the first case on the Mental Capacity Act 2005 to reach the Supreme Court.[43] This case reaffirmed *Bland*. Lady Hale (with whom the other Supreme Court Justices agreed) held that the application of the best interests test requires a careful balancing exercising when considering patients in a MCS, but '[t]here are cases, such as *Bland*, where there is no balancing exercise to be conducted'.[44] In other words, the law has now (almost) definitively concluded that the provision of CANH is not in the best interests of a patient in PVS.

The courts have, however, displayed some openness to developments in medical science and the possibility that a patient could move from a vegetative to a minimally conscious state. In 2006, a judge delayed issuing a declaration on the lawfulness of removing CANH from a woman who had been in PVS for three years to allow time for the effects of a new drug to be assessed.[45] Sir Mark Potter P allowed a three-day course of the new drug to be administered on the back of a report that a momentary neurological response had followed its administration to a restless PVS patient. Since the patient before his Lordship evidenced no increased responsiveness, he subsequently granted the declaration originally sought by the NHS Trust. Five years later, the Court of Appeal refused to issue any declaration on a patient's best interests when asked to rule on the lawfulness of continuing an experimental treatment on a patient who had been left in or near a vegetative state by Creutzfeldt-Jakob Disease (CJD).[46] Crucially,

---

42 See BBC 2011 and Wijdicks 2014, 116–119. After four weeks, a MCS is regarded as a 'continuing' MCS: https://www.nhs.uk/conditions/disorders-of-consciousness.

43 *Aintree University Hospitals NHS Foundation Trust v James* [2013] UKSC 67. The first case concerning a patient in a MCS pre-dates the label: *Re R* [1996] 2 FLR 99.

44 [2013] UKSC 67, [36].

45 *B NHS Trust v J* [2006] EWHC 3152.

46 *AVS v A NHS Foundation Trust* [2011] EWCA Civ 7.

Bland: *patients in a vegetative state*   99

there was no doctor volunteering to provide the treatment and the hospital had not agreed to transfer the patient's case if such a doctor were to be identified. The Court of Appeal therefore refused to issue the declaration simply because it was unwilling for it to be used to 'twist the arm' of a doctor to carry out the procedures or pressurise the Secretary of State to provide a hospital where the procedures could be carried out.[47]

The 'permanence' of PVS may be challenged, because there have been cases of misdiagnosis and recovery to a MCS.[48] Diagnostic difficulties are presented by the fact that the vegetative state and MCS are on a spectrum: both are disorders of consciousness involving sleep-wake cycles with the difference resting on whether there is 'variable *but* reproducible' responsive behaviour that suggests some awareness.[49] Recently a patient who had been in a vegetative state for 15 years displayed evidence of some (minimal) awareness after receiving nerve stimulation.[50] This offers the limited prospect that some patients in a vegetative state could be returned to the least responsive end of a MCS.[51] Such limited prospects are unlikely to lead the courts to reverse their view that provision of CANH is no longer in the best interests of a patient who has been in a vegetative state for many months. The latest guidance from the Royal College of Physicians states that a vegetative state may generally be classified as 'permanent' after a year following traumatic brain injury and after six months following a non-traumatic brain injury, but a further period of targeted monitoring may be appropriate in cases of clinical uncertainty.[52]

4.2.3 The five safeguards

In *Bland*, five safeguards were advanced as a matter of good practice. For the first of these, their Lordships advised that a declaration should be obtained from the Family Division before removal of CANH from patients in PVS.[53] Lord Goff indicated that their Lordships had also agreed on four additional safeguards:

> (1) every effort should be made at rehabilitation for at least six months after the injury; (2) the diagnosis of irreversible PVS should not be considered confirmed until at least 12 months after the injury, with the effect that any decision to withhold life-prolonging treatment will be delayed for that period; (3) the diagnosis should be agreed by two other independent doctors; and (4) generally, the wishes of the patient's immediate family will be given great weight.[54]

---

47 [2011] EWCA Civ 7, [38].
48 See Andrews et al 1996, Dyer 1997, Jennett 2002, Laing 2002, Monti et al 2010, Cruse et al 2011 and Law & Choong 2018, 6–7.
49 Law & Choong 2018, 4.
50 See Corazzol et al 2017.
51 See the detailed discussion of the diagnostic method and diagnosis practice in Halliday et al 2015, 562–565.
52 RCP 2013, 10–11.
53 *Bland*, 859, 873 and 885.
54 *Bland*, 870–871.

100   Bland: *patients in a vegetative state*

Subsequent cases have weakened or departed from all five safeguards.

The recommendation that confirmatory declarations be sought before withdrawal of CANH from patients in PVS was said to be 'until a body of experience and practice has been built up'.[55] The justification for this practice, offered by Sir Thomas Bingham in the Court of Appeal and approved by the Law Lords, was 'the protection of patients, the protection of doctors, the reassurance of patients' families and the reassurance of the public'.[56] As has been subsequently recognised, that rationale would apply to a 'very much larger patient population' than those in PVS.[57] Yet, the declaratory procedure is an expensive process. Lewis points out that going to court 'may cause distress to the patient's family and is expensive for the NHS'.[58] Halliday, Formby and Cookson estimate that 'the overall costs of the declaratory relief process to the NHS per case are, *on average*, about £122,000, comprising around £53,000 in litigation costs and £69,000 in ongoing care costs'.[59]

Bland's supposed temporary measure proved to be long-lasting. Early on, both the Law Commission and the Scottish Law Commission recommended the adoption of a non-judicial process focussed on confirming the medical diagnosis and prognosis.[60] In *Burke*, Munby J held that the Strasbourg case law on Article 8 (the right to respect for private and family life) meant that, at least where there was dispute, 'what was previously only a matter of good practice is now, by reason of the Human Rights Act 1998, a matter of legal requirement'.[61] That ruling was quickly overturned by the Court of Appeal.[62] Now, judicial applications concerning incapacitated adults go before the Court of Protection, set up by the Mental Capacity Act 2005. The Act's Code of Practice declares that a court declaration before withdrawing life-sustaining treatment should be sought 'where there is any doubt about the patient's best interests'.[63] Until December 2017, paragraph 5 of Practice Direction 9E went further by providing that applications that 'should be brought to the court' include 'decisions about the proposed withholding or withdrawal of artificial nutrition and hydration from a person in a permanent vegetative state or a minimally conscious state'. This has led to some judicial and academic suggestion that a declaration had become a matter of legal obligation.[64] With respect, the Code of Practice does not refer to all patients in PVS and the Practice Direction provided procedural guidance rather than imposed legal obligations. In 2017, the Court of Appeal confirmed that a declaration was

---

55 *Bland*, 859.

56 *Bland*, 815 (Sir Thomas Bingham), as approved by their Lordships: 859 (Lord Keith) and 874 (Lord Goff).

57 *Re M* [2017] EWCOP 19, [37].

58 Lewis 2007, 397.

59 Halliday et al 2015, 580 (emphasis added).

60 Law Commission 1995, 90–93, and Scottish Law Commission 1995, 82–84.

61 *R (Burke) v GMC* [2004] EWHC 1879, [200]–[202], relying on *Glass v United Kingdom* [2004] 1 FLR 1019.

62 [2005] EWCA Civ 1003.

63 Department for Constitutional Affairs 2007, para 5.36.

64 See *Re M* [2011] EWHC 2443, [82] (Baker J), and Halliday et al 2015, 558.

Bland: *patients in a vegetative state* 101

not necessary where the doctors and family were in agreement, albeit in a case in which this was not fully argued. Peter Jackson J in the Court of Protection concluded, after receiving written submissions on the point, that a court declaration was not 'necessary as a matter of law, as opposed to as a matter of practice', but the court is always available where there is disagreement or other compelling reason for judicial involvement.[65] This was reaffirmed after oral argument by O'Farrell J in the Queen's Bench Division,[66] from which the Supreme Court is (at the time of writing) hearing an appeal. Thus, 25 years after *Bland*, there is no longer any need for routine judicial approval of the decision to withdraw CANH from patients in PVS.

The move away from the other four safeguards was much quicker. Less than a year after *Bland*, the accidental dislodgement of a patient's feeding tube led to the Court of Appeal issuing a declaration that it need not be replaced, despite some doubts about whether he was truly in PVS and the lack of opportunity for confirmation of diagnosis by independent doctors.[67] Indeed, even in the absence of such time pressures the courts have been willing to depart from all four additional safeguards,[68] so it is apparent that the court now sees its role as simply ensuring that the patient satisfies medical criteria for removal of treatment.[69] This reinforces the view that there is now little need for routine judicial involvement in PVS cases.

4.2.4 Other jurisdictions

Like the courts of England and Wales, the US courts have heard many cases involving the withdrawal of life-prolonging care/treatment from patients in PVS. The most high-profile cases concerned Karen Ann Quinlan, Nancy Cruzan and Terri Schiavo. *Quinlan*, heard by the Supreme Court of New Jersey in 1976, supported the removal of the patient's ventilator at the request of her father.[70] She continued to live in PVS until her death from pneumonia in 1985. In *Cruzan*, heard by the US Supreme Court in 1990, a majority of 5 to 4 held that the state of Missouri could require 'clear and convincing evidence' of an incapacitated patient's wishes before removal of life-sustaining treatment.[71] The four dissenters would have permitted immediate withdrawal of CANH from Nancy Cruzan, but, since they could not persuade the majority, this had to wait until a lower court ruled that her parents had satisfied the specified evidential threshold. All the Supreme Court Justices either implicitly

---

65 *Re M* [2017] EWCOP 19, [37].

66 *An NHS Trust v Y* [2017] EWHC 2866.

67 *Frenchay Healthcare NHS Trust v S* [1994] PIQR P118.

68 See eg *Re G* [1995] 2 FCR 46 (evidence was provided by only one independent doctor and the patient's mother was opposed to withdrawal) and *NHS Trust B v H* [2001] Fam 348 (the patient had only been in a vegetative state for nine months). See further Pattinson 2017b, 525–527.

69 For the most authoritative statement of medical criteria see RCP 2013. New guidance will be issued by the RCP later in 2018 (this manuscript was submitted in April).

70 *In re Quinlan*, 355 A 2d 647 (1976).

71 *Cruzan v Director, Missouri Department of Health* (1990) 110 S Ct 284.

102 Bland: patients in a vegetative state

or explicitly accepted that CANH was medical treatment.[72] This aligns with *Bland*, though only Lord Mustill mentioned *Cruzan* and then only in passing with regard to a different point.[73]

The conflict between the parents and husband of Terri Schiavo over removal of her gastrostomy tube lasted over 11 years and included numerous hearings and appeals and extensive political intervention at both state and federal level.[74] At one point, Florida's Governor, Jeb Bush, arranged for the legislature to rush through 'Terri's Law' to empower him to issue an executive order requiring reinsertion of the gastrostomy tube.[75] A couple of years later, again with the intention of preventing the implementation of a court decision, Republicans in the US Congress took the audacious step of subpoenaing Terri Schiavo to testify at a congressional hearing.[76] It seems that the attempt of Terri's parents to argue that she was not truly in PVS and the release of a selectively edited video of Terri's involuntary movements had persuaded many that she was actually in a MCS.[77] What this all shows is that PVS cases can, if presented in a particular way, very easily elicit public concern and be used as political footballs. As things stand in the US, more than two thirds of states permit the withdrawal of CANH from patients in PVS, but some states prohibit life-shortening withdrawal of CANH unless there is, or in some cases even if there is, an advance refusal.[78]

Bland itself has had considerable influence in other jurisdictions. Its reasoning was, for example, followed in two cases in the 1990s – one in Ireland, the other in New Zealand – involving patients who were in a MCS, rather than PVS.[79] That is not to suggest that every aspect of the case has received universal support. Jennett (who gave evidence in *Bland* and was one of the first to clinically describe PVS) has suggested that 'only in the United Kingdom' was judicial approval required before withdrawal of CANH from patients in PVS.[80] A survey of 22 jurisdictions undertaken by Halliday and his co-authors in 2015 indicates that this was an overstatement.[81] Of the jurisdictions surveyed, 14 did not require a court decision, but four did (England/Wales, Northern Ireland, Ireland and India); two prohibit withdrawal of CANH (Italy and Israel) and the legal position was uncertain

---

72 See eg the dissent of Justice Brennan, in which Justices Marshall and Blackmun joined: 'No material distinction can be drawn between the treatment to which Nancy Cruzan continues to be subject – artificial nutrition and hydration – and any other medical treatment' (*Cruzan* (1990) 110 S Ct 284, 2866).

73 *Bland*, 890.

74 See eg Cerminara 2010.

75 www.myfloridahouse.gov/Sections/Bills/billsdetail.aspx?BillId=12713

76 http://abstractappeal.com/schiavo/HouseSubpoenas.pdf.

77 Cerminara 2010, 85.

78 See Wijdicks 2014, 288.

79 See *In the matter of A Ward of Court (No 2)* [1996] 2 IR 79 and *Re G* [1997] NZFLR 362, respectively.

80 Jennett 1999, 796.

81 See Halliday et al 2015, 574.

Bland: *patients in a vegetative state* 103

in Scotland. All this shows is a degree of legal plurality from which it is not clear that anything of significance follows.

4.3 Application of the PGC

Modified law as integrity indirectly applies the PGC. The precautionary thesis advanced as a direct application of the PGC in Chapter 1 (1.3.3) holds that our actions must respect the possibility (however remote) that other beings are agents. Since 'ought implies can', only those who behave like agents ('ostensible agents') can meaningfully be granted rights according to the will conception ('will-rights').[82] For the same reason, only those who display at least some agency-like behaviour (beings who approach being ostensible agents) can meaningfully be granted rights to the generic capacities of agency under the interest conception of rights ('interest-rights'). We are therefore required to grant will-rights to ostensible agents and interest-rights to those who approach being ostensible agents. These rights are only correlative to positive duties where the presumed agent cannot defend his or her generic capacities without assistance (the own unaided effort proviso), and the provision of assistance does not deprive the provider of the same or more important generic capacities (the comparable cost proviso). The weight of these rights is to be determined by the criterion of avoidance of more probable harm: assessed by the degree to which the relevant presumed generic capacity is needed to act successfully or at all (the criterion of degrees of needfulness for action) and the degree to which the being in question approaches ostensible agency.

As noted at the beginning of this chapter, Tony Bland was considered to have irretrievably lost *all* awareness. Lady Athena does not have access to a time machine, so cannot consider subsequent evidence that a small number of those thought to be in a vegetative state were in, or could be returned to, the bottom end of the minimally conscious state (see 4.2.2). In any event, under the principle of proportion under precaution, those at the bottom end of the MCS have only marginally greater moral status than those in a vegetative state.

On the facts as understood by the House of Lords, even under precaution Tony's rights are limited. He does have a right to life, which in the circumstances would amount to a positive interest-right to the CANH and associated care required to maintain his biological life. Nonetheless, his display of the characteristics of ostensible agency is lower than that of any creature that displays behavioural responses to external stimulus suggestive of sentience. At the point where a patient in a vegetative state is considered to lack any realistic prospect of recovery, he is considered to lack even potential behavioural display of sentience. This is important because the provision of life-sustaining care to a patient in PVS raises resource allocation issues of relevance to the basic generic rights of others. A patient in intensive care for the remaining

---

82 See the discussion in ch 1 (1.3.3).

104 Bland: *patients in a vegetative state*

decades of his life will absorb significant resources: the financial cost alone of treating patients in PVS is estimated to be £90,000 per individual per year.[83] These healthcare resources could be used to save and prolong the lives of others; not merely others of negligible moral status – others in or heading towards PVS and anencephalic babies – but those who behave like agents and therefore have full moral status. Indeed, it is arguable that the House of Lords applied this reasoning behind a veil of denial. As Morgan put the point: 'There is a sense in which Tony Bland is a hostage to the fortune which the British public health service no longer has'.[84]

A further consideration is that most patients in PVS were, prior to entering into PVS, ostensible agents.[85] They could therefore have previously been competent and have expressed views and values concerning the provision of life-sustaining treatment prior to their deterioration into a vegetative state. Any attempt to give effect to a patient's prior views and values will present challenges.[86] The first challenge is determining whether those prior views and values sufficiently represent the patient's will on what should happen in the situation in which he now finds himself. The issue is that the scope and meaning of his wishes needs to be interpreted in a context with potentially unanticipated features without the ability to return to him for further discussion and consideration. Few have expressed a clear view on receiving CANH and associated care when in PVS. The second challenge is the personal identity objection to giving effect to the prior will of a now incompetent patient. According to this objection, the process that renders the individual incompetent will often destroy the conditions necessary for continuity of personal identity and thereby remove the moral authority of prior views and values.[87] This objection has its origins in the view that psychological continuity with one's past self (assessed by apparent retention of interpersonal memories and personality traits) is a necessary condition for personal identity.[88] I have argued elsewhere that English law's rejection of the personal identify objection is supported by the PGC, because the objection (a) invokes and applies criteria for identifying personal identity that are not required to give effect to the generic rights of agents, and (b) requires more assumptions to accept than to reject.[89]

Tony Bland had not given any indication of his wishes.[90] His family did not think that Tony would 'want to be left like that', but that seems to have been little more than a best guess on the basis of their understanding of his general views. He was only 17 at the time that he sustained such devastating damage to his cerebral cortex and had had no reason to direct his mind to such issues.[91] Thus, the doctors who deliberately dehydrated and starved Tony Bland could not defer to his prior will.

---

83 Kitzinger & Kitzinger 2015.
84 Morgan 2001, 220.
85 See Beyleveld & Brownsword 2001, 252.
86 See Pattinson 2017a.
87 See eg Buchanan 1988, esp 280, and Dresser 1995, 35.
88 See Locke 1690, Parfit 1984, 204–209, and the discussion in Pattinson 2017a.
89 See Pattinson 2017a.
90 *Bland*, 798 and 807.
91 cf Hoffman LJ's approach in *Bland*, 827 and 829–830, as discussed in Douglas 2018.

The doctors were also not seeking to give effect to his right to be free of suffering associated with his continued life, because they did not believe that he was in pain or aware to any extent. They were, however, acting in accordance with the wishes of his family and their views on what Tony's wishes would have been. While Tony himself possessed less moral status than any human or animal with at least some apparent awareness, his loved ones have full moral status and the effect of his continued life on them was therefore a morally relevant factor.

In the House of Lords, their Lordships denied that Tony had a positive right to life requiring continued provision of CANH without appealing to his having previously waived the benefit of that right or appealing to the rights of others. This, paradoxically, both undervalues and overvalues Tony's interest-rights. They are undervalued because their Lordships effectively denied that a patient in PVS has a basic positive right to life, and overvalued because their Lordships denied that the interest-rights of a patient with very limited moral status could be over-ridden to protect the basic will-rights of those with full status. Under the PGC, a strong case can be made for the moral permissibility, indeed a moral obligation, to free up finite healthcare resources needed by others in a situation where a patient is considered to be irretrievably insensate and unconscious.

The House of Lords also drew a sharp distinction between killing by an act and killing by an omission. This distinction is rejected by many moral theorists. Rachels challenges the distinction between acts and omissions by asking you to imagine that you are in the same room as a starving child and have a sandwich that you do not need.[92] This analogy has force because it neutralises factors that restrict the imposition of positive duties under the PGC, such as the cost to the actor[93] and the probability that death will result. Finnis and Keown reject the distinction because of the tenets of their sanctity of life position, according to which *intentionally* terminating the life of an innocent human is always wrong irrespective of whether it is done by an act or an omission.[94] We saw in Chapter 2 (2.5) that the sanctity of life position is contrary to the tenets of the PGC. Harris rejects the distinction because he holds that killing by deliberate act is only wrong as such if it is contrary to the will of a 'person' who is capable of valuing his or her own existence.[95] Harris, however, departs from the tenets of the PGC by rejecting rights and appealing to an implicit preference utilitarianism.[96] Under the PGC, the distinction between killing and letting die only has force insofar as it tracks the distinction between positive and negative rights.

In contrast to English law, the PGC does not require the blanket rejection of intentional life-shortening acts. Under the PGC, a case could therefore be made for the conclusion that the rights of Tony and others would be better protected by ending his life quickly by lethal injection, rather than slowly by dehydration

---

92 See Rachels 1979, 160.
93 See discussion of the comparable cost proviso above and in ch 1 (1.3.3).
94 See Finnis 1993 and Keown 1997; see further Finnis 1995a; 1995b; 1995c.
95 See Harris 1985; 1995a; 1995b and 1995c.
96 See Harris 1998, 257; 1985, xvi; and the discussion in Pattinson 2017b, 569–570.

106 Bland: *patients in a vegetative state*

and starvation. We must remember, however, that Lady Athena in the idealised judgment below is not deciding the issue as a legislator. Modified law as integrity requires justification *and fit*. Lady Athena therefore needs to consider the PGC-measured benefits of accelerating Tony's death by lethal injection by reference to the PGC-measured costs of revising or evading common law principles that support the prohibition of the deliberate killing of others by lethal injection. She could not conclude that those in PVS fall completely outside the law of homicide without rendering such individuals valueless things in the eyes of the law. There is no equivalent to the legislative provisions that protect others with only interest-rights, such as embryos, fetuses and various non-human animals.[97] The only potentially relevant basis in the existing common law for upholding the lawfulness of an intentionally life-ending act on those protected by the law of homicide is the doctrine of necessity, as underpinned by the principle of the lesser of two evils and utilised by Lady Athena in *Adams* and *Gillick*. It is not, however, so readily invoked with regard to this aspect of *Bland* because here the legal dilemma is not so clearly weighted in favour of setting aside an otherwise almost absolute legal prohibition. The court in *Bland* was not faced with a direct all-or-nothing choice between permitting an act that deliberately shortened life and permitting a more serious harm. In *Bland*, all those involved merely wanted to withdraw CANH, which would bring an end to the patient's life in a matter of days without disproportionate suffering to either the patient or others. Tony had been in PVS for over three years. Thus, the conclusion of Lady Athena's idealised judgment below will not differ in this regard from that of the other Law Lords.

4.4 Options available to Lady Athena

To enable Lady Athena's judgment to be the ratio of the House of Lords in *Bland*, I have adopted the approach used when revisiting *Gillick* and imagined the judicial panel had seven members. As previously, the two additional members will simply agree with Lady Athena and at least one of the other Law Lords will be treated as agreeing with the views expressed by Lady Athena. Since Lord Goff gave the principal speech, Lady Athena will be assumed to have read a draft of that judgment and thereby able to incorporate aspects and otherwise respond to it.

One of the most prominent critics of their Lordships' reasoning has been Keown,[98] but Huxtable avers that '[e]ven Keown has not indicated precisely what he would decide in a case like Anthony Bland's'.[99] Lady Athena will apply modified law as integrity to support alternative reasoning towards the same overall conclusion. When seeking to discern a legal principle to give effect to the PGC

---

97 See eg the Offences Against the Person Act 1861, Animal (Scientific Procedures) Act 1986, and the Human Fertilisation and Embryology Act 1990. On embryos and fetuses, see ch 5 (5.2.3).
98 See eg Keown 1997 and the discussion in Pattinson 2017b, ch 15.
99 Huxtable 2012, 111; cf Foster 2011.

she has two general options. *Option one* is for her to discern a legal principle that directly articulates the requirements of the PGC. Lady Athena did this in *Gillick* when she discerned the principle that capacity tracks competence and she will adopt this approach below by discerning a principle that recognises that Tony has a lower status than many other human beings. *Option two*, on which she must fall back when the pre-existing law forecloses the first option, is for her to evade the apparent implications of firmly established legal principles by discerning a principle to refashion a recognised exemption. She did this, as Athena J, in *Adams* by refashioning the doctrine of necessity in terms of the principle of the lesser of two evils. Below, she will embrace their Lordships' determination that the removal of CANH is a mere omission when performed by the patient's medical team, while recognising that this is an instance where principle requires a legal fiction.

The judgment below retains the language used at the time. CANH is therefore referred to as 'artificial feeding' and PVS is taken to refer to a 'persistent vegetative state'. This language has limitations. Since both 'persistent' VS and 'permanent' VS abbreviate to PVS, it is easy to confuse a vegetative state that has lasted for at least four months (then called a 'persistent' VS and now called a 'continuing' VS) with what would now be called a 'permanent' VS.[100] In the current terminology, a 'permanent' VS is one that has persisted for more than six months if caused by non-traumatic brain injury or for more than a year if caused by a traumatic brain injury. Lady Athena will refer to a vegetative state that has lasted for long enough to be clinically regarded as permanent as an irreversible VS or irreversible PVS. This, I hope, prevents terminological confusion without anachronistically using the modern terminology.

Some changes have been made to the submissions attributed to the barristers in the case. The safeguards attributed to Robert Francis QC derive from the original judgment.

---

100 See Laudreys 2000, RCP 2013, and www.nhs.uk/conditions/disorders-of-consciousness.

108 Bland: *patients in a vegetative state*

4.5 Idealised judgment: *Airedale NHS Trust v Bland* (HL)

To be cited as:
Airedale N.H.S. Trust v. Bland [1993] R.L.C. 3
3 February 1993

Lady Athena

My Lords, Anthony Bland has been in a vegetative state for over three years. He is in a "persistent vegetative state" (P.V.S) and his vegetative state has persisted for long enough to be considered irreversible. He sleeps and wakes but has tragically and irretrievably lost all awareness. Anthony was only 17 at the time that he sustained such devastating damage to his cerebral cortex, and with continued medical care he could continue in a vegetative state for many years. The facts are not in dispute and I gratefully adopt the detailed summary of the Master of the Rolls, which is incorporated into the opinion of my learned and noble friend, Lord Goff of Chieveley. Airedale N.H.S. Trust, with the support of Anthony's parents, sought declarations in the High Court to resolve uncertainty as to the lawfulness of removing artificial feeding an other measures aimed at prolonging Anthony's life. The judgment of the President of the Family Division granting these declarations was affirmed by the Court of Appeal. I would dismiss the appeal brought on Anthony's behalf by the Official Solicitor, Mr. James Munby. In reaching this opinion, I have been greatly assisted by submissions from Mr. Francis, for the respondents, and Mr. Anthony Lester, as *amicus curiae*, instructed by the Treasury Solicitor.

There is agreement between counsel appearing before your Lordships that authoritative guidance on the lawfulness of discontinuing life-sustaining support (here artificial feeding) may be provided by way of declaratory relief of the kind considered by this House in *In re F. (Mental Patient: Sterilisation)* [1990] 2 A.C. 1. In that case, this House reluctantly accepted that the *parens patriae* jurisdiction no longer enabled the court to give consent on behalf of an incapacitated adult to what would otherwise be a trespass. After considered argument this House nonetheless found that the declaratory jurisdiction enabled the court to provide the necessary guidance to the medical profession. In my view, the principle underlying this House's conclusion that declaratory relief was available is that directly affected individuals should not be left without authoritative guidance in situations of significant legal uncertainty. This includes the situation where the decision of a doctor to act in accordance with her clinical judgment places her at risk of prosecution for a serious crime. That principle applies to the question before this House of whether discontinuing the provision of artificial feeding to Anthony will constitute murder. In my view, this House must approach this case by searching past cases for principles, stripped of missteps and irrelevances, capable of explaining and justifying the law on withdrawing life-sustaining treatment.

The right to life

My Lords, this House has been greatly assisted by detailed submissions on the principles/rights underlying the homicide offences. For my part, I reject the explanatory force of the principle of sanctity of life, at least if understood as the principle that it is always wrong to intentionally kill an innocent human being. I do not accept that this sanctity of life principle can be reconciled with other principles that operate within the law of homicide. It cannot be reconciled with the application of the principle of the lesser of two evils to the law of murder, by which a doctor may deliberately hasten death by administering proper and proportionate pain relief: *Attorney-General's Reference (No. 1 of 1958)* [1958] R.L.C. 1. It cannot be reconciled with the principle of self-determination, according to which a doctor cannot administer life-sustaining treatment contrary to the express wishes of a patient with capacity: *Gillick v. West Norfolk and Wisbech A.H.A.* [1985] R.L.C. 2 and *In re T. (Adult: Refusal of Treatment)* [1993] Fam. 95. It is also potentially in tension with the principle that an extremely negative quality of life can remove the duty to administer life-sustaining treatment to a young child: *In re C. (A Minor) (Wardship: Medical Treatment)* [1990] Fam. 26 and *In re J. (A Minor) (Wardship: Medical Treatment)* [1991] Fam. 33, on which see below.

In my view, the homicide offences protect the right to life. The above cited principles demonstrate that the correlative duties imposed by this right may sometimes be waived or overridden. The case law has, however, unquestionably given the negative right (to non-interference with continued life) greater effect and weight than it has given to the positive right (to the assistance required for continued life). The difference can be discerned from the distinction drawn in the case law between doing an act which causes death and omitting to do the act which would have prevented death. The act/omission distinction, drawn within the *actus reus* requirement of the law of homicide, should not be regarded as one founded in ordinary language, for in ordinary language the same situation may often be described positively or negatively. Not providing something that was previously provided may be described as the inaction of non-provision or the action of removing provision. In either case, any duty to continue to provide would be a positive duty, because both assisting and continuing to assist involve providing something to another. This affords the principled basis for identifying the withdrawal of life-sustaining care as an omission when the assister ceases to assist but as an act when another intervenes to prevent the assistance. I therefore agree with my learned and noble friend, Lord Goff, that, in law, it is an omission for a doctor to withdraw life-sustaining care from her patient.

In the law of homicide, where the accused was under a duty to do something for the deceased that would have prevented death and omits to do that thing, this may constitute the *actus reus* of homicide: either murder (*Rex v. Gibbins* (1918) 13 Cr.App.R. 134) or manslaughter (*Reg. v. Stone* [1977] Q.B. 354) depending upon the *mens rea* of the accused. The issue in the instant case is not whether Anthony's doctors have responsibility for his care, for they clearly do (*Barnett v. Chelsea and Kensington Hospital* [1969] 1 Q.B. 428), but whether discontinuance of artificial feeding would be a breach of duty, which, since this will intentionally cause the

110   Bland: *patients in a vegetative state*

patient's death, would thereby be unlawful. Mr. Munby seeks to rely on a principle discerned from *Rex. v. Gibbins* and *Reg. v. Stone*, which were cases in which the Court of Appeal upheld the homicide convictions of the accused persons for omitting to feed and properly care for the individuals who died as a result while in their care. Mr. Munby submits that those cases instantiate the principle that the provision of food and water is "essential or basic care", which cannot lawfully be withheld from those in one's care. He contrasts "essential care" with "medical treatment", whereby only the latter may be withheld by healthcare professionals on account of an advance refusal (*In re T.*, above) or the patient's best interests (*In re J.*, above). Mr. Munby further submits that even if artificial feeding is regarded as a clinical response to a patient's inability to self-feed, this applies only to the insertion of the nasogastric tube, rather than to its continued use to provide food and water.

I cannot accept these submissions. If they were accepted, then it would follow that artificial feeding through an extant tube would have to continue even if the now incapacitated patient had refused it in advance. It would also follow that it would have to continue whenever it would prolong an incapacitated patient's life, even if its continuation would cause unbearable distress alleviable only by sedation for the rest of the patient's life. In short, I do not accept that the law imposes a duty to continue provision of artificial feeding contrary to the principles of self-determination and best interests. The principle advanced to support the claim that the provision of basic care is not subject to either the recipient's prior will or best interests relies on the (purportedly overriding) rights of those others (healthcare professionals, other patients, and loved ones) who are likely to experience serious distress from its withdrawal. Why, however, must the law assume that the potential distress experienced by others from witnessing the dehydration of an apparently insensate patient in medical care will go beyond that likely to be caused by witnessing withdrawal of a ventilator or antibiotics? The death of a patient in medical care from dehydration, suffocation or infection would seem capable of causing equivalent distress. Thus, for my part, I do not see how reliance on the rights of others could require artificial feeding to be distinguished from ventilation, antibiotics and other forms of medical treatment. It follows that, in this respect, artificial feeding is legally equivalent to medical treatment.

The legal status of those considered to be in an irreversible P.V.S.

No case involving the withdrawal of life-sustaining treatment from a severely cognitively impaired patient has previously reached this House. Those decided by the lower courts have concerned babies and have fallen into two categories: brain stem dead babies and cognitively impaired babies.

The first category is represented by a single case, *In re A.* [1992] 3 Med. L.R. 303, which concerned a 20-month baby boy who satisfies the clinical criteria for brain stem death. This meant that A. lacked any brain function and was only biologically alive due to the reparatory support provided by a ventilator. Johnson J. used the declaratory jurisdiction to confirm, at p. 305, that A. was "dead for all legal, as well as medical, purposes" and it was therefore lawful for the consultant to disconnect him from the ventilator. The judge added, also at p. 305,

"I hold too that it would be wholly contrary to the interests of that child, as they may now be, for his body to be subjected to what would seem to me to be the continuing indignity to which it is subject. Moreover, I hold it to be quite unfair to the nursing and medical staff of this hospital, for the reasons previously given."

It seems to me that this case instantiates the principle that cessation of brain stem function, as determined by clinical criteria, renders the patient legally dead, at which point the patient no longer has any right to the continuation of biological life and the law defers to the interests of others, particularly those providing medical care.

The second category of case considered by the lower courts has concerned newborn babies who (unlike either A. or Anthony Bland) were considered capable of experiencing pain. The first of these was the decision of the Court of Appeal in *In re B. (A Minor) (Wardship: Medical Treatment)* [1981] 1 W.L.R. 1421. This case concerned an infant with Down's syndrome complicated by an intestinal blockage. Her parents refused to consent to the surgery required for her to survive. The test adopted by Templeman L.J., at p. 1424, was "whether the life of this child is demonstrably going to be so awful that in effect the child must be condemned to die". Dunn L.J. added, at pp. 1424–1425, that he agreed with counsel on behalf of the Official Solicitor that "the child should be put into the same position as any other Mongol child and must be given the chance to live an existence". Implicit in the Court of Appeal's reasoning is the principle that a child with Down's syndrome does not have a status less than that of any other child, so treatment decisions are to be made in that child's best interests. Since this child was likely to benefit from decades of post-operative life without intolerable suffering, it followed that surgery was in his best interests.

Earlier I indicated that when searching past cases for principles capable of explaining and justifying the law, it is proper and appropriate to strip out missteps and irrelevances. I therefore think that my Lords should not be distracted by the direction given to the jury in *R. v. Arthur* (1981) 12 B.M.L.R. 1, which was in a case in which a doctor was charged with attempted murder after he had ordered "nursing care only" for a baby with Down's syndrome whose parents did not want him to survive. Farquharson J., at p. 22, instructed the jury that they should "think long and hard before deciding that doctors, of the eminence we have heard . . . have evolved standards which amount to committing crime". With respect to the judge, who does not seem to have been made aware of the Court of Appeal's decision in *In re B.*, the correct standards are those captured by the principle that a child with Down's syndrome has a status equal to that of any other child.

Subsequent cases have applied the best interests test to babies with far more significant impairments. In *In re C. (A Minor)* [1990] Fam. 26, the Court of Appeal held that it was in the best interests of a newborn baby suffering from congenital hydrocephalus, who was hopelessly and terminally ill, for her suffering to be eased and her life not to be briefly prolonged by medical treatment designed to address future infection or feeding difficulties. Under a year later, in *In re J.* [1991] Fam. 33, the Court of Appeal considered the position of a baby who was not dying, but was severely brain damaged, epileptic and likely to be blind, deaf, mute and quadriplegic, but still able to feel pain. He had been ventilated on two previous occasions and the

112 Bland: *patients in a vegetative state*

Court of Appeal supported the doctors' view that it would not be in his best interests to administer ventilation again, should he need it in the future.

Lord Donaldson, at pp. 53–54, indicated that three preliminary principles were not in dispute before the Court of Appeal:

> "First, it is settled law that the court's prime and paramount consideration must be the best interests of the child . . . . Secondly, the court's high respect for the sanctity of human life imposes a strong presumption in favour of taking all steps capable of preserving it, save in exceptional circumstances . . . . Thirdly, and as a corollary to the second principle, it cannot be too strongly emphasised that the court never sanctions steps to terminate life. That would be unlawful. There is no question of approving, even in a case of the most horrendous disability, a course aimed at terminating life or accelerating death. The court is concerned only with the circumstances in which steps should not be taken to prolong life."

Taylor L.J. added, at p. 55, "the correct approach is for the court to judge the quality of life the child would have to endure if given the treatment, and decide whether in all the circumstances such a life would be so afflicted as to be intolerable to that child."

I have already indicated that the principle discerned from *In re A.* is that upon clinical certification of cessation of brain stem function, a patient no longer has any right to the continuation of biological life and the law defers to the interests of others, particularly those providing medical care. The principle discernible from *In re B.*, *In re C.*, and *In re J.* is that babies with a functioning cerebral cortex have a legal right to life, but their rights do not require any steps to prolong their lives that are contrary to their best interests. The presumption in favour of life-prolonging treatment is therefore rebuttable, such as where the quality of life following medical intervention is expected to be so poor as to be intolerable. Baby B. and Baby J., despite their cognitive differences, were both considered sentient, which is not, alas, the case for Anthony Bland. Anthony's condition therefore places him between that of Baby A. (brain stem dead) and Baby J. (severely impaired but nonetheless sentient). The distinguishing characteristic of a vegetative state that has endured long enough to be considered clinically irreversible is that the brain stem remains alive and functioning (in contrast to A.), while the cortex of the brain apparently loses its function and activity (in contrast to J.). There has been no case involving a newborn kept biologically alive, by means of respiratory support or artificial feeding, with a functional brain stem while lacking a functioning cerebral cortex. I doubt that a baby born with such a compromised brain, which could be the result of the serious birth defect known as anencephaly, would be given life-prolonging treatment in the first place.

It seems to me that Anthony's medical and legal status therefore rests between that of a patient who is brain stem dead and a patient evidencing the cortical function required for some awareness of the external world. That is to say that a patient in a clinically irreversible P.V.S. (or an equivalent state of anencephaly) has a *sui generis* legal status. It follows that while Anthony is not legally dead, he does not have equal rights to a patient who displays clear evidence of an ability to feel pain. The law's

Bland: *patients in a vegetative state* 113

starting point when determining the lawfulness of withholding or withdrawing life-sustaining care from a patient in an irreversible vegetative state therefore need not be the patient's interests alone, which is what is required by the best interests test, but may be determined by reference to the overall interests of all affected persons.

My Lords, all parties accept that the consequence of withdrawing artificial feeding will be Anthony's death. I am not persuaded that a meaningful distinction can be drawn between asking whether it is in Anthony's best interests that artificial feeding should be ended and asking whether it is in his best interests that he should die. Further, since his continued life involves neither distress to him nor contravention of his previous wishes (or even his clearly expressed core values), I also cannot see how it can be concluded that he has no interest at all in continued life, however limited that life will be. The alternative conclusion implies that he has no right to life, from which it would follow that he is no longer subject to the protection of the law of homicide at all. If, as I contended, the question is not whether treatment/continued life is in Anthony's best interests but whether it is in the overall interests of all those affected, then we may directly address the question of whether his interest in continued life is sufficient to require that his life be maintained for what could be many decades. This is a difficult question because it hides behind no legal fiction.

My view is therefore that those in an irreversible vegetative state, unlike those who are brain stem dead, have a legal right to life protected by the law of homicide, but that right to life is not equivalent to that of other patients. This means that hospitals and healthcare teams are not required to provide assistance for years or even decades when those limited resources could be used to assist others who have a greater legal status. Once a patient is judged, according to best medical practice, to be irreversibly in a vegetative state, those responsible for his treatment may therefore properly decide to withhold or withdraw continued life-sustaining care. In many cases, as here, this outcome will also accord with the wishes of loved ones who have been kept in an emotional limbo in which they cannot grieve, despite having no realistic hope that the patient will ever recover awareness. For these reasons, I agree with the conclusion reached by the Court of Appeal that Anthony's healthcare team have no continuing duty to keep him in what my learned and noble colleague, Lord Goff, describes as a "living death".

Safeguards

The view taken by the President of the Family Division and the Court of Appeal was that medical decisions to withdraw life-sustaining treatment from patients in a P.V.S. should, as a matter of good practice and until a suitable body of experience and practice has been built up, be confirmed by a declaration from the High Court. Sir Thomas Bingham M.R. considered this approach to be in the interests of the protection of patients, the protection of doctors, the reassurance of the patients' families, and the reassurance of the public. This view was supported before the Appellate Committee by Mr. Munby for the Official Solicitor and Mr. Lester, as *amicus curiae*. For the respondents, Mr. Francis suggested that it would suffice if reference to the court was required only in certain specific cases, i.e., (1) where there is medical disagreement as to the diagnosis or prognosis, and

114 Bland: *patients in a vegetative state*

(2) where there is conflict or disagreement with or between the patient's relatives or loved ones over the recommended course of action.

My Lords, the case before this House demonstrates the important function that the declaratory procedure serves. For my part, I would not restrict declaratory relief to members of the medical profession who seek reassurance before acting on their clinical judgment in a situation of legal uncertainty, and would happily recognise that it has wider utility with regard to other situations of anticipated legal dispute or complexity. It seems to me, however, that a requirement to invoke the declaratory jurisdiction in every case involving discontinuance of life-sustaining care from a patient in an apparently irreversible vegetative state cannot rest on the broad principle articulated by the Master of the Rolls. The general concerns of protecting patients and doctors and reassuring the patients' families and the public are no less relevant to other patients in actual or potential receipt of life-prolonging care. Nor is it clear that those interests are best protected by adopting the blanket expectation that every such case should involve the costly and time-consuming process of instructing legal teams to seek a High Court declaration.

To be clear, I fully support the view that a patient's medical team need to ensure that their diagnosis and prognosis of an irreversible vegetative state complies with best medical practice and has been independently verified. In that vein, Mr. Francis, for the respondents, has suggested four safeguards: (1) every effort should be made at rehabilitation for at least six months after the injury; (2) the diagnosis of irreversible P.V.S. should not be considered confirmed until at least 12 months after the injury; (3) the diagnosis should be agreed by two other independent doctors; and (4) generally, the wishes of the patient's immediate family will be given great weight. While those safeguards might not be applicable in every case, in the absence of medical disagreement or strong objection from the patient's immediate family, they should be enough to remove the need for default judicial approval. Thus, for my part, I would support Mr. Francis' contention that reference to a court should not be triggered by the mere fact that the patient from whom life-sustaining care is to be withheld or withdrawn is in a vegetative state that is medically considered irreversible.

For these reasons, I would dismiss the appeal.

Lord Hercules

I have had the advantage of reading in advance the opinion of my noble and learned friend, Lady Athena. For the reasons she gives, with which I am in full agreement, I too would dismiss this appeal.

Lady Ares

My Lords, I too would dismiss the appeal for the reasons given by Lady Athena.

5 *Re MB*

Refusal of treatment in late pregnancy

5.1 Introduction

The eponymous 'MB' was 40 weeks pregnant when admitted to hospital. Four days later, Hollis J in the Family Division of the High Court granted a declaration that it would be lawful to perform a non-consensual caesarean section, using reasonable force if necessary. The case was heard by the Court of Appeal just over an hour later and the appeal was dismissed after a two-hour hearing with reasons handed down eight days later.[1]

MB had initially consented to the caesarean but then, because of her fear of needles, refused to allow blood samples to be taken or have anaesthetic administered by injection. She then agreed to anaesthesia by mask but later changed her mind. An expert witness described her 'needle phobia' as such that 'at the moment of panic . . . her fear dominated all'.[2] The Court of Appeal ruled that her acute needle phobia deprived her of *capacity*[3] and the administration of the anaesthetic was lawful on the basis that it was in her best interests. She consented after being told the outcome of the hearing.

Butler-Sloss LJ gave the judgment of the Court of Appeal, which did four important things. First, it affirmed and developed the common law test for adult capacity. Secondly, it held that the right of an adult with capacity to refuse treatment for any or no reason[4] applied to a pregnant woman whose refusal would endanger her fetus. Thirdly, it confirmed that the test to be applied to all incapacitated adults was the best interests test, which was 'not limited to best medical interests'.[5] *Fourthly*, it laid down a set of procedural safeguards to ensure that the declaratory procedure was not misused to override the refusal of a competent woman without her involvement.

---

1 *Re MB (Caesarean Section)* [1997] 2 FLR 426, CA (hereafter cited as *Re MB*).

2 *Re MB*, 438.

3 This chapter relies on the distinction between competence and capacity drawn in ch 3 (3.1). A *competent* patient is one judged to possess sufficient cognitive-functional faculties to be able to make a decision with respect to a given situation. A patient with *capacity* possesses the authority to make a legally valid decision.

4 *Re T* [1993] Fam 95, 102.

5 *Re MB*, 439.

116   Re MB: *refusal of treatment in pregnancy*

The chapter below is divided into five sections. The *first* will examine the four aspects of the Court of Appeal's judgment identified above, along with the relationship between refusing life-prolonging treatment and assisted suicide. The *second* section will consider how the approach of English law compares with those adopted in other jurisdictions. The *third* section examines these issues using the Principle of Generic Consistency (PGC). The *fourth* section will provide an explanatory link from the third section to the idealised judgment in the *fifth* section. That idealised judgment will draw on the idealised judgment from *Gillick* to refine the capacity test and discern legal principle to qualify the best interests test.

5.2 Legal principles on capacity and refusal of treatment in late pregnancy

5.2.1 The capacity test

Re MB was a major decision for the common law capacity test. Previous cases had given some guidance on the test for adult capacity, but a decision of an appeal court was needed to bring this guidance together as a coherent whole.

In *Re F*, Lord Donaldson had stated that capacity to make treatment decisions concerned whether a patient was 'mentally competent to appreciate the issues involved' and all three judges in the Court of Appeal had referred to the ability to exercise a 'right of choice'.[6] The House of Lords did not elaborate, save to add the obvious point that capacity required the ability to communicate.[7] The Court of Appeal in *Re T* declared that an adult was presumed to have capacity to make treatment decisions, which could be rebutted by mental illness or temporary factors such as unconsciousness, the effects of shock, fatigue, pain or drugs.[8] More serious decisions were said to require more decision-making ability than less serious decisions – a point to which I will return below.[9] More detailed guidance had to wait for the first instance decision of Thorpe J in *Re C*.[10] Thorpe J accepted the view of an expert witness that there were three-stages to the decision-making process: 'first, comprehending and retaining treatment information, second, believing it and, third, weighing it in the balance to arrive at choice'.[11] The information that the patient needs to be able to understand for this three-stage capacity test was said to concern 'the nature, purpose and effects' of the proposed treatment.[12]

The Court of Appeal in *Re MB* affirmed all these points. Butler-Sloss LJ went further and declared that a patient will only lack capacity if 'some impairment or

---

6 *Re F* [1990] 2 AC 1, 12 and 18 (Lord Donaldson MR), 31 (Neill LJ) and 34 (Butler-Sloss LJ).
7 [1990] 2 AC 1, 52 (Lord Bridge) and 74–75 (Lord Goff).
8 [1993] Fam 95, 112 and 113.
9 [1993] Fam 95, 113.
10 *Re C* [1994] 1 WLR 290.
11 [1994] 1 WLR 290, 295.
12 [1994] 1 WLR 290, 295.

disturbance of mental functioning renders the person unable to make a decision' and the purpose of the three-stage *Re C* test was to determine whether there is such an inability.[13] The information that the patient must be able to understand and retain was said to be that 'which is material to the decision, especially as to the likely consequences of having, or not having, the treatment in question'.[14] This is very similar to the test subsequently enacted in the Mental Capacity Act 2005, which is examined in some depth in Chapter 3 (3.3.2). Three issues require further consideration here: the relevance to the adult capacity test of (a) risk-relativity, (b) the diagnostic requirement and (c) temporary factors.

(a) Risk-relativity

With regard to risk-relativity, Butler-Sloss LJ expressly approved this statement of Lord Donaldson in *Re T*:

> What matters is that the doctors should consider whether at that time he had a capacity which was commensurate with the gravity of the decision which he purported to make. The more serious the decision, the greater the capacity required.[15]

In her words, '[t]he graver the consequences of the decision, the commensurately greater the level of competence is required to take the decision'.[16]

As defined in this book, neither capacity nor competence can be possessed in degrees or levels.[17] These are binary judgments about a specific individual facing a specific task at a specific time: competent or incompetent, capacitated or incapacitated. Lord Donaldson and Butler-Sloss LJ made their comments in the context of discussions about when patients are to be treated as having the legal authority to make their own decisions. Thus, what is said to vary according to the seriousness/ gravity of the decision must be the abilities required for capacity or the level of scrutiny given to a patient's abilities when assessing capacity.

Lord Donaldson and Butler-Sloss LJ were adopting a risk-relative sliding scale of capacity. They apparently considered the threshold criteria for capacity to be higher for refusals of life-saving treatment than, say, the mending of a broken finger and generally higher for refusals of medically-indicated treatment than for consent to the same treatment. Gunn and his co-authors demur by suggesting that Lord Donaldson was referring to the complexity of the decision in a way that is not directly linked to its risks.[18] Lord Donaldson, however, went on to say:

---

13 *Re MB*, 437. Butler-Sloss LJ omitted to refer to the second stage of the *Re C* test, but has subsequently made it clear that the Court of Appeal had approved the full test: *Re B* [2002] EWHC 429, [33].

14 *Re MB*, 437.

15 [1993] Fam 95, 113.

16 *Re MB*, 437.

17 See ch 3 (3.1) and n 3 above, for definitions.

18 See Gunn et al 1999, 273.

118 Re MB: *refusal of treatment in pregnancy*

Doctors faced with a refusal of consent have to give very careful and detailed consideration to what was the patient's capacity to decide at the time when the decision was made. It may not be a case of capacity or no capacity. It may be a case of reduced capacity. What matters is whether at that time the patient's capacity was reduced below the level needed in the case of a refusal of that importance, *for refusals can vary in importance. Some may involve a risk to life or of irreparable damage to health.* Others may not.[19]

Here his Lordship explicitly links seriousness and importance to the 'risk to life or of irreparable damage to health'.

Underlying this discussion is a tension between the two risk-relative approaches: *strong* and *weak* risk-relativity.[20] Both types of risk-relatively vary the threshold criteria for capacity (or procedural safeguards for assessing capacity) according to the risk that the patient will cause herself permanent harm.

Strong risk-relativity takes the risk of harm as its primary concern, rather than seeking to determine whether the patient is capable of making a considered choice to accept that risk or outcome. This approach is incompatible with the competence-based approach, because it can deny capacity to a patient who is genuinely believed to be competent (such as where she is refusing treatment aimed at preventing death or severe permanent harm) and grant capacity to a patient who is genuinely believed to be incompetent (such as where she is consenting to life-saving treatment). An example of this approach can be found in judicial declarations to the effect that a mature child's refusal of life-saving treatment may be overridden by parental or judicial consent, irrespective of the child's competence.[21]

Weak risk-relativity is concerned with the risk that the patient will unwittingly cause herself irreversible harm. This approach seeks to maximise patient autonomy by leaving the decision to the patient where doing so does not unduly risk unintentional self-harm. It therefore seeks to deny capacity to a patient only if she is uncontroversially considered to be incompetent (after appropriate dialogical and supportive interaction) *or* if there is genuine doubt as to the patient's cognitive ability to make a considered choice *and* complying with the patient's views carries non-trivial risk of death or irreversible damage to health. Weak risk-relativity requires capacity to be determined by competence assessment with the procedural safeguards and level of scrutiny given to a patient's decision-making abilities being risk-relative. Accordingly, patients whose competence status is genuinely unclear may be granted legal authority to consent to uncontroversially life-saving treatment but not to a risky experimental treatment, participation in research or to volunteer as an organ donor. Similarly, such patients may be granted the capacity to refuse treatment for minor conditions but not to refuse life-saving treatment of the same level of medical complexity. In Chapter 3,

---

19 *Re T* [1993] Fam 95, 116 (emphasis added).
20 These were briefly distinguished in ch 3 (3.4.1 and 3.4.2).
21 See the discussion of *Re R* [1991] 4 All ER 177 and *Re W* [1993] Fam 64 in ch 3, esp 3.3.1 and 3.4.2.

Re MB: *refusal of treatment in pregnancy*   119

weak risk-relativity was defended as compatible with the PGC and applied by Lady Athena in *Gillick*.[22]

While English law has elements of both strong and weak risk-relativity,[23] the above statements from Lord Donaldson and Butler-Sloss LJ are compatible with weak risk-relativity. The subsequently enacted Mental Capacity Act 2005 makes no reference to the likelihood of a tragic outcome when assessing a patient's capacity, but it does emphasise that capacity assessment must not assume a lack of capacity on the basis of a particular diagnosis or condition.[24] Similarly, s 1(3) states that an individual is not to be treated as lacking capacity 'unless all practical steps to help . . . have been taken without success'. These procedural safeguards reduce the danger that a competent patient will be deprived of capacity solely on the basis that she faces a significant risk to her life or health, while permitting additional precautionary steps in situations of significant risk.

(b) The diagnostic threshold

Butler-Sloss LJ's formulation of the adult capacity test was influenced by the Law Commission's report on *Mental Incapacity*.[25] The Law Commission had proposed that the capacity test should require that a person's inability to make a decision should be linked to a 'disability or disorder of the mind or brain, whether permanent or temporary, which results in an impairment or disturbance of mental functioning'.[26] Butler-Sloss LJ apparently agreed, because she concluded that the patient's inability to make a decision must be as a result of 'some impairment or disturbance of mental functioning'.[27] A very similarly worded diagnostic requirement can now be found in s 2(1) of the Mental Capacity Act 2005.[28]

While Butler-Sloss LJ was not explicit in her reasons for concluding that the common law capacity test had a diagnostic requirement, the Law Commission had argued that it was needed to ensure that those who made 'unusual or unwise decisions' were not ipso facto denied capacity.[29] Halliday has similarly argued that the diagnostic requirement in the 2005 Act, by preventing a finding of incapacity purely on the basis of an inability to comply with the functional aspect of the test, should prevent a pregnant woman from being deprived of capacity on the basis of the ordinary stress and pains of labour.[30] This seems a rather indirect way of ensuring that the capacity assessor does not seek to replace the patient's preferences and values with her own or

---

22 See 3.4.2 and 3.6. See also 5.4.1, below.
23 Strong risk-relativity underpins both the law on the refusals of mature minors (see 3.3.1 and 3.4.2) and mental health law (see Pattinson 2017b, 179–182).
24 See s 2(3)(b) of the 2005 Act and Department for Constitutional Affairs 2007, para 4.48.
25 *Re MB*, 433–434 and 437.
26 Law Commission 1995, [3.12].
27 *Re MB*, 437.
28 See the discussion in ch 3 (3.3.2)
29 Law Commission 1995, [3.8].
30 Halliday 2016, 86, commenting on Johnson J's decision in *Norfolk and Norwich Healthcare Trust v W* [1997] 1 FCR 269 (discussed below in relation to temporary factors).

120 Re MB: *refusal of treatment in pregnancy*

those of the wider community. The 2005 Act also deals with this directly by stating, in s 1(4), that '[a] person is not to be treated as unable to make a decision merely because he makes an unwise decision'.

The diagnostic requirement also presents the risk of an incompetent patient being granted capacity. The Code of Practice to the Mental Capacity Act 2005 suggests that the effect of s 2(1) is that the Act does not apply to those who 'are unable to make the decision for some other reason, for example because they are overwhelmed by the implications of the decision'.[31] As explained in Chapter 3 (3.3.3), if this is so, then it follows that the diagnostic requirement implies that this capacity test departs from a competence-based standard. A patient who is, for example, completely overcome with emotion every time she thinks about her cancer lacks the cognitive-functional ability to make a decision. Even if she is considered cognitively able to make other decisions at an equivalent level of complexity, she is unable to apply those abilities to the situation in which she finds herself. As Lady Athena's opinion will demonstrate, a competence-based test need not require that the patient's inability to make the decision be causally linked to a clinically recognised mental impairment or disorder.

(c) Temporary factors

The third capacity issue from *Re MB* requiring further consideration is the Court's approach to the 'temporary factors' advanced by Lord Donaldson in *Re T* as potential grounds for a lack of capacity. While some of the first instance decisions overruling women's refusals in late pregnancy did not apply a capacity test[32] or invoked s 63 of the Mental Health Act,[33] most had concluded that the pregnant woman temporarily lacked capacity.[34] In the first of two cases heard in a single day, Johnson J held a woman to lack capacity on the basis that she was incapable of weighing up the relevant considerations.[35] The patient had a history of mental illness and, despite obvious indications to the contrary, denied that she was pregnant. His Lordship emphasised the debilitating effects of the 'acute emotional stress and physical pain [that arises] in the ordinary course of labour'.[36] In the second case, Johnson J held the patient to be 'unable to make any valid decision, about anything of even the most trivial kind' because of the pain and emotional stress of labour.[37] She was considered competent by her obstetrician, whose view Johnson J rejected without even setting eyes on her. In *Re MB*, Butler-Sloss LJ (in my view correctly) doubted whether the evidence before Johnson J was sufficient to support his conclusion.[38]

---

31 Department for Constitutional Affairs 2007, [12.13].
32 *Re S* [1993] Fam 123.
33 *Tameside and Glossop Acute Services Trust v CH* [1996] 1 FLR 762.
34 *Re L* [1997] 2 FLR 837; *Norfolk and Norwich Healthcare Trust v W* [1997] 1 FCR 269 and *Rochdale NHS Trust v C* [1997] 1 FCR 274.
35 *Norfolk and Norwich Healthcare Trust v W* [1997] 1 FCR 269, 272.
36 [1997] 1 FCR 269, 272.
37 *Rochdale NHS Trust v C* [1997] 1 FCR 274, 275.
38 *Re MB*, 435.

Perhaps one reason why Lord Donaldson's temporary factors proved so malleable was that the Court of Appeal in *Re T* was actually unclear on their application to the heavily pregnant Miss T at the time of making her advance refusal. Lord Donaldson thought that there was 'abundant evidence' to overturn the first instance judge's conclusion that she had capacity on the basis of her 'physical and mental state', including the fact that she was in 'severe pain' and drugged.[39] Butler-Sloss LJ chose not to overturn the first instance judge's conclusion that she had capacity.[40] Staughton LJ agreed with both. In *Re MB*, Butler-Sloss LJ took the opportunity to make it clear that women were not to be artificially found to temporarily lack capacity by dint of the ordinary pain and stress of labour:

> The 'temporary factors' mentioned by Lord Donaldson MR in *Re T* (confusion, shock, fatigue, pain or drugs) may completely erode capacity but those concerned must be satisfied that such factors are operating to such a degree that the ability to decide is absent.[41]

Nonetheless, MB's acute needle phobia was found to have deprived her of capacity. Butler-Sloss LJ reached this conclusion by relying on an expert witness who claimed that 'at the moment of panic . . . her fear dominated all'.[42] That same expert witness was dismissive of MB's general understanding, describing her as 'a naive, not very bright, frightened young woman'.[43] Morris poignantly asks whether the Court would still have concluded that MB lacked capacity if the expert witness had not considered her naïve and if she had expressed a clear preference for a vaginal delivery.[44]

It is now over 20 years since *Re MB* and we are still waiting for a case in which a woman is recognised to have capacity to refuse a medically recommended caesarean before it takes place.[45] In *St George's Healthcare NHS Trust v S*, a woman obtained a declaration from the Court of Appeal to the effect that her treatment had amounted to trespass, but by that point she had been discharged from hospital with a healthy baby following a caesarean section, which had been supported by a High Court declaration.[46] In *Bolton Hospitals NHS Trust v O*, Butler-Sloss P held another pregnant woman to be temporarily incapacitated on the basis of her overwhelming panic.[47] She was suffering from post-traumatic stress disorder as a result of four previous caesareans and, when another was recommended, her

---

39 [1993] Fam 95, 111.
40 [1993] Fam 95, 118.
41 *Re MB*, 437.
42 *Re MB*, 438.
43 *Re MB*, 430.
44 Morris 2002, 109.
45 cf other jurisdictions below (5.3).
46 *St George's Healthcare NHS Trust v S* [1999] Fam 26.
47 *Bolton Hospitals NHS Trust v O* [2002] EWHC 2871, [15].

122 Re MB: *refusal of treatment in pregnancy*

panic was found to have left her unable to 'see through the consequences of the act'.[48] More recent cases – one heard by the Court of Protection in 2012 and the other in 2013 – concerned heavily pregnant women with serious mental illnesses who, all expert witnesses agreed, clearly lacked competence.[49]

5.2.2 The assisted suicide issue

Before addressing the prioritisation of the woman's interests over those of the fetus, I want to briefly consider the fact that English law permits refusal even where the life of the patient herself is endangered. The Court of Appeal in *Re MB* held that an adult who satisfies the capacity test was entitled to refuse to consent to any medical treatment, 'even though the consequence may be death or serious handicap of the child she bears, or her own death'.[50] The right of an adult with capacity to refuse life-saving treatment was already well established[51] and its application in late pregnancy (technically obiter in *Re MB* on the basis that she lacked capacity) was soon after confirmed by the Court of Appeal.[52]

Given the statutory prohibition of assisted suicide in the Suicide Act 1961, it might be thought that life-endangering refusals are subject to the patient not intending to commit suicide or at least the doctor not intending to assist in such a suicide. In no case of life-endangering refusals of caesarean sections has the woman apparently been intending to commit suicide, but what if her refusal was the result of such an intention? Is a doctor who withdraws treatment in response to the refusal of a suicidally motivated patient assisting in her suicide?

Under s 2(1) of the Suicide Act 1961, as amended, it is an offence to *intentionally* encourage or assist the suicide or attempted suicide of another, punishable by up to 14 years' imprisonment. The courts have hitherto refused to interpret the refusals of life-sustaining treatment that have come before them as suicidal, let alone view the doctor as intending to assist in the patient's suicide. In *Bland*, Lord Goff was explicit that a patient with capacity who refuses life-saving treatment was simply doing what she was entitled to do and 'there is no question of the patient having committed suicide, nor therefore of the doctor having aided or abetted him in doing so'.[53]

A doctor who complies with a suicidally motivated refusal need not, of course, have the purpose of assisting the patient's suicide. The doctor may have come to the conclusion that the life-sustaining treatment should not be provided anyway (perhaps on the basis that it is futile or too burdensome) or may merely wish to

---

48 [2002] EWHC 2871, [15].
49 *Re AA* [2012] EWHC 4378 and *Re P* [2013] EWHC 4581.
50 *Re MB*, 437.
51 See *Re T* [1993] Fam 95, esp 102 (obiter); *Bland* [1993] AC 789, esp 857 and 864 (obiter); *Re C* [1994] 1 WLR 290 (ratio).
52 *St George's Healthcare NHS Trust v S* [1999] Fam 26.
53 [1993] AC 789, 864.

respect the patient's legal right to refuse treatment. But what if a doctor believes a refusal to be suicidally motivated and also believes that if she were to act on that refusal her own intention (purpose) would be to assist in that suicide? In theory, she cannot remove the life-sustaining treatment without committing assisted suicide and cannot continue to treat the patient without committing assault and battery. That doctor would therefore seem to be required to immediately transfer the patient to the care of another who is capable of acting on the refusal without intending to assist in the patient's suicide. In practice, it would be very difficult to persuade a jury that the doctor's intention was to assist in suicide. In any event, the consent of the Director of Public Prosecutions is required for prosecution under s 2(4) of the Act, and that consent is unlikely to be forthcoming. Thus, this issue is more of a theoretical than a practical concern. It will not be addressed by Lady Athena in the idealised judgment below on the basis that it was very clear on the facts that MB's life was not at risk.

5.2.3 The interests of the fetus

The fetus[54] could be granted three types of legal protection: (a) direct protection, (b) retrospective protection when born alive, or (c) indirect protection as a result of protection of the pregnant woman. As will be shown below, English law grants all three forms of protection. While the fetus is not a legal person, it is not treated as a valueless thing.[55]

English law therefore cannot be aligned to the view that the fetus is owed direct moral duties of the same weight as those owed to you or me (full status), which would imply legal personhood. Nor can English law be aligned with the view that the fetus is owed no direct moral duties at all (no status), which would imply no direct legal protection. Instead, the law aligns with a view between these extremes, according to which the fetus is owed direct duties that have less weight than those owed to you or me (limited status). The most popular limited status position holds that the fetus' value to be gradualist or proportional to gestational development until it obtains full moral status at birth or beyond. This proportional status view, it will be shown below, most easily explains the direct legal protection granted by English law to the developing human.

An embryo outside the body falls within the Human Fertilisation and Embryology Act 1990. The fetus inside the woman's body falls within ss 58 and 59 of the Offences Against the Person Act 1861 and s 1 of the Infant Life (Preservation) Act 1929, subject to s 1(1) of the Abortion Act 1967, as amended. Before implantation the embryo may be lawfully destroyed without relying on any of the grounds in the abortion legislation. In fact, it must be destroyed if

---

54 Technically, the term 'fetus' only applies from 8 weeks' gestation, but for convenience I will adopt this term for the entity within the woman's body at all points of development.
55 See Pattinson 2002a, ch 4; Scott 2004; Pattinson 2006/2017b, chs 7–9; Cornock & Montgomery 2011.

124 Re MB: *refusal of treatment in pregnancy*

either gamete provider withdraws consent to its storage or use.[56] The fetus has greater protection within the womb. The most permissive ground for abortion only applies up to 24 weeks,[57] but the more restrictive grounds for abortion apply up to birth.[58] Legal personality is only acquired at birth.[59] The result is that English law grants increasing protection to the developing human according to four legally relevant thresholds: (a) preimplantation (currently up to the development of the primitive streak or 14 days, whichever is earlier);[60] (b) implantation to 24 weeks; (c) post-24 weeks; and (d) birth.[61]

In *Re MB*, Butler-Sloss LJ pointed out that the Abortion Act 'gives precedence to the health of the mother over the unborn child'.[62] Three of the four grounds for abortion do indeed concern the mother's health or life: abortion is permitted up to 24 weeks where the continuance of the pregnancy would involve risk, greater than if the pregnancy were terminated, of physical or mental injury to the pregnant woman (s 1(1)(a)), and up to birth where necessary to prevent grave permanent injury to her health or serious risk to her life (ss 1(1)(b)/(c)). But the fetus is still protected against less pressing maternal interests and desires. Under the current law, a pregnant woman without a defence under the Abortion Act may be convicted of unlawfully procuring a miscarriage.[63]

In addition to direct legal protection during its development, the fetus is given retrospective protection. The law of tort enables a child who is born alive to sue for damages in respect of injuries inflicted before birth. Under the Congenital Disabilities (Civil Liability) Act 1976, the right to sue materialises at birth and requires a breach of duty owed to its parents.[64] A child born before this Act came into force on 22 July 1976 has a similar action at common law in negligence.[65] The criminal law has also been prepared to grant retrospective protection to the fetus. In *A-G's Reference (No 3 of 1994)*, which was pending at the time of *Re MB*, the House of Lords held that the requirements of manslaughter could be made out when a child's death could be shown to have been caused by injuries inflicted before birth.[66] Lord Mustill declared that a fetus was 'an organism *sui generis*', neither simply part of its mother nor as a legal person.[67]

---

56 Subject to a cooling off period: Human Fertilisation and Embryology Act 1990, Sch 3, para 4A.

57 Abortion Act 1967, s 1(1)(a).

58 Abortion Act 1967, s 1(1)(b)–(d).

59 eg *Paton v BPAS* [1979] QB 276, *In Re F (In Utero)* [1988] Fam 122, *C v S* [1988] QB 135, *Burton v Islington Health Authority* [1993] QB 204.

60 Human Fertilisation and Embryology Act 1990, s 3(3)(a).

61 See further Pattinson 2002a, ch 4; 2017b, chs 7–10; 2017c.

62 *Re MB*, 441.

63 Under the Offences Against the Person Act 1861, s 58: *R v Catt* [2013] EWCA Crim 1187.

64 ss 1(1), 1(3) and 2.

65 *Burton v Islington HA* and *De Martell v Merton and Sutton HA* [1993] QB 204. Similar decisions have been reached in other jurisdictions: see Todd 2017, 241–242.

66 *Attorney-General's Reference (No 3 of 1994)* [1998] AC 245.

67 [1998] AC 245, 255–256 (Lord Mustill, with whom their Lordships agreed).

The retrospective protection granted to the fetus is, however, principally against third parties *other than its mother*. The 1976 Act explicitly grants maternal immunity, except in the context of negligent driving where there is compulsory insurance.[68] While the English courts have not yet definitively ruled out a claim against the mother at common law, it has been ruled out by the Supreme Court of Canada.[69] In *A-G's Reference (No 3 of 1994)*, there was no conflict between the interests of the mother and her fetus. She was stabbed in the stomach by a third party, which resulted in her premature labour and seriously premature child surviving for only 121 days. More recently, the Court of Appeal has held that a child who had been injured before birth by her mother's excessive alcohol consumption could not claim compensation from the Criminal Injuries Compensation Authority.[70] The Court reasoned that at the time of the injury the fetus was not a legal person, so could not be regarded as being 'any other person' for the purposes of s 23 of the Offences Against the Person Act 1861. This enabled the Court of Appeal to declare that it had reached a conclusion that was consistent with maternal immunity from tort under the 1976 Act.[71] *AG's Reference (No 3 of 1994)* was distinguished on the basis that the actus reus of manslaughter was not complete until death took place, by which time the child was a legal person, whereas the actus reus of the s 23 offence was not made out because it required the administration of poison to a person and there was no person at the relevant time.[72] Retrospective protection granted to the fetus therefore has little purchase against the pregnant woman.

In *Re MB*, Butler-Sloss LJ concluded:

> Although it might seem illogical that a child capable of being born alive is protected by the criminal law from intentional destruction, and by the Abortion Act from termination, otherwise than as permitted by the Act, but is not protected from the (irrational) decision of a competent mother not to allow medical intervention to avert the risk of death, this appears to be the present state of the law.[73]

This rejects Lord Donaldson's obiter caveat in *Re T* to the 'absolute' right of an adult with capacity to refuse treatment: '[t]he only possible qualification is a case in which the choice may lead to the death of a viable foetus'.[74] Butler-Sloss LJ went on to declare that the fetus did not have any legal interests until birth that were 'capable of being taken into account when a court has to consider an application for a declaration in respect of a caesarian [sic] section operation'.[75] It followed

---

68 Congenital Disabilities (Civil Liability) Act 1976, s 1(1). See further Law Commission 1974 and Pattinson 2017b, 326–329.
69 See *Burton* [1993] QB 204, 232 (Dillion LJ) and *Dobson v Dobson* [1999] 2 SCR 753, respectively.
70 *CICA v First-tier Tribunal (Social Entitlement Chamber)* [2014] EWCA Civ 1554.
71 [2014] EWCA Civ 1554, [47] (Treacy LJ) and [67] (Lord Dyson MR).
72 [2014] EWCA Civ 1554, esp [63].
73 *Re MB*, 441.
74 [1993] Fam 95, 102; followed in *Re S* [1993] Fam 123.
75 *Re MB*, 444.

126 Re MB: *refusal of treatment in pregnancy*

that the lawfulness of performing a caesarean on the incapacitated MB was to be determined solely by reference to her legal interests, which the Court of Appeal assessed by applying the best interests test (see 5.2.4). In a more recent decision of the Court of Protection, Mostyn J followed *Re MB* and accordingly declared that 'the interests of this unborn child are not the concern of this court as the child has no legal existence until he or she is born, other than in respect of tortious acts committed on him or her'.[76]

In *St George's Healthcare*, Judge LJ recognised that the fetus does have legal interests: '[w]hatever else it may be a 36-week foetus is not nothing: if viable it is not lifeless and it is certainly human'.[77] He went on to affirm, as part of the ratio of the case before the Court of Appeal, the view that a woman with capacity was entitled to refuse treatment for herself or her fetus. This was because the fetus' 'need for medical assistance does not prevail over her rights'.[78] If we accept the decision in *Re MB*, this surely follows. It would be perverse if the fetus' interests could not prevail over the rights of an incompetent woman but could prevail over the rights of a competent woman.

5.2.4 Best interests

MB was willing to consent to the caesarean section, but had withdrawn that consent because her fear of needles led her to object to the taking of blood samples and the administration of anaesthetic. She had been offered and initially consented to anaesthesia by mask, but later withdrew that consent (it seems because of the risk of regurgitating and inhaling stomach contents following use of the mask). Her agreement to the most invasive part of her treatment simplified the Court of Appeal's assessment of her best interests. The Court of Appeal therefore chose to consider whether the administration of anaesthesia was in her best interests without providing guidance on the application of the best interests test to other cases.

Caesareans are major operations. They expose women to risks of haemorrhage, infection and damage to their abdominal organs.[79] Michalowski, in her commentary on *Re MB*, points out that 9 to 15 per cent of caesareans lead to serious side effects and the risk of maternal mortality is between 2 and 11 times higher than for vaginal delivery.[80] Other sources concur: Hall and Bewley cite figures indicating that maternal death is three times more likely to occur following an elective caesarean than vaginal delivery and nine times more likely following an emergency caesarean.[81] A woman who has had a

---

76 *Re AA* [2012] EWHC 4378, [5].
77 *St George's Healthcare NHS Trust v S* [1999] Fam 26, 45.
78 [1999] Fam 26, 50.
79 See Halliday 2016, 16.
80 Michalowski 1999, 122.
81 Hall & Bewley 1999; see also Donohoe 1996, 200–202.

Re MB: *refusal of treatment in pregnancy*   127

caesarean will often need to deliver any future child in the same way and the procedure can hinder maternal-fetal bonding and leave a scar.[82]

Since weight was implicitly placed on MB's desire to have a healthy child and her support for the caesarean,[83] this case could be considered a missed opportunity to revisit *Bland*'s dismissive dicta on the substituted judgment test.[84] The substituted judgment test seeks to treat an incompetent patient by reference to that patient's core values and thereby seeks to reach the decision the patient would have made had she been competent; whereas the best interests test asks whether the proposed course of action is the best one for the patient, all things considered. The Court of Appeal went straight to the best interests test on the basis of the decision of the House of Lords in *Re F*,[85] although *Re F* was not a case in which the substituted judgment test could have been applied, because F had never been competent to make the type of decision in question.

The Court of Appeal's reliance on *Re F* was, nonetheless, selective.[86] The House of Lords in *Re F* had relied on the *Bolam* test, whereby what is in the patient's best interests was to be determined by reference to a responsible body of medical opinion.[87] Yet, Butler-Sloss LJ did not mention *Bolam* or the negligence standard and instead declared that best interests were 'not limited to best medical interests'.[88] Butler-Sloss LJ was, in effect, following the judgment of the Court of Appeal (of which she was a member) in *Re F* over that of the House of Lords.[89] Later cases, led by her Ladyship, affirmed that the determination of a patient's best interests was only to start with responsible medical opinion and was ultimately a legal decision to be made by reference to all the medical, emotional and other welfare issues.[90] In this way *Re MB* began the move towards the best interests test as it now appears in s 5 of the Mental Capacity Act 2005.

On the facts, the Court of Appeal could not support the caesarean as a means of protecting MB's physical health. The court accepted that while vaginal birth presented a risk of 50 per cent to the fetus, 'there was little physical danger to the mother'.[91] The Court of Appeal therefore relied on the predicted psychological effects of her child being born injured. Reliance was placed on an expert witness

---

82 See Robertson 1983, 454.

83 *Re MB*, 439.

84 *Bland* [1993] AC 789, 871–871 (Lord Goff) and 895 (Lord Mustill). See further below (5.5).

85 [1990] 2 AC 1.

86 See Pattinson 2006, 142–144.

87 See, in particular, [1990] 2 AC 1, 54 (Lord Bridge) and 67–68 (Lord Brandon, with whom Lord Jauncey agreed), citing *Bolam v Friern Hospital Management Committee* [1957] 1 WLR 582.

88 *Re MB*, 439.

89 The House of Lords had explicitly rejected the Court of Appeal's view that the law required something more stringent than *Bolam*: [1990] 2 AC 1, 54, 67–68. Such willingness to depart from a problematic precedent will be defended in ch 6 (6.2).

90 *Re A* [2000] 1 FLR 549, 555; *Re S* [2001] Fam 15, 28 and 29; *Simms v Simms* [2002] EWHC 2734, [42]; *A Hospital NHS Trust v S* [2003] EWHC 365, [43].

91 *Re MB*, 439.

128 Re MB: *refusal of treatment in pregnancy*

to support the conclusion that 'she was likely to suffer significant long-term damage if there was no operation and the child was born handicapped or died'.[92] The same expert witness had also concluded that MB was unlikely to suffer psychiatric harm from imposing the procedure upon her. He had, however, reached that conclusion on the basis that she was not against the caesarean, rather than by consideration of the likely impact of ignoring her needle phobia.

Once a finding of incapacity has been made, the courts have been consistently willing to issue a declaration to the effect that a medically recommended caesarean is lawful. In *Bolton Hospitals NHS Trust v O*, Butler-Sloss P issued such a declaration without even mentioning the best interests test.[93] There was also no mention of the substituted judgment test, yet the declaration was apparently issued on the basis that the patient wanted it issued so that the decision could be 'taken out of her hands'.[94] More recently, in *Re AA*, Mostyn J found a planned caesarean to be in the best interests of an incapacitated woman on the basis that a vaginal birth presented a significant risk of uterine rupture with concomitant physical and psychiatric consequences for the woman.[95] His Lordship went on to opine:

> I would also add, I hope not at variance with *Re MB*, that I would have thought it was in her best interests, that is, her mental health best interests, that her child should be born alive and healthy and that such result should be, if possible achieved, and such risks attendant should be avoided. I think, looked at from her point of view, there is also a significant mental health advantage in her unborn child not being exposed to risk during his or her birth.[96]

That passage is worth re-reading. Mostyn J seems to be indicating that he would have declared the caesarean to be in her best interests even in the absence of any risk to her physical health. Crucially, his declared willingness to rely on her 'mental health best interests' makes no mention of the need for supportive psychiatric evidence specific to this particular patient. There seems to be a keen judicial desire to find an unwanted caesarean to be lawful.

5.2.5 Procedural safeguards

The judgment in *Re MB* concluded by setting down procedural guidance 'to be followed when the medical profession feel it necessary to seek declarations from the courts'.[97] Butler-Sloss LJ advised that:

---

92 *Re MB*, 439.
93 [2002] EWHC 2871.
94 [2002] EWHC 2871, [14].
95 [2012] EWHC 4378, [4].
96 [2012] EWHC 4378, [5].
97 *Re MB*, 445.

Re MB: *refusal of treatment in pregnancy* 129

(1) the court's jurisdiction turned on capacity;
(2) a declaration should be sought where there were doubts as to capacity;
(3) a potential problem should be identified as early as possible to enable the hospital and patient to obtain legal advice;
(4) it was highly desirable that any judicial involvement occurs before it becomes an emergency;
(5) any hearing should be inter partes;
(6) the pregnant woman should be represented, unless exceptionally, she does not wish to be;
(7) the Official Solicitor be notified of all applications and invited to act as guardian ad litem or amicus curiae;
(8) there should be evidence on competence, preferably from a psychiatrist;
(9) the Court of Appeal's advice in this judgment be made available to persons providing evidence; and
(10) information about the patient and her circumstances should be provided to the judge to enable evaluation of the patient's best interests.

Despite the care taken with this ten-point guidance, almost every point had been ignored in the next case to be brought before the Court of Appeal. In *St George's Healthcare NHS Trust v S*, a woman who refused an induced delivery was sectioned under the Mental Health Act 1983 and the hospital authorities applied for, and obtained, an ex parte declaration that the treatment could be administered against her will.[98] Not only did those treating her accept that she understood the risks and still wanted a natural delivery, she never received treatment for any mental illness, the court hearing had been arranged without her or her solicitor being informed, and the judge had been falsely led to believe that this was an emergency situation in which the patient was actually in labour. The Court of Appeal reiterated and re-expressed the guidance in *Re MB* and emphasised that a hearing without the patient being involved or represented could in no way protect the hospital.[99] It is deeply concerning that it took two Court of Appeal judgments to give practical effect to matters as straightforward as ensuring that any hearing is not entirely one-sided and involves the judge being accurately and fully informed of the facts.

Halliday points out that some of these procedural safeguards 'appear to have been circumvented' in *Re AA*.[100] The application was characterised as 'urgent' and counsel apologised for putting incomplete documentation before the judge, suggesting a failure to follow procedural requirements 3, 4 and 10, above.[101] It is also striking that the judge's declaration that the caesarean was lawful was to be kept from the patient until after it had been performed![102]

---

98 [1999] Fam 26.
99 [1999] Fam 26, 63–65.
100 See *Re AA* [2012] EWHC 4378 and Halliday 2016, 69–70.
101 [2012] EWHC 4378, note by Mostyn J, and exchange between the judge and Ms Burnham.
102 Declaration 5.

5.3 Other jurisdictions

A shocking illustration of the brutality of a forced caesarean can be found in the US case of *Re AC*. Angela Carder was in the late stages of terminal cancer and pregnant. Despite medical advice that a caesarean was likely to hasten her death and unlikely to save the fetus, the hospital sought a declaration that this invasive procedure could be performed without her consent. The District Court of Washington DC granted the declaration.[103] In the eloquent words of Faludi:

> So instead of treating her cancer, they jammed a tube down her throat, pumped her with sedatives, a strategy to delay the hour of death. Carder tried to fight this 'treatment', her mother says, remembering how her daughter thrashed and twisted on the bed fending off the doctors. 'She said, "No, no, no. Don't do that to me".' But Carder lost the battle and was, quite literally, silenced. With the tube in place, she couldn't speak.[104]

The District of Columbia Court of Appeals refused to stay this decision on appeal,[105] but later vacated its earlier judgment following the death of both the mother and fetus.[106] Ultimately, and too late for Angela, a pregnant woman was held to have the right to refuse treatment. Terry J added a potential caveat by conceding 'the possibility' that the patient's wishes might yield to 'a conflicting state interest' in an 'extremely rare and truly exceptional' case.[107] This caveat has been eagerly invoked by courts wishing to reach a different conclusion.[108]

US case law is, however, divided. Halliday has pointed out that while the Appellate Court of Illinois has expressly supported the right of a competent woman to refuse a caesarean,[109] other state courts have been willing to authorise, and even order, treatment to protect the fetus on the basis of the state's interest in potential life, which has been regarded as compelling at viability.[110] Many US states have also been prepared to compel a pregnant woman to undergo a blood transfusion for the benefit of the fetus.[111]

Review of the US jurisprudence highlights a further point that perusal of the English case law could lead us to overlook: medical experts can wrongly predict the likely effects of vaginal childbirth when recommending a caesarean section. In one case before a federal district court, Hinkle J accepted the 'clear and uncontradicted evidence' that a previous caesarean section had created a

---

103 114 Daily Wash Law Rptr 2233 (DC Super Ct July 26, 1986), reprinted as an appendix to *Re AC*, 573 A2d 1235, 1262 (DC App 1990).

104 Faludi 1992, 469; also quoted in Fox & Moreton 2015, 161.

105 533 A2d 611 (DC, 1987).

106 573 A2d 1235 (DC App, 1990).

107 573 A2d 1235, 1252.

108 See eg *Pemberton v Tallahassee Memorial Regional Medical Centre*, 66 F Supp 2d 1247 (ND Fla 1999), 1254 (n 18) and the English law case of *Re S* [1993] Fam 123, 124.

109 *In re Baby Boy Doe, a Fetus v Mother Doe* 632 NE 2d 326 (1994).

110 See Halliday 2016, 38.

111 See Halliday 2016, 8–16, 38.

Re MB: *refusal of treatment in pregnancy*   131

'very substantial risk' that vaginal delivery would result in uterine rupture and fetal death.[112] Yet, Halliday points out, in subsequent pregnancies the woman in question went on to have four successful vaginal deliveries.[113] English medical law cases outside the context of refused caesareans are similarly replete with mistaken medical predictions.[114]

Germany and Ireland present an interesting contrast to the approach in this jurisdiction and in the US. Despite the German constitutional court ruling that the fetus is a beneficiary of the constitutional guarantee of human dignity and the right to life, and German law's recognition of positive duties to the fetus, 'there are no reported cases of German courts ordering obstetric intervention against the wishes of a pregnant woman'.[115] Similarly, although Article 40.3.3° of the Irish Constitution expressly recognised the 'right to life of the unborn', in the first caesarean refusal case to go before the Irish High Court it was held that a competent woman could not be forced to have a caesarean section against her will.[116] A woman who had had three previous caesareans was thereby held to have capacity to refuse an elective caesarean notwithstanding the consequent increased risk of injury and death to both her and her fetus. This serves as a useful reminder that recognising the fetus to be worthy of protection does not automatically lead to forced caesarean sections.

5.4 Application of the PGC

5.4.1 Capacity

I examined above Butler-Sloss LJ's assertion that the level of 'competence' (by which she meant decision-making abilities) required to make a legally valid decision is proportional to the gravity of the consequences of that decision.[117] This invited consideration of a risk-relative approach to capacity, which varies the threshold criteria and procedure according to the expected harm/benefit from complying with the patient's expressed view, and will thereby err towards non-interference where the risk of harm is low and towards interference where the risk of harm is high. It was argued in Chapter 3 (3.4.2) that strong risk relativity is incompatible with the PGC. This is because a patient has a basic generic right to decide for herself whether to accept interference with her bodily integrity and all generic rights have waivable benefits. But to reject all forms of risk-relativity is to claim that no account should ever be taken of the consequences of making a

---

112 *Pemberton v Tallahassee Memorial Regional Medical Centre*, 66 F Supp 2d 1247 (ND Fla 1999), 1254.
113 See Halliday 2016, 25.
114 See eg the discussion of *Re C* [1994] 1 WLR 290 and *R v Portsmouth Hospitals NHS Trust ex p Glass* [1999] 2 FLR 905 in Pattinson 2017b, 563.
115 Halliday 2016, 93.
116 *Health Service Executive v B* [2016] IEHC 605. For critique of the High Court's reasoning, notwithstanding support for its conclusion, see Wade 2017. In May 2018, a referendum overwhelmingly passed to replace Article 40.3.3° with the phrase 'Provision may be made by law for the regulation of termination of pregnancy'.
117 *Re MB*, 437 and 5.2.1.

132   Re MB: *refusal of treatment in pregnancy*

mistake either way. Rejection of risk-relativity as such would imply that cases of genuine doubt as to the patient's competence (which can persist even after appropriate dialogical and supportive interaction) are to be treated as if no doubt exists and no account is to be taken of the level of harm faced in such circumstances. This risks preventable generic harm to patients and a good faith attempt to apply the PGC must therefore allow reliance on weak risk-relativity. This reasoning informed Lady Athena's opinion in the idealised *Gillick* judgment.

The discussion of strong risk-relativity in Chapter 3 focussed on its rejection of the decisive authority of the patient's competent decision where giving effect to her will is likely to result in her death or serious harm to her health. Strong risk-relativity can also take account of the risk to others, thereby disempowering a competent patient where the more important interests of others are at stake. This second element arises if the fetus has moral interests capable of outweighing those of the pregnant woman. It will, however, be argued in the next section that the woman's basic generic rights outweigh the fetus' right to life (5.4.2). From this it follows that strong risk-relativity in either form is to be rejected when assessing capacity to refuse invasive treatment during pregnancy. Care must therefore be taken to ensure that weak risk-relativity is not used to mask concerns that support or imply rejection of the competence-based approach to capacity, as per strong risk-relativity.

The caesarean section cases that have been addressed by the courts of England and Wales were brought in high-pressured circumstances in which almost instant decisions were required. That was the reason why *Re MB* went from the High Court to the Court of Appeal in just over an hour. Even more pressing urgency faced Johnson J when he interrupted the hearing in *Norfolk* to hear the application in *Rochdale* at 5.15 pm on the basis that a caesarean would need to be carried out by 5.30 pm to save the life of the fetus and avoid harm to the woman's health.[118] Such pressures are not invariably unavoidable. In *Re MB*, MB's counsel pointed out that 'the problem of MB's needle phobia had been apparent for some time' and there had therefore been 'adequate time' to assess and address her competence 'before the court was called on to make a decision'.[119] This is a powerful point. There will be circumstances where it should be anticipated that a currently competent pregnant woman will reach a point at which she will be unable to make decisions with regard to her own body, such as where it is known that she has a needle phobia (as in *Re L* and *Re MB*) or post-traumatic stress disorder (as in *Bolton Hospitals NHS Trust v O*).[120] In such circumstances, all practicable steps need to be taken to enable the patient to remain competent, or at least to make an advance decision. Otherwise, she is denied the power to exercise her rights and others are unavoidably granted decision-making authority over her body. Two of the safeguards advanced by Butler-Sloss LJ were designed to address this issue: potential problems should be identified as early as possible and judicial involvement

---

118 *Rochdale NHS Trust v C* [1997] 1 FCR 274, 275, referring to *Norfolk and Norwich Healthcare Trust v W* [1997] 1 FCR 269. These cases were considered above (5.2.1).

119 *Re MB*, 436.

120 These cases – *Re L* [1997] 2 FLR 837, *Re MB* and *Bolton Hospitals NHS Trust v O* [2002] EWHC 2871 – were discussed above. See also Halliday 2016, 60 and 221.

Re MB: *refusal of treatment in pregnancy* 133

should occur before it becomes an emergency (see 5.2.5). Lady Athena will go further, by placing greater weight on facilitating patient decision-making and on the prior wishes and values of an incompetent patient.

5.4.2 The weight of the rights of the fetus

It was argued in Chapter 1 (1.3.3) that the PGC must be applied according to a set of meta-principles. It was, in particular, argued that giving effect to the categorical PGC in light of the impossibility of knowing whether or not another is an agent requires a specific type of moral precaution. The PGC thereby implies what may be called the principle of proportion under precaution. Accordingly, the moral status of the fetus is proportional to its approach to ostensible agency (that is, to it displaying the characteristics and behaviour expected of an agent). Another way of putting that point is that closeness to ostensible agency is relevant to moral status. This is because the closer to ostensible agency, the fewer speculative (but coherent) hypotheses are needed 'to account for a hypothetical presumption that the being actually is an agent but is not able to display apparent [/ostensible] agency, or else makes more plausible speculative hypotheses that would provide such an account'.[121]

This principle implies that evidence of *potential ostensible agency* is relevant to its moral status. That is to say that in a single variable conflict between a fetus predicted to have the potential to develop into a cognitively functional adult human being and one predicted to lack this potential, the former will count for more than the latter. Holm and Coggon have denied the relevance of potential to the precautionary thesis. They claim that 'it is not clear that general potential to become an agent has any bearing on something's being an agent'.[122] But that is not the claim being made. It is true that potentially being X is not equivalent to being X. That is true whether X is 'being an agent' or 'being an ostensible agent'. But the claim being made by the precautionary thesis is *neither* that:

(a) potential for agency has any bearing on being an agent *nor*
(b) potential for ostensible agency has any bearing on being an ostensible agent.

Rather, the claim is that:

(c) potential ostensible agency has a bearing on *closeness* to being an ostensible agent.[123]

Imagine two otherwise identical fetuses (fetus A and fetus B) with only one material difference: only fetus A is predicted to have the developmental potential to

---

121 Beyleveld & Pattinson 2010, 265.
122 Holm & Coggon 2008, 302.
123 Remember that 'ostensible agent' is shorthand for the conclusion that another being displays the characteristics and behaviour expected of an agent, so 'potential ostensible agent' refers to evidence of ability to develop into a being displaying such characteristics and behaviour.

134 Re MB: *refusal of treatment in pregnancy*

become an ostensible agent. The claim is that fetus A is closer to being an ostensible agent than fetus B. This is simply because the precautionary thesis requires account to be taken of any evidence of closeness to ostensible agency and the evidence suggests that fetus A could develop into an ostensible agent, whereas fetus B could not.

Perhaps an alternative scenario can make this point clearer. Imagine that you are faced with two people (P1 and P2) who both claim to be President of the United States (hereafter POTUS). Imagine further that you are required to treat both as POTUS insofar as this is possible, but find yourself in a position in which you must prioritise the claim of one to being POTUS over the claim of the other. You know that eligibility for being POTUS currently *includes* being an adult who was born in the US. The only relevant difference between P1 and P2 that you can discern is that P1's official birth certificate shows that he was born in the US, whereas P2's official birth certificate shows that he was born in the UK to British parents. One way of expressing this difference is to say that P1 is potentially POTUS. That does not make P1 POTUS or even close to being POTUS, but it is legitimate to conclude that P1 is closer to being POTUS than P2. Thus, if you are required to give greater weight to the claim of the one who is, on the evidence, closest to being POTUS, then you would give greater weight to P1's claim.

Since the moral status of the developing human is proportional to its closeness to ostensible agency, it follows that the fetus is entitled to greater protection in late pregnancy than at conception. There are, however, practical and moral hurdles presented by attempts to convert abstract moral principles into legal rules and principles. Effective legal recognition and enforcement requires complex moral evaluations to be converted into simple workable rules and principles. The gradualist moral status implied by the principle of proportion under precaution, therefore, converts into thresholds of legal protection.[124] We saw above (in 5.2.3) that English law adopts a threshold approach, whereby increased legal protection is granted at four thresholds. The key threshold for the gestating fetus is 24 weeks, which has been linked to viability, and differs from the key threshold in other jurisdictions.[125]

Complexity is presented by the fact that the woman within whose body a fetus is gestating will almost invariably have greater moral status. Indeed, she will usually be an ostensible agent who is competent to make decisions with regard to what is to happen to her body. This presents a potential conflict between her will-rights (rights under the will conception of rights) and the fetus' interest-rights (rights under the interest conception).[126] Some theorists wish to reject descriptions of the mother-fetus relationship as potentially involving a conflict of rights or interests.[127] But if, as I contend, the fetus has moral status that is not dependent on the mother's status or her recognition of the fetus, then there will inevitably be situations in which such conflict arises.

---

124 See Pattinson 2002a, ch 4.
125 See Pattinson 2017b, 246–247.
126 Ch 1 (1.3.2 and 1.3.3).
127 See further Fox & Moreton 2015, 163–165.

Re MB: *refusal of treatment in pregnancy* 135

Multivariable disputes are likely to require the criterion of avoidance of more probable harm to be applied procedurally.[128] Elsewhere, I have argued that not all morally relevant variables – moral status, degree of harm and probability of harm manifesting – share the same degree of intimacy to the probability of harm, because '[f]or a being to be capable of suffering PGC-relevant harm at all, of any degree of severity or risk of occurrence, it must be an agent'.[129] Further, 'workable regulatory policy requires practical solutions and assumptions, even where the relevant variables appear to be incommensurable or uncertain'.[130] I went on to argue that the PGC requires a very different approach to beings that display qualitatively different levels of displayed behaviour and characteristics.[131] Bricks and tables cannot meaningfully be granted any generic rights, because they exhibit no behavioural capacities of ostensible agency.[132] Bacteria and other very simple organisms can meaningfully be granted interest-rights, but those rights must be regarded as overridden by *any* generic need of an ostensible agent. The developing fetus initially has only a marginal status but that status increases with gestational development. Even just before birth, it may properly be concluded that the basic generic conditions of a pregnant woman who is an ostensible agent should be presumptively treated as at least as valuable as the fetus' most basic generic condition (ie its life).[133] English law adopts an approach consistent with this illustration of a good faith attempt to give effect to the PGC. Under the Abortion Act 1967, the life and health of the pregnant woman take priority over the life of the fetus.[134]

In addition to the potential conflict between the rights of the woman and the rights of the fetus, there is the question of whether the woman herself owes duties to assist the fetus. All positive duties are limited by the 'comparable cost' proviso.[135] Accordingly, a positive right cannot impose on another a duty to deprive herself of the same or more important generic capacities, as measured by the degree of needfulness for action. It follows that no one can be required to sacrifice his or her life or health to protect another's rights, even if that other is an ostensible agent. Since a fetus is not close to being an ostensible agent, a woman cannot be under a duty to accept basic harm to herself to assist its presumed generic needs. She may, of course, choose to accept such harm to herself.[136]

Caesareans are major operations, involving cutting into the woman's abdomen and exposing her to significantly increased risk of serious complications and death over vaginal delivery (see 5.2.4, above). Many other procedures performed

---

128 See ch 1 (1.3.4).
129 Pattinson 2002a, 72.
130 Pattinson 2002a, 72.
131 Pattinson 2002a, 71–75.
132 See also Beyleveld & Pattinson 2010, 262–363.
133 See also Rodrigues & van den Berg 2012, 153–154.
134 s 1(1)(a)–(c), as discussed in 5.2.3.
135 See further ch 1 (1.3.3).
136 See Wade 2013, esp 20–21, for the view that 'mutual persuasion' between a healthcare professional and a patient is needed to facilitate good decision-making.

136 Re MB: *refusal of treatment in pregnancy*

for the benefit of the fetus, such as fetal surgery, also subject women to basic generic harm.[137] Inflicting basic generic harm on a pregnant woman does not violate her generic rights if it is inflicted with her consent or, if she is incompetent, performed in accordance with what is legitimately believed to be her likely will. That follows from the fact that her rights are will-rights, so have waivable benefits, and the continued moral authority of a competent ostensible agent over her future incompetent self.[138] With regard to an incompetent patient whose likely will is unclear, any basic harm inflicted on her would have to be justified as an attempt to prevent her suffering more likely or greater basic harm.[139]

Harm to the health of the fetus can also result from a pregnant woman's actions that are not connected to her basic right to refuse invasive surgery. Where, for example, a pregnant woman drinks excessive alcohol or ignores her low intake of folic acid, the fetus she is carrying faces notable risk of being born with fetal alcohol syndrome or a neural tube defect.[140] She is thereby risking basic harm to her fetus by actions that do not track her own basic generic interests. However, as noted earlier, identifying something as a morally relevant factor or even a moral obligation does not automatically require that it be treated as a legally relevant factor or legal obligation, because there are practical and moral costs involved in converting a moral principle into a legal principle or rule. Some social and regulatory measures taken towards pregnant woman are easier to reconcile with the PGC than others. Information campaigns about the negative effects to the fetus of certain actions during pregnancy are at the less problematic end of the scale. While information campaigns could influence a pregnant woman to limit her alcohol intake or increase her folic acid intake, they do not interfere with her basic generic rights but provide information that could aid the exercise of her rights. Imprisonment and forced folic acid injections are at the other end of the scale, because they involve pregnant women being subjected to basic harm and thereby indefensibly prioritise the fetus' interests over those of the woman. In short, any measure taken to protect the fetus needs to be assessed for its impact on the pregnant woman and every other potentially affected ostensible agent. Not only do the basic will-rights of the woman override the basic interest-rights of the fetus, but enforcing the rights of the fetus can itself cause basic harm to women. *Re MB* is, of course, a case concerned with invasive surgery for the benefit of the fetus.

5.5 Options available to Lady Athena

Situating Lady Athena in the Court of Appeal requires me to move her from the House of Lords, where she sat when revisiting *Gillick* and *Bland*. This can

---

137 See Rodrigues & van den Berg 2012.

138 On authority of over one's incompetent future self, see Pattinson 2017a.

139 In other contexts, the infliction of basic harm on an incompetent patient will sometimes also be justifiable as a necessary mean of giving effect to another's more important basic generic rights.

140 See NHS 2017a; 2017b.

Re MB: *refusal of treatment in pregnancy* 137

be achieved by promoting her to Master of the Rolls. Once in the Court of Appeal, it is relatively simple to construct a scenario in which her judgment represents the majority judgment because in the actual case there was only one judgment of the Court given by Butler-Sloss LJ. I therefore only need to have Lady Athena replace Saville LJ or Ward LJ and have the other agree with her judgment.

The idealised judgments in *Adams, Gillick* and *Bland* took different approaches to those in the original cases. She has therefore changed the law's trajectory.

Lady Athena's opinion in *Gillick* adopts a cognitive-functional test for capacity for both adults and children. She therefore avoided phrases such as 'sufficient maturity',[141] which are likely to result in a child being deprived of capacity in a situation in which an adult with the same level of cognitive-functional ability would be granted capacity. Further, she dealt more fully with the informational component of capacity and emphasised that the patient's reasoning was not to be assessed by reference to the values of others. This means that developments between *Gillick* and *Re MB* – the case law, and perhaps even the Law Commission's report on *Mental Incapacity* – would be likely to be different.

Lady Athena's opinion in *Bland* relies on the overall interests test instead of the best interests test used in the original decision. This means that she no longer has to deal with the actual decision in *Bland* in which Lord Goff relied on *Re F*[142] to reject the substituted judgment test and Lord Mustill dismissed that test as 'simply a fiction'.[143] These responses were problematic. Lord Goff's approach fails to recognise that the substituted judgment test presupposes previous competence, so could never have applied to F. Lord Mustill's approach mistakenly treats the substituted judgment test as a mechanism for obtaining the patient's consent, rather than for promoting that person's autonomy interests.

As in previous chapters, and for obvious reasons, no references are provided in the judgment below to later materials from which ideas and inspiration have been drawn.[144] The majority of the arguments attributed to the barristers in the case are based on those summarised in the actual judgment. An exception is the argument for the substituted judgment test attributed to Robert Francis QC (for MB) and opposed by John Grace QC (for the NHS Trust) below – the original decision in *Bland* had foreclosed this debate. The idealised judgment also spells 'fetus' as 'foetus', which is the spelling adopted in the case reports, though it is not etymologically correct or as simple.[145]

---

141 *Gillick* [1984] QB 581, 189.
142 [1990] 2 AC 1.
143 [1993] AC 789, 871–871 (Lord Goff) and 895 (Lord Mustill).
144 The discussion of the best interests test logically yielding only one answer is attributable to Butler-Sloss LJ, who was accepting a submission advanced by James Munby QC, in *Re S* [2001] Fam 15, 27.
145 See further Williams 1994, 71 (n 1) and Grace 1999, 57.

138 Re MB: *refusal of treatment in pregnancy*

5.6 Idealised judgment: *Re MB (Medical Treatment)* (CA)

To be cited in later judgments as:
Re MB (Medical Treatment) [1997] R.L.C. 4
26 March 1997

Lady Athena M.R.

MB was 40 weeks pregnant and the foetus was in breech position. She had initially consented to a caesarean section but then, because of her fear of needles, refused to allow blood samples to be taken or have anaesthetic administered by injection. She then agreed to anaesthesia by mask, but later changed her mind in response to discussion of the increased risk that she may regurgitate and inhale stomach contents. The evidence before us is that a vaginal delivery poses little danger to MB but presents a 50 per cent risk that the foetus will receive insufficient oxygen and thereby suffer death or brain damage. A more detailed summary of these facts is set out in the judgment of Butler-Sloss L.J., which I gratefully adopt.

The judge granted the declarations sought by the hospital to the effect that it was lawful for MB's delivery to take place by caesarean, including the insertion of needles for the purposes of intravenous infusions and anaesthesia. We dismissed the appeal after the hearing and I now provide my reasons for that decision.

In the process of addressing the issues raised by this appeal, I will search past cases for principles, stripped of missteps and irrelevances, capable of explaining and justifying the law on which this appeal turns, as per *Gillick v. West Norfolk and Wisbech A.H.A.* [1985] R.L.C. 2 and *Airedale N.H.S. Trust v. Bland* [1993] R.L.C. 3.

The legal status of the foetus

Mr. Grace, on behalf of the hospital, sought to persuade us that, even if MB is competent, the court could and should take account of the interests of the foetus and weigh those against MB's interests. I will deal with this submission first because it has implications for both the capacity of a woman who is competent to refuse treatment during pregnancy and the lawfulness of treatment performed on a pregnant woman who is incompetent to refuse that treatment.

The only support for the view that the foetus' legal interests are capable of overriding those of the pregnant woman can be found in the *obiter* statement of Lord Donaldson M.R. in *In re T. (Adult: Refusal of Treatment)* [1993] Fam. 95, at p. 102, and in Sir Stephen Brown P.'s decision to prioritise the interests of the foetus over the woman's religious objections to a caesarean section in *In re S. (Adult: Refusal of Treatment)* [1993] Fam. 123. I will return to *In re S.* below.

The foetus does, of course, receive protection from the law. The Offences Against the Person Act 1861, ss. 58 and 59, makes it an offence to procure an abortion and the Infant (Life Preservation) Act 1861, s. 1, makes it an offence to intentionally destroy a child, capable of being born alive, before birth. Similarly,

Re MB: *refusal of treatment in pregnancy* 139

s. 1 of the Congenital Disabilities (Civil Liability) Act 1976 provides retrospective protection to a foetus by virtue of the cause of action granted to a child born disabled as a result of injuries wrongfully inflicted in the womb, albeit not against the mother except in the context of negligent driving.

There are, however, significant limits to the legal protection granted to the foetus. The rights associated with legal personality vest at birth: *Paton v. B.P.A.S.* [1979] Q.B. 276, *In re F. (in Utero)* [1988] Fam. 122, *C. v. S.* [1988] Q.B. 135, *Burton v. Islington Health Authority* [1993] Q.B. 204. In *Attorney-General's Reference (No. 1 of 1958)* [1958] R.L.C. 1, when confirming the decision in *R. v. Bourne* [1939] 1 K.B. 687, the Court of Appeal declared that "the mother's right to life outweighs the right to life of the unborn child". Under the Abortion Act 1967, s. 1 (as amended by the Human Fertilisation and Embryology Act 1990), three of the four grounds for abortion prioritise the mother's health or life. Abortion is permitted up to 24 weeks where the continuance of the pregnancy would involve risk, greater than if the pregnancy were terminated, of physical or mental injury to the pregnant woman (s. 1(1)(a)) and up to birth where necessary to prevent grave permanent injury to her health or serious risk to her life (s. 1(1)(b) and (c)).

Thus, while the foetus has interests recognised by the law, those interests do not take priority over the rights of the woman. The rights of legal persons include the right to bodily integrity from which it follows that a competent person is entitled to refuse life-saving treatment and an incompetent person is entitled to be treated in accordance with her interests. Few medical invasions of bodily integrity are as dramatic as a caesarean section, which involves major abdominal surgery. In my view, the foetus' interests are not sufficient to either deprive a competent woman of capacity to make decisions with regard to her own body or, if she lacks competence, to require that her interests be subservient to those of the foetus. It is important to note that the conclusions with regard to competent and incompetent women are interlinked. That is to say that a foetus' interests cannot prevail over those of a competent woman unless they could also prevail over those of an incompetent woman. It follows that, even though I will go on to conclude below that at the time of the hearing MB was temporarily incompetent, my conclusion that a competent woman has the right to refuse treatment even if it will result in the death of the foetus cannot properly be regarded as *obiter* to this decision.

The capacity to consent to or refuse treatment

An individual has capacity to consent to or refuse medical treatment if she is competent in the sense of having the "cognitive-functional ability" to make that decision: *Gillick v. West Norfolk and Wisbech A.H.A.* [1985] R.L.C. 2. It was suggested to us during argument that the cognitive aspect of cognitive-functional ability could be regarded as insufficient to make a decision only when there is a medically recognised condition or disorder. It was submitted that such a "diagnostic threshold" for incapacity was required to ensure that a patient was not deprived of capacity merely because her decision is unusual or unwise, or not one that the person assessing capacity would have made. A mere impairment or

140 Re MB: *refusal of treatment in pregnancy*

deficiency in cognitive ability below this threshold would therefore not do. It was further suggested that Johnson J. in *Rochdale N.H.S. Trust v. C.* [1997] 1 F.C.R. 274, at p. 275, had overlooked this diagnostic threshold when suggesting that a pregnant woman could be deprived of capacity purely on the basis of the ordinary pain and stresses of labour. For reasons that I will articulate presently, I would also question the conclusion reached by Johnson J. that the woman before him lacked capacity, but not on the basis of such a narrowly defined diagnostic requirement. In my view, such a narrow threshold is not required by the principle that capacity tracks cognitive-functional ability. In fact, such a threshold would require capacity to be granted to individuals who lack the cognitive-functional ability to make that decision, despite not possessing a medically recognised disorder. Consider the situation of an individual who is functionally unable to make a particular decision at a particular time as a result of cognitive difficulties that are attributable to an immature brain that in no way deviates from what is medically expected for her young age. Alternatively, consider functional inability that is attributable to temporarily overpowering emotions that are not connected with a phobia, trauma or other medically recognised disorder.

I made it clear in *Gillick* that "[t]he right to decide whether or not to consent to medical treatment is meaningful because it is not dependent upon others agreeing with the decision that is made." This does not change merely because the individual happens to be pregnant or in labour, because that would elevate the foetus' rights over those of the pregnant woman. We must therefore continue to apply the capacity test without qualification, according to which the patient has capacity if she is able to understand and process or weigh the relevant information.

In *Gillick*, I distinguished between the "straightforward" consent situation and situations where the "nature, purpose or implications of what is proposed are more complex". In the former, the patient need only broadly understand and process the medical information and risks of what is proposed. In the latter, the presumption of capacity is rebuttable where she is unable to sufficiently understand the implications of the options before her to enable her to evaluate those implications by reference to her considered values.

Refusing a medically recommended caesarean falls into this second category. It falls outside the "straightforward situation . . . where a patient seeks to consent to non-experimental medical treatment recommended by a healthcare professional on the basis that it is required to protect her medical interests". A decision either way on whether to accept a caesarean section has potentially profound implications for a pregnant woman. The decision to refuse a caesarean section requires understanding of the likely effects of that recommendation relative to the alternatives, including vaginal delivery, and the considered weighing of those implications by the patient. In the process, she will need to consider the content and effect of her overall values.

In none of the cases cited to this court was a woman recognised to have capacity to refuse a medically recommended caesarean before it took place. In my view, the proper application of the correct capacity test casts serious doubt on the outcome of two of those cases.

Re MB: *refusal of treatment in pregnancy* 141

In re S. (Adult: Refusal of Treatment) [1993] Fam. 123 was a case in which no doubts were expressed about the patient's competence. The patient, Mrs. S., was in spontaneous labour following admission to hospital with ruptured membranes and refused to consent to a caesarean on the basis of her religious beliefs. With respect to Sir Stephen Brown P., who was required to make an urgent decision in an unexplored legal situation, I can find no basis to support his declaration that the operation could be performed lawfully without Mrs. S.'s consent.

Rochdale N.H.S. Trust v. C. 1997] 1 F.C.R. 274 was another case heard in a situation of great urgency. The consultant obstetrician was of the opinion that a caesarean section would need to be carried out urgently if the foetus was to survive and if risk of damage to the patient's health was to be avoided. Johnson J., at p. 274, noted:

> "The patient's objection to Caesarian section was that she had had a previous delivery in this way and had suffered backache and pain around the resulting scar. She had told the consultant: 'I would rather die than have a Caesarian section again'."

The judge went on to note that the consultant obstetrician held the view that the "mental capacity of the patient was not in question and that she seemed to him to be fully competent". He nonetheless concluded, at p. 275:

> "the patient was not capable of weighing-up the information that she was given . . . . The patient was in the throes of labour with all that is involved in terms of pain and emotional stress. I concluded that a patient who could, in those circumstances, speak in terms which seemed to accept the inevitability of her own death, was not a patient who was able properly to weigh-up the considerations that arose so as to make any valid decision, about anything of even the most trivial kind, surely still less one which involved her own life."

There are a number of striking features about this paragraph. First, the views of the consultant obstetrician were dismissed without the judge having had the time to either speak to the patient or receive alternative expert opinion. Secondly, the basis for concluding that the patient was incapable of weighing up the relevant information seems to have been the ordinary pains and stresses of labour, rather than evidence of their disabling severity at every instance at which the patient's wishes were sought. Thirdly, the patient's willingness to accept her own death over another caesarean was not regarded as evidence of the firmness and sincerity of her views, but of her failure to be able to weigh up the relevant considerations. Fourthly, at p. 275, the patient was said to be "unable to make any valid decision, about anything of even the most trivial kind" and then, at p. 276, the judge inferred from the fact that the patient had changed her mind by the time the case reached the court that "the operation was in fact performed with her consent". If she was unable to make decisions of "even the most trivial kind", then it must follow that she was also unable to consent, as opposed to acquiesce.

142   Re MB: *refusal of treatment in pregnancy*

While recognising the incredible haste in which the judge was forced to make his decision, any one of these four points would lead me to question the finding of incompetence on the facts as presented in his judgment.

MB's capacity

There was no suggestion that MB did not understand the implications of the options before her, nor was she refusing to consent to a caesarean section because she considered vaginal delivery to be more closely aligned with her core values. MB was in favour of the operation and her refusal was purely a question of needle phobia. Affidavit evidence from Dr. F., the consultant psychiatrist, in response to the question as to whether MB was competent was that:

> "Away from the need to undergo the procedure, I had no doubt at all that she fully understood the need for a caesarian [sic.] section and consented to it. However in the final phase she got into a panic and said she could not go on. If she were calmed down I thought she would consent to the procedure. At the moment of panic, however, her fear dominated all."

While an aversion to needles could, in principle, be the product of a considered choice, panic that "dominates all" prevents considered choice. During her moment of panic she was unable to weigh the implications of her refusal by reference to her overall values.

In *Gillick v. West Norfolk and Wisbech A.H.A.* [1985] R.L.C. 2, it was held that before a determination of incapacity is made "all practicable steps [must be taken] to assess capacity and assist a patient with the process of decision making". At the time of the hearing, the opportunities to assist MB to overcome her needle phobia were limited and, though we indicated that all practicable efforts were to be taken in the limited time before she is anaesthetised, we could see no alternative but to agree with the judge's conclusion that she temporarily lacked capacity. I accept, however, Mr. Francis' submissions that the problem of MB's needle phobia had been apparent for some time and there appears to have been many missed opportunities for its effect on her ability to make a decision to be assessed and for measures to be considered to address that phobia. The hospital's actions in failing to take all practicable steps to assist MB to overcome her problems may therefore have had a detrimental effect on MB's decision to make her own autonomous decision. I cannot emphasis enough the need for such anticipatory action to be taken before the situation becomes one of such urgency that no efforts to assist the patient are likely to yield results in time.

Overall interests, best interests, and substituted judgment

Three tests were suggested to us for the determination of the lawfulness of treatment performed on a woman in late pregnancy who lacks competence to make that decision: the overall interests test (as per *Airedale N.H.S. Trust v. Bland*

[1993] R.L.C. 3), the best interests test (as per *In re F.* [1990] 2 A.C. 1), and the substituted judgment test.

The overall interests test requires that what is lawful is to be determined by reference to the overall interests of all affected persons. This test applies in relation to patients in an irreversible vegetative state: *Airedale N.H.S. Trust v. Bland.* MB, unlike a patient in an irreversible vegetative state, has full legal status. We have seen that the interests of a patient who lacks capacity but still has full legal status cannot be outweighed by the interests of the foetus. It follows that the lawfulness of treating MB, as an incompetent woman in late pregnancy, must be determined by her interests alone.

It was suggested to us by Mr. Grace on behalf of the hospital that once the foetus' interests are excluded from consideration, the proper test was the best interests test. This test asks whether the proposed course of action is the best one for the patient, all things considered. Further, it was submitted, that a patient's best interests were to be determined by reference to the negligence standard as laid down in *Bolam v. Friern Hospital Management Committee* [1957] 1 W.L.R. 582. That is to say that what is in the patient's best interests must accord with the view of a responsible body of medical opinion: *In re F.*, above, pp. 54 and 67–68.

Mr. Francis on behalf of MB suggests that the best interests test is not to be reduced to the negligence standard and only applies if the substituted judgment test is inapplicable or yields unclear answers. The substituted judgment test seeks to treat an incompetent patient by reference to her core values and thereby seeks to reach the decision the patient would have made had she been competent.

I cannot accept the submissions made by Mr. Grace. *In re F.* is not, in my view, authority for the proposition that the substituted judgment test does not apply to any incompetent patient. The House of Lords was concerned with a patient who had never been competent to make complex treatment decisions, so the substituted judgment test could not meaningfully be applied to her. Further, where the best interests test does apply, it cannot be reduced to the *Bolam* test. *Bolam* operates in the law of negligence to prevent a judge from selecting one expert view over another to support a finding of negligence in a situation where both views are supported by a responsible body of medical opinion. It follows that there can be bodies of responsible medical opinion with mutually incompatible views. Since the *best* interests test can logically provide only one answer, it follows that the *Bolam* test can be no more than the first stage of the best interests test.

The test applying to incapacitated patients must be compatible with the principle that a relevant refusal made by a patient at the time of possessing capacity (an advance refusal) is binding. This principle was expressed by Lord Donaldson in *In re T. (Adult: Refusal of Treatment)* [1993] Fam. 95, at p. 103: "an anticipatory choice, . . . if clearly established and applicable in the circumstances – two major 'ifs' – would bind the practitioner". This principle justifies and explains the declaration given by Thorpe J. on the lawfulness of an "advance directive as to the future medical treatment" of C. in *In re C. (Adult: Refusal of Medical Treatment)* [1994] 1 W.L.R. 290, at p. 295. In my view, normative consistency with this principle requires adoption of the substituted judgment test over the

144   Re MB: refusal of treatment in pregnancy

standard best interests test in those cases where the patient had previous views and values that fall just short of the procedural clarity required for a binding advance refusal. That is not to suggest that the best interests test has no role to perform. Indeed, such a conclusion could not explain or justify the decision of the House of Lords in *In re F*. When the substituted judgment is inapplicable or yields unclear answers, then we must seek to determine what is in the patient's interests by taking account of all other relevant factors.

Another way of expressing my conclusion, indeed my preferred way, is to say that the substituted judgment test operates as the first stage of the best interests test and we move to the second stage only when it is inapplicable or yields unclear answers. This second way of expressing the point is not inconsistent with the view expressed by Hoffman L.J. on the ambit of the best interests tests in *Airedale N.H.S. Trust v. Bland* [1993] A.C. 789, at p. 833:

> "The patient's best interests would normally also include having respect paid to what seems most likely to have been his own views on the subject. To this extent I think that what the American courts have called 'substituted judgment' may be subsumed within the English concept of best interests."

The substituted judgment test requires that every effort be made to apply the patient's core beliefs and values. Where the matter comes to court, even outside the context of a medically recommended caesarean, all practicable steps should be taken to hear from the patient and her loved ones directly to ascertain any core beliefs and values. The patient might, for example, be a lifelong adherent to a faith with particular views on the treatment in question, such as a lifelong adherent to the Jehovah's Witnesses faith who is opposed to blood transfusions. It follows that in *In re S. (Adult: Refusal of Treatment)* [1993] Fam. 123, even if Mrs. S. had temporarily lacked capacity, the decision on whether to subject her to a caesarean section would need to take full account of her firm beliefs as a "Born Again Christian", which she shared with her husband.

In practice, many decisions concerning incapacitated patients are made without court guidance. Healthcare professions act lawfully when they act in accordance with a reasonable belief on the application of the correct legal test to a patient: *Gillick v. West Norfolk and Wisbech A.H.A.* It is therefore important to emphasise that a reasonable belief that treatment may be lawfully administered will be one reached after taking all practicable steps to take full account of the now incapacitated patient's core values.

Substituted judgment and MB

Mr. Francis submitted that the judge did not find, and there was no evidence to find, that the medical intervention was in MB's best interests. Applying the law as explained above, since MB lacked capacity, the starting point was the substituted judgment test. We needed to consider whether performing the caesarean section was likely to accord with her core values and, if so, whether that

Re MB: *refusal of treatment in pregnancy* 145

remained the case in this situation where it required her needle phobia to be overridden. On the evidence, it was clear that MB wanted her foetus to be born alive and was in favour of the operation, subject only to her needle phobia. MB had a firm and considered wish to deliver a healthy child and the consultant psychiatrist's expert view was that she would not suffer lasting harm from the anaesthesia being administered to her to achieve that desired result. Her desire to avoid needles represented the only part of that decision-making process that did not align with her core values, which is to say that she had no principled objection to needles. Someone applying the substituted judgment test to MB could therefore reasonably conclude that she would, if competent, have permitted her needle phobia to be overridden to enable performance of a caesarean section in the interests of the foetus. There was therefore no need on the facts for considered analysis of other factors that would come into a best interests assessment in a situation where there is uncertainty as to the patient's core values or their application to the situation in which she subsequently finds herself. In such a situation, the best interests test would be applied from the point of view of the patient, but, *ex hypothesi*, no clear direction would be provided by her views and values from when she was competent.

Procedure

I respectfully agree with the ten points of procedure presented in the judgment of Butler L.J. and adopt those points without qualification. By way of particular emphasis, a court declaration from a hearing that is *ex parte*, in which the pregnant woman was not given the appropriate opportunity to be represented, could not provide meaningful guidance on the application of the law. Such a declaration would be worthless.

I would therefore dismiss this appeal.

6 Conclusion

Revisiting five further cases

6.1 Introduction

This book has so far revisited four landmark cases in English medical law. For each, a new leading judgment has been attributed to Athena J/Lady Athena, which relies on an alternative set of legal principles to those in the original case or extends the principle relied on further. The combined effect of these judgments is, I contend, a small web of legal principle that has greater internal coherence and moral defensibility. Readers who have got this far may well wonder whether judges in future cases could realistically adopt such an approach and re-spin extant judicial threads into a more coherent and defensible web. Some commentators considered Dworkin's Hercules to operate 'at too high level of abstraction to assist the resolution of real cases'.[1] My confidence in the approach of this book is bolstered by the existence of cases in which the leading judgments are appropriately compatible with rights-based legal idealism of the type applied to the selected landmark cases.

A recent example is the decision of the UK Supreme Court in *Montgomery v Lanarkshire Health Board*, which is now the leading case on the standard of care for disclosure of medical risks to patients.[2] A seven-member court overturned a decision of the House of Lords of 30 years' standing.[3] Lord Kerr and Lord Reed, with whom the other Supreme Court Justices agreed,[4] directly appealed to a rights-based perspective:

> One development which is particularly significant in the present context is that patients are now widely regarded as persons holding rights, rather than as the passive recipients of the care of the medical profession.[5]

---

1 Lee 1988, 28. Lee also criticised 'Dworkin's failure to examine the detail of British law' (ibid, 27). See also Campbell 2007, 296. Other critics have wider concerns: see eg the materials cited in Stavropoulos 2017, 2084.

2 [2015] UKSC 11.

3 *Sidaway v Board of Governors of the Bethlem Royal Hospital* [1985] AC 871.

4 Lady Hale give a speech of her own, but concluded by declaring that were anyone to detect any difference to the approach of the joint judgment she would 'instantly defer to their way of putting it': [2015] UKSC 11, [117].

5 [2015] UKSC 11, [75].

This provided a step towards the following conclusion:

> The doctor is therefore under a duty to take reasonable care to ensure that the patient is aware of any material risks involved in any recommended treatment, and of any reasonable alternative or variant treatments. The test of materiality is whether, in the circumstances of the particular case, a reasonable person in the patient's position would be likely to attach significance to the risk, or the doctor is or should reasonably be aware that the particular patient would be likely to attach significance to it.[6]

This new test replaced a standard of care resting on what a reasonable doctor would do with one tracking maximal patient autonomy.[7] Lord Kerr and Lord Reed argued that 'respect for the dignity of patients requires no less'.[8] Lady Athena would (had she been in the Supreme Court) have concurred with this reasoning, because the PGC similarly recognises rights grounded on an autonomy-based conception of dignity.[9]

There are, of course, some hurdles to Athenian web spinning. One potential obstacle is that, starting in the time period in which my fictional Athena sits as a judge, medical law has changed from being principally a subject of the common law to being largely a creature of statute. Many recent medical law statutes have formalised the common law position with additional mechanisms to fill gaps and resolve problems. The Mental Capacity Act 2005, for example, gave statutory effect to the common law test for capacity and added provisions dealing with matters previously dealt with by the common law doctrine of necessity. This means that some of the routes open to my Athena have been closed or hindered by statutory developments. But, conversely, some additional paths have now opened – below I will revisit *Quintavalle* to show how legislation can itself provide principles for judicial application. The coming into force of the Human Rights Act 1998 in October 2000, which is after the four cases revisited in the preceding chapters, is a rich source of more wide-reaching principles. This Act makes the language of rights de rigueur,[10] which may partly explain the reasoning process of the Supreme Court in *Montgomery*. It thereby provides many opportunities for a judge seeking to give effect to the PGC.[11]

Other contextual developments are in play in the revisited cases. *Gillick* is an example of a case brought by parties other than healthcare professionals/bodies or patients with the goal of reshaping the law and *Re A* (which will be revisited

---

6 [2015] UKSC 11, [87].

7 See the discussion prior to *Montgomery* in Pattinson 2014, 120–122.

8 [2015] UKSC 11, [93].

9 See ch 3 (esp 3.4.1) and Beyleveld & Brownsword 2001.

10 To which those of a utilitarian persuasion object: see eg Purshouse 2018, esp n 8.

11 Lady Athena would consider the Convention rights to be enforceable between individuals (ie horizontally effective), which she could do without direct appeal to the PGC, as per Beyleveld & Pattinson 2002; cf Phillipson & Williams 2011.

148 *Conclusion: revisiting five further cases*

below) is an example of a case in which third party interventions were allowed. I have not reopened the question as to standing to bring an application or the limits to third party interventions, because I see no reason to object to judges dealing with the gateway to a full hearing before the court on an ad hoc basis, as long as the judges hold the parties to the limits of justifiable legal principle.

Before reviewing the principles derived and applied in the four idealised judgments and before addressing five additional medical law cases, I first want to expand on the position taken towards the common law method and judgment writing. Readers will have noticed that I have neither treated existing precedents as if they have statutory force nor treated them as if they carried no legal weight. I have also attempted to act within the confines of the customs and conventions of the English common law.

6.2 The role of precedent and judgment writing

The doctrine of stare decisis is widely considered to be 'a cornerstone of our legal system' and 'woven into the essential fabric of the common law'.[12] It is classically expressed as the norm that the precedents set by the appeal courts *bind* the lower courts.[13] In the English legal system, we are routinely told, all the courts below the highest appeal court are bound by its decisions[14] and the Court of Appeal's decisions bind the court itself (with narrow exceptions)[15] and all courts below. Is such a view an accurate portrayal of the operation of stare decisis in practice or a justifiable theory on how it ought to operate? The simple answer is that it is neither.

English law is widely considered to adhere more closely to the formal dictates of stare decisis than other common law systems, but that adherence is not quite what the formal language of the courts would suggest. The case law is indeed replete with the language of 'binding authority' or 'binding precedent'[16] and the associated language of following, distinguishing and separating the ratio decidendi from obiter dicta. But you do not need to look far to find cases where judges have knowingly departed from a precedent of a superior court without distinguishing it,[17] treated (historically) 'persuasive' Privy Council decisions as far more authoritative than

---

12 *Kay v Lambeth LBC* [2006] UKHL 10, [42], and Harris 2002, 412, respectively. See also the discussion of precedent and the Human Rights Act 1998 in Pattinson 2015a.

13 See Montrose 1958, 125; Duxbury 2008, 12; and Hernández 2014, 167.

14 On the highest appeal court see *Practice Statement (Judicial Precedent)* [1966] 1 WLR 1234 (declaring willingness to depart from *London Tramways Company v London County Council* [1898] AC 375) and *Austin v Southwark LBC* [2010] UKSC 28, esp [25]. See also *Willers v Joyce* [2016] UKSC 44, esp [5].

15 *Davis v Johnson* [1979] AC 264, 324 and 328 (approving *Young v Bristol Aeroplane* [1944] KB 718) and *R (RJM) v Secretary of State for Work and Pensions* [2008] UKHL 63.

16 See eg *Société Générale v Geys* [2012] UKSC 63, [93] and [141], *Mills v HSBC Trustee (CI) Ltd* [2011] UKSC 48, [40] and *Willers v Joyce* [2016] UKSC 44, [1], [12], [16] and [22].

17 See eg the discussion of *Re F* [1990] 2 AC 1 in ch 5 (5.2.4).

Conclusion: revisiting five further cases **149**

formally 'binding' domestic decisions[18] or treated what could plausibly be considered obiter as the ratio, or vice versa.[19] In practice, in the English legal system precedents are treated as carrying no more than significant presumptive authority.

Legal theory cannot support strict adherence to past decisions.[20] As Duxbury has argued, no single principle or theory can explain or justify anything more than 'a strong rebuttable presumption that earlier decisions be followed'.[21] Arguments supporting precedent divide into two types.[22] The first are the consequentialist arguments appealing to the predicted beneficial effects of adherence to past decisions. Examples include claims that following precedent saves the time and effort of working through the same points, generates legal stability, facilitates certainty and predictability, and curbs arbitrary judicial discretion. Such arguments are inevitably subject to counter examples of situations where such effects are unlikely to occur or did not in fact occur. The second are arguments appealing to the intrinsic value of supporting a decision that comes first in time. The classic example is the principle that like cases should be treated alike, which appeals to fairness and equality.[23] Such arguments require greater specification because what is worth honouring is what is good about prior decisions, not prior decisions as such. We saw in Chapter 1 that the PGC cannot support *strict* adherence to precedent, because only the PGC itself is categorically binding, and previous judges may have ignored the requirements of the PGC or have acted with less insight or fewer resources than are now available.

The 'fit' and 'justification' of the modified version of 'law as integrity', detailed in Chapter 1, provides the means by which weight can be vested in past decisions. *Modified law as integrity* envisages judges surveying past decisions and utilising the PGC to discern or construct a principle or underlying reason to explain those decisions. Prior cases that cannot be interpreted as plausible indirect applications of the PGC must be discarded. Past and present cases can then be brought together as a consistent whole under the PGC. This method grants legal authority to a precedent that is proportional to its fit (with existing rules and rulings) and justification (moral defensibility). Athena values internal coherence or 'fit' because she is applying the PGC indirectly and is cognisant of the likely consequences of explicit

---

18 See eg *Smith v Leech Brain* [1962] 2 QB 405, esp 415 (CA), in which *The Wagon Mound* [1961] AC 388 (PC) was followed in preference to *Re Polemis* [1921] 3 KB 560 (CA); and *R v James and Karimi* [2006] EWCA Crim 14 in which *Attorney General for Jersey v Holley* [2005] UKPC 23 was followed in preference to *R v Smith (Morgan)* [2001] 1 AC 146 (HL). The Privy Council can now 'expressly direct' the courts of England and Wales to treat their decisions as binding: *Willers v Joyce* [2016] UKSC 44, [21].

19 See eg the discussion of *Hedley Byrne v Heller* [1962] 1 QB 396 in Duxbury 2008, 70.

20 cf Alexander & Sherwin 2007, who argue that the ends of the legal system are best served by treating rules announced in past cases as 'binding'.

21 Duxbury 2008, 183.

22 See Schauer 1987, Maltz 1988 and Duxbury 2008, esp ch 3.

23 See eg Schauer 1987, 595–597. cf Kronman 1990, 1031–1036, who appeals to 'traditionalism' in the form of the claim that the past deserves to be respected 'for its own sake' merely because it is the past. Accepting the contestable idea of intrinsic *respect* for the past does not, however, imply the conclusion that precedents ought to be followed: see Duxbury 2008, 171.

150 *Conclusion: revisiting five further cases*

appeal to the PGC. The indirect application of the PGC is consistent with a range of substantive legal rules and principles and it is not the role of a judge to replace an established set of legal materials with a set that has no greater claim to consistency with the PGC. The reasons often cited for giving weight to past judicial decisions – such as the value of legal stability, predictability and equality before the law – are relevant to the protection of the generic rights of those operating within a particular polity. Explicit adherence to internal coherence also enables Athena to act in a context in which she is the only judge who is conscientiously attempting to give effect to the PGC. In such a context, explicitly declaring adherence to the PGC as the supreme overarching principle is likely to undermine a judge's ability to give effect to it. Modified law as integrity thereby enables Athena to operate within the language of the English legal system (or any common law system) and treat her own previous idealised judgments as particularly authoritative.

Alexander and Sherwin have criticised the 'legal principles' approach of Dworkin and others as a failed attempt to provide a happy compromise between two alternative models of precedent.[24] These two models are (i) 'ATC moral reasoning', which attempts to make every decision afresh in terms what is morally best 'all-things-considered', and (ii) 'binding precedent rules', which treats rules announced in past cases as serious and binding. Alexander and Sherwin provide two arguments for their claim that 'legal principles' combine the worst features of these two approaches.

First, they argue, 'principles tend to be more vague and more dependent on value-laden terms than posited rules that prescribe results for future cases'.[25] They contrast the principle that no one should profit from a wrong with the rule stating that an heir convicted of murdering an ancestor may not claim a share of that ancestor's estate. They argue that the rule may be 'inconveniently underinclusive', such as when the murderer kills herself before the trial, but that is preferable to reliance on 'open-ended' concepts, such as the concept of wrongdoing that is required to identify a wrong and a profit.

Secondly, they argue, '[m]ultiple principles may qualify as plausible explanations for existing legal materials', and even when this is not so competing principles need to be weighed.[26] They argue that existing legal materials are also in a state of flux and a workable threshold is required below which judges are free to discard 'recalcitrant' cases.[27]

Modified law as integrity differs from Alexander and Sherwin's target in that the criteria required to respond to their criticisms can be found in the PGC as the overarching principle. Athena is required to do her competent best to give effect to the PGC in light of the conditions under which she operates, and it is this obligation that guides her efforts to discern legal principles from existing

---

24 Alexander & Sherwin 2007.
25 Alexander & Sherwin 2007, 43.
26 Alexander & Sherwin 2007, 43.
27 Alexander & Sherwin 2007, 44.

Conclusion: revisiting five further cases   151

legal materials that are capable of explaining and justifying her decisions. The PGC provides the anchor for her determination of the permissible level of open-endedness to discerned legal principles, the criteria for weighing competing principles and the criteria for discarding irreconcilable cases. This book has presented four examples of how modified law as integrity could have been applied and five further examples will be provided below.

6.2.1 Some idiosyncrasies of appellate judgments

As I was writing the idealised judgments, I was frequently irritated by some of the idiosyncrasies of appellate judgment writing within the customs and conventions of the legal system of England and Wales. One issue stems from judicial insistence on use of the male pronoun in the absence of an unambiguous gender neutral singular pronoun in the English language. Support can be offered for this approach in legislative language on the basis of the need for consistency of singular pronouns and the convention of statutory construction that 'he' refers to all genders. But judges have too often insisted on using male pronouns, even when the person to whom they are applying the law is female![28] Consider, for example, Lord Donaldson's discussion of capacity in *Re T*:

> What matters is that the doctors should consider whether at that time *he* had a capacity which was commensurate with the gravity of the decision which *he* purported to make. The more serious the decision, the greater the capacity required. If the patient had the requisite capacity, they are bound by *his* decision.[29]

This was a case in which the patient whose case was before the court, 'Miss T', was female. The patients/applicants in three of the four revisited cases identified as female (*Adams, Gillick* and *Re MB*), whereas all the doctors and most of the judges identified as male. This is one of the reasons why, despite my own male gender, my ideal judge identifies as female. At the time of writing, the Supreme Court remains almost exclusively populated by white, privately educated men and there have been no exceptions to the first of these identifiers.

Another irritation is the paucity of references to academic materials in judgments, particularly in older judgments. I have provided those references in my commentary to partly address the limitations of referencing in judgments.

A third irritation is the tendency of judges to reject coherent legal theory in favour of pragmatic conclusion-based reasoning. In a media interview, Lord Sumption proudly declared: 'I don't have a judicial ideology'.[30] That statement

---

28 In this vein, see the wonderful satire of the concept of the 'reasonable *man*' in the fictional case of *Fardell v Potts* by Herbert 1932, 8ff.

29 [1993] Fam 95, 113 (emphasis added).

30 Quoted in Steavenson 2015.

152 *Conclusion: revisiting five further cases*

was incorrect. His Lordship does follow a set of ideas and ideals; what he doesn't have is fully developed legal theory.

6.3 Legal principles identified and applied in the idealised judgments

My imagined judge provides the majority judgment in one imaginary appeal and three actual appeals. This enables her to discern and construct a number of legal principles. The use of an imaginary appeal is necessitated by the fact that Devlin J's direction to the jury in *Adams* has been continually accepted as good law, despite never being directly relevant to the facts of any subsequent appeal case. It has been possible to simply situate Athena in the other cases by making her a Lord of Appeal in Ordinary and then placing her in the Court of Appeal as Master of the Rolls. Had Athena actually held those posts, Lady Hale would not have been the first female *Lord* of Appeal in Ordinary in 2004, and maybe gender-neutral titles would have been adopted much earlier.

The first case is a fictional Attorney General's reference to the Court of Appeal from *Adams*, which was heard in 1957. Athena J's judgment in *Attorney-General's Reference (No 1 of 1958)* substitutes Devlin J's (version of the) principle of double effect with the principle of the lesser of two evils. This moves the legal response to life-shortening pain relief from mens rea (intention) and actus reus (causation) to the defence of necessity, thereby allowing a doctor to openly administer opioids even if one of her purposes is to hasten death. This alternative principle complies with the requirements of fit and justification: it explains and justifies past decisions and Athena J's conclusions. Crucially, it enables Athena J to limit the ambit of a legal wrong (intentional killing) so that it more closely tracks the protection of generic rights. It also widens a legal avenue to which she later returns. Indeed, the reason for starting with this case is that a robust legal principle of necessity is required to give effect to the justification component of modified law as integrity in a legal system that does not treat the PGC as an overarching constitutional norm.

The second case, *Gillick*, was heard by the House of Lords in 1985. Lady Athena's judgment first applies the principle from *Adams* – the lesser of two evils – to avoid having to rely on a narrow interpretation of intention and thereby deal with problems of fit with the extant law. This also enables her to make it clear that this principle deals with the conflict between two important rights, whereby the 'lesser evil' is the infringement of the less important right or the lower risk of violating an equivalent right. She then discerns a principle of competence-based capacity applying to both adults and children. This second principle supports the conclusion that a child under 16 with sufficient cognitive-functional abilities may consent to treatment, while enabling unity of principle with regard to refusal of treatment and adult capacity. Legal principle is thereby re-spun to support a greater integral whole for the common law approach to consent.

The third case, *Bland*, was heard by House of Lords in 1993. Lady Athena discerns a principle that accords humans with extremely limited cognitive prospects and abilities a lower legal status. This is the principle of sui generis status for those with no apparent cortical function. From this it follows that patients

Conclusion: revisiting five further cases   153

in an apparently irreversible vegetative state (PVS) have less than full legal status and the applicable legal test is an 'overall interests' test. The principles relied on by Lady Athena support the conclusion that assisted nutrition and hydration may be lawfully withdrawn from Tony Bland without reliance on unprincipled legal fiction and with closer affinity to the PGC than the actual judgments in *Bland*.

The fourth case, *Re MB*, was heard by both the High Court and Court of Appeal just over an hour apart on 18 February 1997. Lady Athena, now as Master of the Rolls, discerns a principle of limited legal status with regard to the developing human, but explains why the principle of competence-based capacity from *Gillick* grants the woman capacity over her body even where it is likely to result in the fetus' death. Having further elaborated the capacity test (rejecting, as contrary to principle, a diagnostic requirement accepted by Butler-Sloss LJ in the actual case), Lady Athena discerns substituted judgment as the first principle for lawful treatment of an incapacitated patient.

6.3.1 The principles

- The principle of the lesser of two evils (*Adams, Gillick* and, below, *Re A*).
- The principle of sui generis/reduced status for those with no cortical function (*Bland*, and developed further in *Re A*).
- The principle of competence-based capacity (*Gillick* and *Re MB*).
- The principle of limited/proportional status for the developing human (*Re MB*, and developed further in *Quintavalle*).
- The substituted judgment principle as the starting point for the treatment of an incompetent patient (*Re MB*).

The chapters preceding the idealised judgments sought to defend the above principles within modified law as integrity. The 'fit' component sometimes removes the option of seeking the more direct path towards giving effect to the PGC. Lady Athena would not, for example, have needed to rely on the defence of necessity in *Adams* had the ambit of the crime of murder been more closely aligned with the generic rights of agents.

6.4 Revisiting five further cases

This book has revisited only a handful of focal cases. This section will apply modified law as integrity to five additional cases:

(1) *Re A (Children) (Conjoined Twins: Surgical Separation)*[31] – on the lethal separation of conjoined twins;
(2) *U v Centre for Reproductive Medicine*[32] – on undue influence in the context of medical treatment;

---

31 [2001] Fam 147 (CA, September 2000).
32 [2002] EWCA Civ 565 (CA, April 2002).

154   *Conclusion: revisiting five further cases*

(3) *R (Quintavalle) v Secretary of State for Health*[33] – on the interpretation of legislation in the face of unanticipated developments in medical science;

(4) *R (Burke) v General Medical Council*[34] – on advance requests for life-prolonging treatment; and

(5) *Yearworth v North Bristol NHS Trust*[35] – on property in human sperm.

These cases are referred to as (1) *Re A*, (2) *U*, (3) *Quintavalle*, (4) *Burke* and (5) *Yearworth*. Placing Lady Athena in these cases would necessitate extending her career by a further 12 years, imagining that some of these cases were heard by the House of Lords and making her the Senior Lord of Appeal in Ordinary. Not all of this is unrealistic: Lords Bingham, Phillips and Neuberger have had similar career profiles, albeit over a shorter time frame. Alternatively, and more realistically in terms of career longevity, we could simply imagine other judges reasoning these cases according to modified law as integrity.

6.4.1 Re A: *lethal separation of conjoined twins*

Re A was heard by the High Court in August 2000 and the Court of Appeal a month later.[36] All four judges agreed that the separation of the conjoined twins given the pseudonyms Jodie and Mary was lawful, even though it would result in the death of the weaker of the two. The twins were joined at the lower abdomen. Mary, the weaker of the twins, was being sustained by their shared aorta. She had a very impaired heart and brain and no lung function. Without separation it was predicted that Jodie's heart would fail in the months ahead. Jodie's chances of survival were estimated at only 40 per cent following emergency separation and at 94 per cent following elective separation, but an elective separation would kill Mary.[37] The parents refused to consent to elective separation, considering such action to contravene the tenets of their Roman Catholic faith. The hospital made an application to the High Court for a declaration that separation would be lawful. Johnson J issued that declaration on the basis that it was not in the interests of either child to remain conjoined and the operation would be a legal omission analogous to withdrawing clinically assisted nutrition and hydration. In the Court of Appeal, the majority concluded that the separation was only strictly in the best interests of the stronger twin (Ward and Brooke LJJ) and that it would not be murder because of the doctrine of necessity (Brooke and Walker LJJ).

---

33 [2003] UKHL 13 (HL, March 2003).

34 [2005] EWCA Civ 1003 (CA, July 2005).

35 [2009] EWCA Civ 37 (CA, February 2009).

36 [2001] Fam Law 16 and [2001] Fam 147, respectively.

37 Unless put on a heart and lung machine, which McEwan (2001) points out was not considered by their Lordships.

Conclusion: revisiting five further cases   155

On the necessity point, their Lordships were at pains to distinguish *R v Dudley and Stephens*[38] on the basis that the choice here as to who was to die was not arbitrary and unfair. According to Brooke LJ, 'Mary is, sadly, self-designated for a very early death. Nobody can extend her life beyond a very short span'.[39] The courts had, however, insisted in other cases (notably in *Adams*) that a few moments of life are not disposable and it is therefore just as much murder to intentionally deprive someone of minutes as it is to deprive them of years.[40] It would seem to follow, as Harris points out, that both twins could plead necessity 'with equal force and plausibility'.[41] This was not how the matter was perceived by Brooke and Walker LJJ. Yet, Brooke LJ's reasoning would not seem to apply in a case involving two unconscious but otherwise unimpaired adults – such as a situation where a third party acts to save an unconscious stranger by throwing another off a raft that is incapable of supporting their combined weight for a prolonged period. The judgment, in effect, treated the weaker twin as having less value.

Applying the PGC, under the precautionary thesis Jodie has a greater moral status than Mary.[42] While at the time of the Court of Appeal's decision neither Jodie nor Mary could be granted more than interests-rights, Mary's interests-rights would be more limited. Jodie had the cognitive functioning and developmental potential of a typical neonate, whereas Mary was said to have 'very severe' brain abnormalities, including a 'very poorly developed "primitive" brain' rendering it 'uncertain' to what extent she was capable of registering pain.[43] All things being equal, the criterion of avoidance of more probable harm therefore favours Jodie over Mary, which implies that it is morally preferable to act to maximise Jodie's chances of survival over maximising the duration of Mary's short life. But were all things equal? It could be contended that this was not simply a choice between the lives of two beings with unequal moral status, because the parents were profoundly invested in the decision. They were likely to suffer the basic harm of emotionally disabling grief irrespective of whether the separation was elective or emergency, so the question is whether any additional distress resulting from actions contrary to their religiously based preference would be sufficient to tip the scales in favour of an emergency separation. On the criterion of degrees of needfulness for action, however, rejection of elective separation posed much greater harm to Jodie than to her parents.[44]

If Lady Athena or another judge applying modified law as integrity had led the Court of Appeal, she would have applied the doctrine of necessity, underpinned by the principle of the lesser of two evils from the idealised judgment in *Adams*.

---

38 (1884–85) LR 14 QBD 273.
39 [2001] Fam 147, 239.
40 A point also made by Michalowski 2002, 389.
41 Harris 2001, 227–228.
42 A point also made by Clucas & O'Donnell 2002.
43 [2001] Fam 147, 161 and 183.
44 See Clucas & O'Donnell 2002. cf the weight given to the parents' views as proxy decision-makers by Gillon 2001 and Hastings 2010.

156 Conclusion: revisiting five further cases

To apply that principle in a binary case of this type, she would extend the sui generis legal status principle from the idealised judgment in *Bland* to capture those with very little cortical function where an either/or choice is required. The revisited judgment in *Re A* could thereby support saving the life of Jodie by sacrificing Mary without having to both assert and deny that the twins have equal value in law; and without having to reinvigorate the principle of double effect.[45]

6.4.2 U: undue influence

U is the second of two English law cases to address the voluntariness of a patient's decision made under considerable pressure from another.[46] In the first, *Re T*, the Court of Appeal had held that Miss T's refusal of a blood transfusion did not apply to her when subsequently unconscious and in need of a transfusion.[47] Overruling the first instance decision on the issue of undue influence, it was held that it was legitimate to conclude that her mother's influence had overborne her will on the basis that she had been left alone with her Jehovah's Witness mother when in a weakened state, resulting in a change of heart with regard to her views on blood transfusions. In *U*, neither Butler-Sloss P at first instance nor the Court of Appeal were willing to find that Mr U's withdrawal of written consent for the posthumous storage of his sperm had been unduly influenced. The Court claimed to be merely applying the principle established by *Re T*, which was a case on which Butler-Sloss (then LJ) had sat.

Butler-Sloss P had found that the nursing sister had placed 'considerable' pressure on Mr U to alter the form on which he had consented to posthumous storage of his sperm to comply with the clinic's 'ethical policy' against posthumous insemination.[48] The President of the Family Division nonetheless concluded that 'an able, intelligent, educated man of 47, with a responsible job and in good health' would not be expected to have had his will overborne by such pressure.[49] The Court of Appeal noted that the couple 'had already committed themselves, mentally, emotionally and financially, to the course of treatment' and 'were both very vulnerable'.[50] But Hale LJ, when giving the judgment of the Court of Appeal, concluded that the President had not applied too strict a test for undue influence, nor should she have applied the test differently to the facts.[51]

U seems wrong on its facts, because Mr U's position and characteristics would not render him immune to the degree of trust typically vested in the medical profession and the emotional vulnerability of most patients.[52] Also, even a small amount

---

45 cf Robert Walker LJ's judgment in *Re A* and the rewritten judgment in Ost 2017.
46 [2002] EWCA Civ 565.
47 [1993] Fam 95.
48 [2002] EWHC 36, [22].
49 [2002] EWHC 36, [28].
50 [2002] EWCA Civ 565, [21].
51 [2002] EWCA Civ 565, [27].
52 See Pattinson 2002b and Scott et al 2012, 282. cf Grubb 2002a, 206 ('One can only agree with the President's conclusion') and Morgan & Devenney 2003, 78 ('it is difficult to be over-critical of the decision').

Conclusion: revisiting five further cases 157

of pressure would have been sufficient to overbear his will in this context, because the costs of his not withdrawing consent appeared to be high and the consequences of withdrawing consent appeared to be very remote. Mr U did not anticipate his sudden death and seems to have feared withdrawal of treatment if he did not follow the advice given at this meeting,[53] which took place only two days before his wife was due to begin treatment but nearly seven weeks after his own sperm had been stored and four and a half months after their initial consultation with the clinic.[54]

If this case had been appealed to a court led by Lady Athena, or another judge applying modified law as integrity, she would have had the opportunity to both challenge the conclusion reached by Butler-Sloss P and Hale LJ on the facts and to refine the common law approach to undue influence in light of legal principle. On this latter point, Lady Athena could draw on the wider case law on undue influence to better protect the generic rights of patients. This case law recognises that it is sometimes appropriate for the courts to protect the autonomy of the particularly vulnerable by adopting an 'evidential rebuttable presumption', which shifts the onus of proof from the party alleging undue influence to the party who is denying it.[55] This case law was not concerned with medical treatment, but with various types of financial or proprietary transaction. In that context, an evidential shift in the burden of proof operates where the relationship is one of trust and confidence (which is presumed in the case of medical adviser and patient) *and* the nature of the transaction 'calls for an explanation' or 'is not readily explicable by the relationship of the parties'.[56] The weight of the presumption and the evidence needed to rebut it depends on the nature of the relationship and the nature of the transaction.[57]

In *Re T*, Butler-Sloss LJ denied the relevance of the 'probate line of cases' and 'the donor line of cases'[58] and agreed with Staughton LJ, who held:

> The cases on undue influence in the law of property and contract are not, in my opinion, applicable to the different context of consent to medical or surgical treatment. The wife who guarantees her husband's debts, or the widower who leaves all his property to his housekeeper, are not in the same situation as a patient faced with the need for medical treatment.[59]

Accordingly, counsel in *U* conceded that the situation was not one in which undue influence could be presumed.[60] Lady Athena would not have left the matter there. The reasoning in the idealised judgments in *Gillick* and *Re MB* (which

---

53 [2002] EWHC 36, [13], and [2002] EWCA Civ 565, [15].
54 [2002] EWCA Civ 565, [12] and [21].
55 See *Barclays Bank v O'Brien* [1994] 1 AC 180, *Royal Bank of Scotland v Etridge* [2001] UKHL 44, esp [16] and [153], and the discussion in Pattinson 2002b, 307–308.
56 [2001] UKHL 44, [18], [21] and [24].
57 [2001] UKHL 44, esp [153].
58 [1993] Fam 95, 119.
59 [1993] Fam 95, 121.
60 [2002] EWCA Civ 565, [20].

158 *Conclusion: revisiting five further cases*

seek to give effect to the PGC) recognised that the law should seek to ensure that decisions properly left to patients respect the patient's autonomy. In *Etridge*, the House of Lords expressly recognised that the law on undue influence seeks to 'ensure that the influence of one person over another is not abused'[61] and that an evidential presumption may be invoked by the particularly vulnerable (identified by reference to a relationship of trust and confidence and an outcome calling for an explanation). Decisions made in a medical context are different from transaction decisions, but they are at least as important – consider the significance of the decisions in *Re T* and *U*.[62] Patients are particularly vulnerable to pressure from medical advisers and a decision made in deference to the *ethical* views of the medical adviser calls for explanation.

Medical advisers are defined by their *medical* expertise. It is an abuse of position for them to use their post to impose their ethical or religious objections to a legally available treatment or service (as opposed to merely refusing to participate in such activities).[63] Medical advisers lack authority to provide directive advice to patients on matters falling outside their expertise, because they are not appointed by a PGC-compliant procedure to provide such advice and do not act with the consent of the patient on such matters.

Lady Athena would seek to recognise the particular vulnerability of patients by requiring an evidential shift in the burden of proof where a patient alleging undue influence can show that (a) the relationship between the parties is one of patient and medical adviser, (b) the medical adviser has put pressure on the patient to make that particular decision, and (c) the persuasion is not directed at addressing the patient's failure to understand the medical details of the relevant treatment or care. Criterion (a) defines a relationship where one party, the patient, is particularly vulnerable because it is formed where that party seeks to rely on the expertise of the other at a time of need, uncertainty and, often, ill health. Criteria (b) and (c) specify circumstances in which the patient's decision calls for an explanation, so that it is appropriate for the medical adviser to bear the burden of showing that her evidenced influence has not been undue.

These criteria are satisfied by the facts of the *U* case, so this reasoning would support a presumption of undue influence. Lady Athena, noting the factors pertaining to Mr U highlighted above and Butler-Sloss P's ruling that the 'evidence was finely balanced', could readily infer that the Centre for Reproductive Medicine had not rebutted this evidential inference. On other facts, this might not be the case. Rebuttal of a presumption where the three

---

61 [2001] UKHL 44, [6].

62 Lady Athena will (even if she does not state this) measure importance in terms of relevance to the affected individual's possession of the generic capacities of agency.

63 They may refuse to participate in the provision of some treatments or services to which they conscientiously object: see Human Fertilisation and Embryology Act 1990, s 28, and Abortion Act 1967, s 4. The leading case on conscientious objection to abortion is *Doogan and Another v Greater Glasgow and Clyde Health Board* [2014] UKSC 68.

Conclusion: revisiting five further cases 159

criteria are satisfied would, if we are to adhere to the principles underpinning those criteria, require clear and compelling evidence, such as proof that the patient has been provided with independent advice and details of an appropriate alternative supplier of the treatment or service. What is sufficient must vary according to the circumstances. In Mr U's case, for example, rebutting such an inference should be very difficult indeed in light of the fact that the pressure was applied at a point when the couple were deeply 'mentally, emotionally and financially' invested in treatment at that clinic.[64] A change of heart consequent on ethical pressure applied well into a long and taxing treatment process supports a strong inference of improper pressure.

Lady Athena's judgment would also need to consider whether the principles underlying the Human Fertilisation and Embryology Act 1990 render it inappropriate for a presumption of undue influence to operate in the context of that Act. Hale LJ emphasised that the only lawful justification for continuing to store human sperm provided by the Act was the man's effective consent, so the courts 'should be slow' to use equitable concepts 'to supply a centre with a consent which they would not otherwise have'.[65] But the Centre *had* received Mr U's effective consent and had only altered that consent many weeks after his sperm had been stored because he was asked to do so by the Centre's nursing sister. The court in *U* was not being asked to sidestep the importance that the Act places on consent – in contrast to *ex parte Blood* where a different panel of the Court of Appeal had happily proceeded in the absence of the required written consent on the basis that the case raised an 'unexplored legal situation'.[66]

Perhaps some support for the Centre's ethical policy against posthumous use of sperm can be found elsewhere in the 1990 Act. Section 13(5) then required that account be taken of the welfare of the child who will be born or affected as a result, *including the need for a father* of any child born as a result of treatment, and another provision rendered any child born as a result of posthumous insemination *legally fatherless.*[67] But posthumous insemination remains lawful under the Act, clinics are not directed to take account of the welfare of the future child before storing sperm under s 14 of the Act, and the clinic can transfer sperm that it objects to using to another clinic. Thus, Lady Athena could properly conclude that neither the Act's effective consent requirements nor its s 13(5) requirement provide statutory resistance to her approach. It is therefore open to her to use evidential inferences of undue influence to protect the decision-making authority granted to the sperm provider by the 1990 Act.

---

64 [2002] EWCA Civ 565, [21].
65 [2002] EWCA Civ 565, [26], and the discussion in Pattinson 2002b, 312.
66 *R v Human Fertilisation and Embryology Authority, ex parte Blood* [1997] 2 All ER 687, 695, and the criticism in Morgan & Lee 1997.
67 s 28(6)(b). Both provisions have been modified by the Human Fertilisation and Embryology Act 2008.

160 Conclusion: revisiting five further cases

6.4.3 Quintavalle: *cloning and interpreting legislation*

In *Quintavalle*, the courts were asked to rule on whether a licence would be required under the Human Fertilisation and Embryology Act 1990 to create a human embryo using the technique used to produce Dolly the sheep. Crane J in the Administrative Court held that the technique fell outside the 1990 Act; this was reversed on appeal to the Court of Appeal and the House of Lords dismissed the appeal.[68] The conclusion of the appeal courts was widely condemned by academics on the basis that it ignored the clear wording of the 1990 Act.[69] The appeal courts adopted a purposive approach to statutory construction in this case and again in a later case, which concerned the application of the 1990 Act to pre-implantation genetic diagnosis and tissue typing.[70]

The 1990 Act, which has subsequently been amended,[71] imposed a licensing requirement on the creation, storage and use of embryos outside the body and prohibited some specific activities in connection with human gametes and embryos. When enacted, it was envisaged that human embryos would continue to be created by fertilisation involving a sperm joining with an egg. It was then known that if an embryo splits at an early stage – before the development of the so-called primitive streak – the resulting embryos will be genetically identical. That is to say, that embryos produced by embryo splitting will be clones, which is how identical twins occur. Dolly was produced by a method not envisaged in 1990 but was a clone in the sense of being (almost) genetically identical to another sheep. She was the product of part of an egg joining with a body (somatic) cell. In her case, that somatic cell was taken from the mammary gland of a sheep, but any somatic cell would have done. The nucleus was first removed from an egg. The nucleus-free (enucleated) egg was then fused with the mammary gland cell by electric stimulation and chemical signals were used to trigger the onset of embryonic development.

The cloning technique used to produce Dolly was referred to as 'cell nuclear replacement' (CNR) in the *Quintavalle* case and the standard nomenclature is 'somatic cell nuclear transfer' (SCNT). My preferred label is the 'Dolly technique', because this avoids suggesting that an isolated nucleus from a somatic cell (as opposed to the whole somatic cell) is transferred into the enucleated egg. The Donaldson report, issued by the Chief Medical Officer the year before the decision of Crane J, expressly refers to the technique as one 'in which the *nucleus* of an adult cell is fused with an egg which has had its nucleus removed'.[72] There is even a picture showing a 'nucleus taken from an adult (somatic) cell' being inserted into an enucleated

---

68 *R (Bruno Quintavalle) v Secretary of State for* Health [2001] EWHC 918; [2002] EWCA Civ 29; [2003] UKHL 13.

69 See Plomer 2002, Grubb 2002b and Morgan & Ford 2004.

70 *R (Josephine Quintavalle) v HFEA* [2005] UKHL 28.

71 Principally, by the Human Fertilisation and Embryology Act 2008. The unamended 1990 Act is referred to below in the present tense.

72 DH 2000, [1.2]; see also [2.2.6]

egg.[73] It is therefore no surprise that this definition is adopted in *Quintavalle* by both Crane J – who refers to CNR as a process by which the 'nucleus . . . *from* one cell is transplanted' into an enucleated egg[74] – and Lord Phillips on appeal. Yet, the 'methods' section of the scientific paper in which Dolly's successful birth was announced to the world, published in *Nature* in February 1997, describes the procedure as involving the '[f]usion of the donor cell to the enucleated oocyte'.[75] This refers to the fusion of the whole donor cell to the enucleated egg, rather than the isolated nucleus of the donor cell, and this reading is confirmed by other sources.[76] This interpretation of the science was brought to my attention by an expert who participated in an engagement project for which I was the principal investigator, and is examined in depth elsewhere.[77] It forms no part of my revisiting of the *Quintavalle* litigation. Indeed, it cannot because this book has taken the facts of the revisited cases as presented by the contemporary court as given.

Counsel on behalf of the ProLife Alliance advanced two arguments. Their principal argument was that the application of the Dolly technique to human cells would not fall within the Act, because an embryo is defined to mean 'a live human embryo where fertilisation is complete' (s 1(1)(a)), including 'an egg in the process of fertilisation' (s 1(1)(b)), and the Dolly technique does not involve an act of fertilisation. Their argument in the alternative was that the Dolly technique is prohibited by s 3(3)(d), which prohibits 'replacing a nucleus of a cell of an embryo with a nucleus taken from a cell of any person, embryo or subsequent development of an embryo'.

At first instance, Crane J accepted the ProLife Alliance's principal argument. The appeal courts were prepared to accept that the Dolly technique did not involve an act of fertilisation, but they were not prepared to hold that it thereby fell outside the 1990 Act. The House of Lords held that the 1990 Act was to be interpreted purposively in light of its purpose of regulating live human embryos created outside the body. According to Lord Bingham (with whom Lords Hoffmann and Scott agreed):

> the four words ['where fertilisation is complete'] were not intended to form an integral part of the definition of embryo but were directed to the time at which it should be treated as such . . . . The essential thrust of section 1(1)(a) was directed to such embryos, not to the manner of their creation.[78]

Lord Steyn was prepared to accept the Court of Appeal's attempt to read the words 'if produced by fertilisation' into s 1(1)(a), but preferred to treat the restrictive wording of the provision 'as merely illustrative of the legislative purpose'.[79]

---

73 DH 2000, 23 (figure 2).
74 [2001] EWHC 918, [15]; [2002] EWCA Civ 29, [4], [11] and [35].
75 Wilmut et al 1997, 813.
76 eg Gee 1999; Trounson & DeWitt 2013, 638 (figure 1); Egli & Chia 2014; Wolf et al 2017, 28 (figure 1); Liu et al 2018, 882 and graphical abstract.
77 See Pattinson & Kind 2017, 116–118.
78 [2003] UKHL 13, [14].
79 [2003] UKHL 13, [26].

162 Conclusion: revisiting five further cases

Lord Millet held that s 1(1) was not intended to define 'the word "embryo" but to rather limit it to an embryo which is (i) live and (ii) human'.[80] In other words, their Lordships ruled that the provision was to be read as specifying no more than when a fertilised egg was to be regarded as an embryo. It followed that the 1990 Act applied to a functional embryo created by the Dolly technique.

Their Lordships made short shrift of the ProLife Alliance's argument in the alternative. Lord Bingham held that the Dolly technique 'does not involve "replacing a nucleus of a cell of an embryo" because there is no embryo until the nucleus of the recipient cell is replaced by the nucleus of the donor cell'.[81] The other Law Lords agreed.[82] Thus, the House of Lords ruled that s 3(3)(d) of the 1990 Act did not prohibit the application of that technique to human cells by, in effect, adhering to the strict wording of the provision.

Cloning is routinely dismissed as immoral and subject to blanket prohibition.[83] This is despite cloning for reproductive purposes (reproductive cloning) being the only means for some to have children who are genetically connected to themselves, and despite stem cells derived from cloned human embryos (non-reproductive cloning) having the potential to treat a wide range of diseases for which there is currently no cure, such as diabetes, Parkinson's disease and macular degeneration.[84] These possibilities make it difficult to align blanket prohibition with the PGC. The relatively low moral status of the embryo, compared to that of humans who are ostensible agents, means that we must be careful to take proper account of the potential of cloning technology to address the basic needs of others. The principal argument against cloning for reproductive purposes is that it may in some sense harm the resultant clone, but even a terrible existence would not automatically mean that the clone's generic rights have been violated by its existence.[85] For an individual's rights to have been violated that individual would have to have been deprived of an alternative existence in which her rights were fulfilled; bringing an individual into existence cannot by itself violate our duties to that individual. Of course, a violation of the clone's rights could occur after the clone comes into existence, such as by forcing her to live as if she were someone else (the cloned person), and the cloning activity itself could sometimes be characterised by an intention to violate the clone's rights in the future. Similarly, no conceptual difficulty is created by the idea that their bringing about the creation of a clone can violate the rights of others. But it is not clear that such considerations would support a blanket prohibition of cloning, rather than close regulation of the technology. What is clear is that cloning technology cannot be left unregulated in a society in which it is likely to take place.

80 [2003] UKHL 13, [45].
81 [2003] UKHL 13, [18].
82 [2003] UKHL 13, esp [28], [36] and [50].
83 See the regulatory overview in Pattinson & Caulfield 2004.
84 See eg Sample 2014 and the discussion in Pattinson & Kind 2017, 113–114.
85 The following is a summary of the argument in Pattinson 2002c.

Conclusion: revisiting five further cases 163

Under modified law as integrity, individual rights of sufficient weight trump decisions yielded by majoritarian politics. It therefore follows that the doctrine of parliamentary sovereignty cannot be interpreted in such a way as to trump the direct application of the PGC. The PGC is sovereign, rather than Parliament. We are not, however, faced with such an issue here, because the purposive approach enables Lady Athena to bring cloning within the 1990 Act to protect generic rights and give effect to a PGC-compliant Parliamentary will. Lady Athena would therefore support the purposive approach to statutory construction, but she would follow through the logical implications of such an approach beyond the point reached in the actual case.[86]

The specific purposive approaches taken by the appeal courts left gaps, which were recognised and dismissed.[87] The first of the two most significant gaps can be found in the Act's prohibition of 'keeping or using an embryo after the appearance of the primitive streak' (s 3(3)(a)), which is taken to have appeared in an embryo not later than 14 days from 'when the gametes are mixed' (s 3(4)). If gametes are defined as sperm and eggs, then this provision does not apply to the Dolly technique, so such embryos are not subject to statutory restriction on the time during which they may be kept and used. The second significant gap can be found in the Schedule 3 requirement that written consent be obtained from those providing 'gametes' for the creation of an embryo. If gametes are defined as sperm and eggs, this is another provision that does not apply, as consent would not be required from the person who provides the somatic cell and is thereby cloned. The appeal courts dismissed these gaps on the basis that they could be filled by the Licensing Authority imposing equivalent requirements.

The gaps identified by counsel for the ProLife Alliance could have been avoided by construing the terms 'fertilisation' and 'gametes' purposively to give effect to the Act's underlying position on the status of the embryo. The Warnock Report upon which the 1990 Act was based explicitly took the view that 'the embryo of the human species ought to have a special status', albeit not the 'same status' as a living child or an adult,[88] and the long title of the 1990 Act states that its purpose is to 'make provision in connection with human embryos and any subsequent development of such embryos'. Invoking the purpose of regulating the use of embryos in recognition of their special status would require 'fertilisation' to be interpreted as the creation of a functional embryo by the joining of genetic material and a 'gamete' to be defined accordingly. The purpose of protecting the embryo can also explain s 3(3)(d), thereby enabling that provision to be interpreted purposively. Replacing the nucleus of an embryo involves the destruction of an embryo, whereas creating an embryo using the Dolly technique does not. An alternative purpose of either prohibiting cloning or prohibiting nuclear

---

86 Below I develop arguments first presented in Beyleveld & Pattinson 2000b, 233–234; 2004, 185–202, and Pattinson 2005.
87 [2002] EWCA Civ 29, [43]–[49]; [2003] UKHL 13, [16].
88 Warnock et al 1984, para 11.7.

164 *Conclusion: revisiting five further cases*

replacement as such would evoke a boot-strap problem: we are required to read words into a section to fulfil the purpose of that section when that purpose itself is said to derive from that very section. In any event, s 3(3)(d) could not have been intended to prohibit cloning as such, because embryo splitting was not prohibited by Parliament.

6.4.4 Burke: *advance requests for life-prolonging treatment*

Burke is currently the only case dealing with a patient's request for 'assisted nutrition and hydration' (ANH) to be continued.[89] Leslie Burke had a degenerative brain condition that would eventually remove his ability to swallow and require him to receive ANH to survive. The evidence indicated that in the final days of his life he would move from being able to interact (stage 1) to being aware but no longer able to communicate (stage 2), before lapsing into a coma (stage 3).[90] He was concerned that the General Medical Council's guidance permitted ANH to be withdrawn while he remained aware (in stages 1 and 2) and he emphatically did not 'want to die of thirst'.[91] He therefore sought declarations to the effect that the GMC's guidance was incompatible with his Convention rights as given effect by the Human Rights Act 1998. While Munby J was willing to declare that parts of GMC guidance were unlawful,[92] Lord Phillips (giving the unanimous judgment of the Court of Appeal) rejected this view[93] and Burke's subsequent application to the European Court of Human Rights was unanimously dismissed as 'manifestly ill-founded'.[94] An appeal to a Supreme Court led by Lady Athena would have supported much of Munby J's reasoning, which was more closely aligned with Burke's generic rights, and thereby prevented the case going to Strasbourg.

Both Munby J and the Court of Appeal accepted that, *while Burke has capacity*, the medical staff responsible for his care have a duty to provide him with ANH for as long as it prolongs his life and is in accordance with his expressed wishes. Munby J's analysis of the case law led him to identify and apply a key set of legal and ethical principles in the sanctity of life (protected by Article 2), dignity (protected by, in particular, Article 3) and autonomy or self-determination (protected by, in particular, Article 8). Munby J concluded that while Burke had capacity he had the *right* to insist on receiving life-prolonging ANH. In contrast, the Court of Appeal ruled that the common law authorities cited by his Lordship were concerned solely with the 'paramount right to refuse treatment' and 'the right to self-determination does not entitle the patient to insist on receiving a

---

89 [2004] EWHC 1879; [2005] EWCA Civ 1003: see Pattinson 2015b. ANH would now be referred to as CANH (clinically assisted nutrition and hydration): see ch 4 (4.1). The old label is used in this section to avoid anachronistic terminology.

90 [2004] EWHC 1879, [170].

91 [2004] EWHC 1879, [6].

92 GMC 2002, [13], [16], [32], [42] and [81].

93 [2005] EWCA Civ 1003.

94 *Burke v UK* (Application No 19807/06), 11 July 2006.

Conclusion: revisiting five further cases   165

particular medical treatment'.[95] The common law was said to impose a positive duty to care for a patient accepted into a hospital, which would not override the wishes of a patient with capacity who refuses ANH, but where a patient wishes to be kept alive by ANH 'this will not be the source of the duty to provide it'.[96] Thus, Burke would merely be the *beneficiary of a duty* to provide such treatment, whose only right was to refuse it.

The courts also had a different response to a counterfactual situation in which during the final stages of Burke's life ANH would hasten his death, rather than prolong his life. Munby J's appeal to the patient's determinate right to autonomy implies that, where it is the patient's wish, ANH should be provided during these final stages.[97] In contrast, the Court of Appeal ruled that 'a patient cannot demand that a doctor administer a treatment which the doctor considers is adverse to the patient's clinical needs'.[98] Thus, Munby J empowered the patient to prioritise relief from thirst over a marginally extended life, whereas the Court of Appeal empowered the doctors to prioritise a marginal extension of life over the patient's wishes. This is not a purely clinical decision; it is a decision to be made solely by reference to the patient's interests. Where the generic rights of others are not engaged, it is for the patient to determine which of his interests take priority. Lady Athena would therefore have sought to return this particular decision to the patient, which is in line with her recognition in *Adams* that palliative care may legitimately be prioritised over a marginal extension of a patient's life and her recognition of the principle of patient autonomy in *Gillick* and *Re MB*.

Many academic commentators reject the suggestion of a *right* to insist on 'ordinarily available' life-prolonging treatment[99] or even ANH. Gillon opines that such an approach is 'non-beneficial and wasteful'.[100] Mason and Laurie similarly bemoan Munby J's support for a rights-based approach over a communitarian/duty-based approach.[101] But the provision of ANH to someone in Burke's position, for as long as he is not comatose, raises no resource allocation difficulties additional to those raised by the Court of Appeal's position. Lady Athena would have insisted that Burke was asking for no more than the power to make a self-regarding decision when no one else has a plausible overriding right.[102]

The Court of Appeal was particularly dismissive of Munby J's declarations on the position of *incapacitated patients*. Munby J recognised that Burke's concerns extended to the final stage of his life, which the Court of Appeal (in my view

---

95 [2005] EWCA Civ 1003, [31].

96 [2005] EWCA Civ 1003, [31]–[32].

97 [2004] EWHC 1879, [116].

98 [2005] EWCA Civ 1003, [55].

99 Munby J was very clear that he was not addressing situations concerned with the prioritisation or allocation of scarce resources, or the provision of experimental or untested forms of treatment, because those issues did not arise in the context of ANH: [2004] EWHC 1879, [27]–[28].

100 Gillon 2004, 810.

101 Mason & Laurie 2005, esp 127 and 131.

102 See also Biggs 2007.

166 Conclusion: revisiting five further cases

perversely) denied.[103] The courts then took divergent approaches to the law. Munby J gave significant weight to assessing the patient's interests 'from the patient's point of view'.[104] In contrast, Lord Phillips refused to provide guidance beyond dismissing the approach of Munby J and asserting that 'it is best to confine the use of the phrase "best interests" to an objective test'.[105] This view runs contrary to the revisited decision in *Re MB*, which discerned the principle of substituted judgment as the first stage of any best interests evaluation.[106] As Lady Athena argued in that case, it is difficult to reconcile an approach that marginalises the patient's prior wishes when assessing what is in his best interests, yet defers to those wishes when they satisfy the requirements for a valid and applicable advance refusal.[107] As it happens, the courts have subsequently (within the confines of the best interests test) moved towards a substituted judgment test, which seeks to make the decision that the patient would have made by applying the patient's views and values, and thereby sided with the approach of Munby J over that of Lord Phillips.[108]

An additional reason advanced by the Court of Appeal for dismissing the extent of Munby J's declarations was that 'they address the effect of an advance directive, sometimes referred to as "a living will", when Mr Burke has made no such directive'.[109] Burke was, however, just as concerned with his expected future as a locked-in but aware patient as he was with the position that he was in at the time of the litigation. He therefore ought to have been taken to be making an *advance request* to the effect that ANH should continue until his death. The Court of Appeal was, perhaps, misled by Munby J's statement that certain issues '[m]ay turn upon the precise terms of the claimant's advance directive'.[110] Munby J was not, however, stating that Burke had not made an advance directive, but recognising that the precise form of that directive could well have changed by the time that Burke loses capacity, some years hence.

The Court of Appeal dismissed Munby J's reliance on Burke's rights to support the conclusion that an advance request 'which is both valid and relevant to the treatment in question' is determinate as to whether a patient should be provided with ANH 'which he believes is necessary to protect him from what he sees as acute mental and physical suffering'.[111] This was another step too far for the Court of Appeal, which considered the common law on advance requests to be identical to that under the Mental Capacity Act 2005.[112] Lord Phillips declared that

---

103 cf [2004] EWHC 1879, [6] and [2005] EWCA Civ 1003, [22], as discussed in Pattinson 2015b, 262–263.
104 [2004] EWHC 1879, [116].
105 [2005] EWCA Civ 1003, [29].
106 See ch 5 (5.6).
107 See Mental Capacity Act 2004, s 26(1), discussed below.
108 See *Aintree University Hospitals NHS Foundation Trust v James* [2013] UKSC 67, esp [45], and the discussion in Pattinson 2017a, 99–101; 2017b, 533–535.
109 [2005] EWCA Civ 1003, [22].
110 [2004] EWHC 1879, [175].
111 [2004] EWHC 1879, [169].
112 [2005] EWCA Civ 1003, [57].

advance requests are an important consideration when assessing what is in the best interests of a patient, under s 4(6)(a) of the 2005 Act, but do not have the binding force granted to advance refusals under s 26. It is worth noting that the 2005 Act does not explicitly state that advance refusals are binding. Section 26(1) states that the legal force of a valid and applicable advance refusal is the same as a valid contemporaneous refusal, and the common law considers a valid contemporaneous refusal to be binding.[113] Similarly, s 4(6)(a) does not explicitly mention advance requests, but states that the patient's past 'wishes and feelings (and, in particular, any relevant written statement made by him when he had capacity)' must be given consideration 'so far as is reasonably ascertainable'. Just as s 4(6)(a) does not prevent greater legal force being attached to valid and applicable advance refusals, it does not prevent greater legal force attaching to specific types of advance request. As alluded to earlier, a later Supreme Court decision on the 2005 Act read the entire best interests test by reference to s 4(6) by declaring that '[t]he purpose of the best interests test is to consider matters from the patient's point of view'.[114] Lady Athena would use the principles articulated above to give significant weight to an advance request for the continuation of ANH.

The final issue of great divergence between the decision at first instance and on appeal was over the involvement of the court. Munby J held that there were some situations where it would be unlawful to withdraw ANH from an incapacitated patient without judicial sanction.[115] His Lordship then placed into this category the situation where a doctor wishes to withhold ANH contrary to the views expressed by the patient when he had capacity.[116] The Court of Appeal held that there was no such duty to seek court approval; in some situations it was merely 'advisable' for a doctor to seek court approval. The House of Lords in *Bland* had given withdrawal of ANH from a patient in PVS as an example of where court approval should be obtained '*as a matter of good practice*'.[117] To extend this using Munby J's criteria would, it was estimated by the Intensive Care Society, lead to around 10 applications a day being made to the courts.[118] Burke was therefore not entitled to impartial adjudication if stage 2 were to give rise to a conflict between his previously expressed wishes and clinical opinion on the continued provision of ANH. Not only did Burke not have a right to ANH, he did not even have a right to judicial consideration of his case. The Court of Appeal did not consider it necessary to express a view on when a step would be sufficiently controversial to render it good practice to seek a declaration, but was emphatic that Burke would not have brought his case before the court had he been 'well

---

113 See eg *Re T* [1993] Fam 95 and *Re B* [2002] EWHC 429.
114 *Aintree University Hospitals NHS Foundation Trust v James* [2013] UKSC 67, esp [45].
115 [2004] EWHC 1879, [202] and [214]. Munby J relied on *Glass v United Kingdom* [2004] 1 FLR 1019.
116 [2004] EWHC 1879, [214].
117 [2005] EWCA Civ 1003, [71] (emphasis in original).
118 [2005] EWCA Civ 1003, [69].

168 *Conclusion: revisiting five further cases*

advised'.[119] Lady Athena would not support a conclusion whereby withdrawing ANH from patients in PVS is given closer judicial scrutiny than the withdrawal of ANH from patients in what would now be called a 'a minimally conscious state'. Burke, during stage 2 of his condition, would have a much greater moral status than a patient in PVS. Any protective steps that properly apply to those in PVS must also apply to those with a greater display of abilities approaching ostensible agency where previously expressed views on their interests conflict with the current view of the treating physicians.

6.4.5 Yearworth: *property in sperm*

In *Yearworth*, the Court of Appeal held that men whose sperm had been negligently allowed to thaw had an ownership interest in the damaged sperm sufficient to found an action in negligence.[120] Ownership of the sperm was held to vest in the men because (a) it had been generated and ejaculated by their bodies alone and (b) the 'sole object of the ejaculation of the sperm was that, in certain events, it might later be used for their benefit'.[121] The Court presented two reasons as to why it did not matter that the men could not 'direct' the use of their sperm once it had been removed.[122] First, numerous statutes limit a person's ability to use property, such as a pharmacist's ability to sell his medicines, without removing his ownership of it. Secondly, the Human Fertilisation and Embryology Act 1990 'assiduously preserves the ability of the men to direct that the sperm be *not* used in a certain way: their negative control over its use remains absolute' (emphasis in original). The Court of Appeal did not expressly articulate a theory of property and restricted itself to the facts before it, stating that it was not, for example, considering bodily materials donated for use by other persons.

It has long been a maxim of the common law that there is no property in a dead body or its parts. Despite the dubious origins of this maxim,[123] the no property rule was confirmed by the Court of Appeal in *Dobson v North Tyneside Health Authority* and *R v Kelly*.[124] An exception to this applies if the corpse or body part has 'acquired different attributes by virtue of the application of skill, such as dissection or preservation techniques, for exhibition or teaching purposes'.[125] The brain preserved in paraffin for autopsy in *Dobson* did not thereby become property, but the conviction for theft of two men who took body parts from the Royal College of Surgeons was upheld in *Kelly*. These decisions are reconcilable if property is understood to be acquired by the application of work and skill *with*

---

119 [2005] EWCA Civ 1003, [13].
120 [2009] EWCA Civ 37.
121 [2009] EWCA Civ 37, [45].
122 [2009] EWCA Civ 37, [45].
123 See Matthews 1983.
124 [1997] 1 WLR 596 and [1999] QB 621, respectively.
125 *R v Kelly* [1999] QB 621, 631; following *Doodeward v Spence* (1908) 6 CLR 406 and *Dobson v North Tyneside HA* [1997] 1 WLR 596, 601–601.

an appropriate intention. That is to say that without an intention to assert ownership, the object's attributes are not regarded as changed by preservation alone. In *Dobson* the preservation had been to comply with the Coroners Rules without the intention of retaining it for any other purpose,[126] whereas in *Kelly* the preservation had been for the purpose of exhibition and teaching.

The Court of Appeal in *Yearworth* opined that the 'easiest course' available to it would be to uphold the claims of the men to have ownership in their sperm by reference to the work-skill exception.[127] As Price notes, however, the work and skill exception 'would have served to have conferred rights on the Unit not the men themselves'.[128] In any event, the Court of Appeal chose a different path. Without rejecting the work-skill principle,[129] the Court of Appeal noted that it was 'devised as an exception to a principle, itself of exceptional character, relating to the ownership of a human corpse'.[130] It therefore preferred to rely on the principle articulated above to the effect that property vested because the sperm was generated by the men's bodies and was removed for the sole purpose of using it for their benefit. The Court did not, however, fully explain how these principles fit together. The most coherent answer is that the *Yearworth* principle applies to the source and the work-skill principle applies to others who come into lawful possession of material no longer subject to the ownership claims of the source. But if Lady Athena is to defend this response, she must first identify a *unifying* principle and satisfy herself that that principle is compatible with the PGC.

A unifying principle can be found in the 'rule-preclusionary' conception of property advanced by Beyleveld and Brownsword as an application of the PGC.[131] Under this conception, ownership is a prima facie right to use or exclude others from using an object, precluding the need to offer a case-by-case justification. Accordingly, once it is established that I have property in an object, the burden of proof is on those who wish to use or otherwise restrict my use of that object. This conception only permits others to use my property where they have my consent or a right that overrides my property right (on the basis that their right protects an interest that is more important than that justifying my proprietary claim in the first place). The ownership interest that the men were recognised to have over their sperm in *Yearworth* was a rule-preclusionary right of just this type: a prima facie right to exclude others from using or damaging their sperm without their consent and that right, granted on the basis of their relationship to the sperm, was one that precluded them having to provide a case-by-case justification for opposing damage to the sperm or its use by others.

---

126 [1997] 1 WLR 596, 602.
127 [2009] EWCA Civ 37, [45].
128 Price 2009, 257.
129 This principle has the support of precedent and is given statutory recognition by the Human Tissue Act 2004, s 32(9)(c).
130 [2009] EWCA Civ 37, [45].
131 Beyleveld & Brownsword 2001, ch 8, and the discussion in Pattinson 2011.

170 *Conclusion: revisiting five further cases*

The rule-preclusionary conception of property, however, has implications that could be considered contrary to other common law principles. Beyleveld and Brownsword have argued that this conception directly implies ownership over my living body and its attached parts.[132] Yet, the Court of Appeal in *Yearworth* cited a common law principle to the effect that a person does not own his or her living body or its parts.[133]

The rule-preclusionary conception does indeed imply ownership of my living body and its attached parts, because if I do not stand in that relationship to my living body then I cannot stand in that relationship to any other object.[134] I act through my body (however it is metaphysically related to me) and it is therefore more important for my purposes (whatever those purposes are) than any other object.[135] Thus, Beyleveld and Brownsword argue, *if* anything stands in such a relation to me that it is necessary for the protection of my primary rights that I be granted rule-preclusionary control over it, it is my body and its attached parts. Having rule-preclusionary control over any object would therefore imply, as a matter of justificatory consistency, that I have such control over my living body.

Beyleveld and Brownsword argue that giving effect to the PGC requires that I be granted rule-preclusionary control over my living body and its attached parts.[136] They start by pointing out that since to deprive me of my attached body parts generically affects my ability to act successfully or at all, to do so against my will infringes my generic rights. Granting me rule-preclusionary control is *required* to protect my generic rights. This is because having no necessary presumption against use of my body and its attached parts by others would place the onus to justify control on me against others who wished to use it. Yet, my reliance on my body and its parts is such that that itself would place my agency under threat and this reliance makes persons particularly prone to attach legitimate and deep emotional significance to their bodies and its parts.

In *Yearworth*, the Court of Appeal accepted that the law had an elaborate series of rules for the protection of the body and bodily autonomy, but declared that the common law has 'always adopted' the principle that 'a living human body is incapable of being owned' and there is an 'allied principle that a person does not even "possess" his body or any part of it: *R v Bentham*'.[137] In *Bentham*, the House of Lords held that a man was not in possession of an imitation firearm within the Firearms Act 1968 when he pushed his fingers into the material of his jacket to give the impression that he had a gun. It was reasoned that an individual 'cannot possess something which is not separate and distinct from himself', because if they were regarded as property for the purposes of section 143 of the Power of Criminal Courts (Sentencing) Act 2000, then 'the court could,

---

132 Beyleveld & Brownsword 2001, 182–183.
133 [2009] EWCA Civ 37, [30].
134 Beyleveld & Brownsword 2001, 182–183.
135 Beyleveld & Brownsword 2001, 186.
136 Beyleveld & Brownsword 2001, 186–188.
137 [2009] EWCA Civ 37, [30].

Conclusion: revisiting five further cases 171

theoretically, make an order depriving the offender of his rights to them and they could be taken into the possession of the police'.[138]

At first sight, the notion of property in English law is therefore not compliant with the rule-preclusionary conception.[139] Notice, however, the Court of Appeal's reference to the elaborate series of legal rules protecting the body and bodily autonomy. The torts of trespass to the person and the crimes of assault are examples of such rules granting rights over one's body and its attached parts that satisfy the substantive and functional features of rule-preclusionary control. That is to say that the law recognises that persons have a prima facie right to exclude others from using, damaging or even touching their body without the need for them to offer a case-by-case justification. In law, these are classified as personal rights. The law therefore simply restricts the terminology of property and ownership to a sub-class of objects that may be subject to rule-preclusionary control – namely, those objects that can, in practical terms, be treated as separate and distinct from living persons. Control over this sub-class is properly distinguished because these objects are not attributes of a person's physical integrity, and adopting different terminology and a different set of specific rules facilitates this expression of hierarchy between the living body and other objects.[140] The PGC does not require that all objects subject to rule-preclusionary control are dealt with by the same legal rules or designated as property. It is entirely appropriate for English law to apply a specific, less protective set of 'property law' rules to a class of objects that stand in a weaker relationship to persons than their living bodies and attached parts.

Revisiting the *Yearworth* decision by reference to the rule-preclusionary conception has explanatory and justificatory force; it complies with the fit and justification requirements of modified law as integrity. Once it is accepted that I have rule-preclusionary control over my living body (including attached body parts and unreleased bodily products), it becomes simple to explain why I have rule-preclusionary control over bodily material that has been removed from my body with the intention of controlling its subsequent lawful use. In such circumstances, the removal of bodily material was for a particular purpose and involved no attempt to abandon it. I therefore retain rule-preclusionary control over it. Use of excised bodily material without my consent is generally not on a par with harm to that bodily material when attached and it follows that theft is not on a par with slavery, trespass to goods is not on a par with trespass to the person, and so on. This is consistent with the earlier decision of a Magistrates' Court to convict a man, who cut hair from the back of a girl's head without her consent, of assault and *larceny*.[141] If bodily material is removed for another purpose, my future intentions towards it may sometimes be such that I can properly be said to

---

138 *Re Bentham* [2005] UKHL 18, [8] (Lord Bingham, with whom the other Lords agreed).
139 The argument below was first presented in Pattinson 2011.
140 cf Hardcastle 2007, 146–150, and Price 2009, 240–241 and 267.
141 *R v Herbert* (1961) JCL 163.

172 *Conclusion: revisiting five further cases*

have abandoned it. Others may then acquire rule-preclusionary control over it as a product of their legitimate labour and exercise of their productive agency,[142] as captured by the work-skill principle.

6.5 Concluding remarks

Athena has remained faithful to many features of Dworkin's 'law as integrity'. She has continued to seek 'integrity' in the law in terms of conformity with both moral principle and the integral whole of the legal system. I have, of course, revised Dworkin's law as integrity to utilise the PGC when seeking those legal principles that provide 'fit' and 'justification'. My thesis is that had the majority judgment in the cases revisited in this book utilised an alternative set of legal principles, then the law would now have better fit and justification. My hope – which is perhaps too idealistic to be realistic – is that future courts could be persuaded to apply this method or, perhaps, some of the specific arguments advanced, as they continue to develop the common law. Real judges cannot select their cases in the way that I have done for Athena, but they do get to sit on far more of them. Athena's cases – even if we add the five cases examined in the last section to the four for which there is a dedicated chapter – pale in comparison to Lord Denning's couple of thousand.[143] But Lord Denning was not a typical judge. In his two decades as Master of the Rolls, he famously did select both his cases and fellow panel members.

Throughout I have directly and indirectly referred to what may be called a 'principle of charitable interpretation', which requires that we interpret those we criticise so as to render what they say as rational as possible.[144] It was in a similar vein that Mill started his review of Sedgwick by declaring that a 'doctrine is not judged at all until it is judged in its best form'.[145] Whether I have remained faithful to this principle is for others to judge, but I contend that it is central to rational debate. I therefore invite you to bring this principle to bear when considering the arguments advanced in this book. Readers are, in particular, invited to remember that identifying mistakes in the application of a theory does not, in itself, establish that that theory is mistaken. Similarly, readers should remember that this book's idealised judgments are not presented as definitive applications of the PGC, but as examples of permissible indirect applications in the context of the extant English legal system. Athena would fashion very different judgments if she were sitting as an appeal judge in a system in which the PGC had explicit status as the supreme constitutional norm.

---

142 See further Gewirth 1996, ch 5, and Beyleveld & Brownsword 2001, 183–188.
143 See Lee 1988, 144.
144 eg in chs 1 (1.2.2) and 2 (2.3). See Beyleveld & Pattinson 2010, 271–272.
145 Mill 1835 (2008, 124).

Bibliography

Adams, John and Brownsword, Roger (2006) *Understanding Law* (4th edn, Sweet & Maxwell).

Adcock, Mike and Beyleveld, Deryck (2007) 'Purposive Interpretation and the Regulation of Technology: Legal Constructs, Legal Fictions, and the Rule of Law' 8(4) *Medical Law International* 305–324.

Alderson, Priscilla and Goodwin, Mary (1993) 'Contradictions within Concepts of Children's Competence' 1 *International Journal of Children's Rights* 303–314.

Alexander, Larry and Sherwin, Emily (2007) 'Judges as Rule Makers' in Douglas E Edlin (ed) *Common Law Theory* (Cambridge University Press), 43–44.

Andrews, Keith, et al (1996) 'Misdiagnosis of the Vegetative State: Retrospective Study in a Rehabilitation Unit' 313 *British Medical Journal* 13–16.

Aquinas, Thomas (1225–1274) *Summa Theologiae* (translated by Fathers of the English Dominican Province) (Benziger Bros, 1947).

Archard, David (2015) *Children: Rights and Childhood* (3rd edn, Routledge).

Arlidge, Anthony (2000) 'The Trial of Dr David Moor' *Criminal Law Review* 31–40.

Bainham, Andrew (1999) 'Lord Denning as a Champion of Children's Rights: The Legacy of *Hewer v. Bryant*' *Denning Law Journal* 81–91.

Balkin, Jack (ed) (2007) *What Roe v. Wade Should Have Said: The Nation's Top Legal Experts Rewrite America's Most Controversial Decision* (NYU Press).

Barkham, Patrick (2008) 'Hannah's Choice' *The Guardian*, 12 November, www.theguardian. com/society/2008/nov/12/health-child-protection

Bartlett, Peter (1997) 'Doctors as Fiduciaries: Equitable Regulation of the Doctor-Patient Relationship' 5(2) *Medical Law Review* 193–224.

Bauhn, Per (ed) (2016a) *Gewirthian Perspectives on Human Rights* (Routledge).

Bauhn, Per (2016b) 'The Gewirthian Duty to Rescue' in Per Bauhn (ed) *Gewirthian Perspectives on Human Rights* (Routledge), 212–226.

Baumann, Holger (2008) 'Reconsidering Relational Autonomy. Personal Autonomy for Socially Embedded and Temporally Extended Selves' 30 *Analyse & Kritik* 445–468.

BBC (2000) 'Fighting for the Right to Die' *BBC News*, 28 November, http://news.bbc. co.uk/1/hi/health/background_briefings/euthanasia/332464.stm

BBC (2010) 'Teenage Jehovah's Witness "Died after Refusing Blood"' *BBC News*, 18 May, http://news.bbc.co.uk/1/hi/england/west_midlands/8690785.stm

BBC (2011) 'Q&A: What is a Minimally Conscious State?' *BBC News*, 28 September, www.bbc.co.uk/news/health-14992607

BBC (2013) 'Transplant-Refusal Girl Hannah Jones Backs Donors' *BBC News*, 20 August, www.bbc.co.uk/news/uk-england-hereford-worcester-23770583

174 *Bibliography*

Beauchamp, Tom L and Childress, James F (2013) *Principles of Biomedical Ethics* (7th edn, Oxford University Press).

Beever, Allan (2007) *Rediscovering the Law of Negligence* (Hart Publishing).

Bentham, Jeremy (1776) *A Fragment of Government.* Reprinted in JH Burns and HLA Hart (eds) *The Collected Works of Jeremy Bentham: A Comment on the Commentaries and A Fragment of Government* (Clarendon, 1977), 391–551.

Bentham, Jeremy (1780) *An Introduction to the Principles of Morals and Legislation* (T Payne and Son). Reprinted as JH Burns and HLA Hart (eds) *The Collected Works of Jeremy Bentham: An Introduction to the Principles of Morals and Legislation* (University of London, The Athlone Press, 1970).

Bentham, Jeremy (1843) *Rationale of Judicial Evidence* in John Bowring (ed) *The Works of Jeremy Bentham*, vol 7 (Simpkin, Marshall and Co, 1843).

Berg, Jessica W, et al (2001) *Informed Consent: Legal Theory and Clinical Practice* (Oxford University Press).

Beyleveld, Deryck (1991) *The Dialectical Necessity of Morality: An Analysis and Defence of Alan Gewirth's Argument to the Principle of Generic Consistency* (Chicago University Press).

Beyleveld, Deryck (1996) 'Legal Theory and Dialectically Contingent Justifications for the Principle of Generic Consistency' 9 *Ratio Juris* 15–41.

Beyleveld, Deryck (2012) 'The Principle of Generic Consistency as the Supreme Principle of Human Rights' 13 *Human Rights Review* 1–18.

Beyleveld, Deryck (2017a) 'What Is Gewirth and What Is Beyleveld? A Retrospect with Comments on the Contributions' in Patrick Capps and Shaun D Pattinson (eds) *Ethical Rationalism and the Law* (Hart Publishing), 233–255.

Beyleveld, Deryck (2017b) 'The Sheffield Natural Law School' in Mortimer Sellers and Stephen Kirste (eds) *Encyclopedia of the Philosophy of Law and Social Philosophy* (Springer), 1–8, https://doi.org/10.1007/978-94-007-6730-0_58-1

Beyleveld, Deryck and Bos, Gerhard (2009) 'The Foundational Role of the Principle of Instrumental Reason in Gewirth's Argument for the Principle of Generic Consistency: A Reply to Andrew Chitty' 20 *King's Law Journal* 1–20.

Beyleveld, Deryck and Brownsword, Roger (1986) *Law as a Moral Judgment* (Sweet & Maxwell; reprinted Sheffield Academic Press, 1994).

Beyleveld, Deryck and Brownsword, Roger (1987) 'Practice Made Perfect': Review of *Law's Empire*, by Ronald Dworkin. 50 *Modern Law Review* 662–672.

Beyleveld, Deryck and Brownsword, Roger (2001) *Human Dignity in Bioethics and Biolaw* (Oxford University Press).

Beyleveld, Deryck and Brownsword, Roger (2006) 'Principle, Proceduralism and Precaution in a Community of Rights' 19(2) *Ratio Juris* 141–168.

Beyleveld, Deryck and Pattinson, Shaun D (1998) 'Proportionality under Precaution: Justifying Duties to Apparent Non-Agents' (unpublished paper available).

Beyleveld, Deryck and Pattinson, Shaun D (2000a) 'Precautionary Reasoning as a Link to Moral Action' in Michael Boylan (ed) *Medical Ethics* (Prentice-Hall), 39–53.

Beyleveld, Deryck and Pattinson, Shaun D (2000b) 'Legal Regulation of Assisted Procreation, Genetic Diagnosis and Gene Therapy' in Hille Haker and Deryck Beyleveld (eds) *The Ethics of Genetics in Human Procreation* (Ashgate), 215–276.

Beyleveld, Deryck and Pattinson, Shaun D (2002) 'Horizontal Applicability and Horizontal Effect' 118 *Law Quarterly Review* 623–646.

Beyleveld, Deryck and Pattinson, Shaun D (2004) 'Globalisation and Human Dignity: Some Effects and Implications for the Creation and Use of Embryos' in Roger Brownsword (ed) *Global Governance and the Quest for Justice. Volume IV: Human Rights* (Hart Publishing), 185–202.

Bibliography   175

Beyleveld, Deryck and Pattinson, Shaun D (2010) 'Defending Moral Precaution as a Solution to the Problem of Other Minds' 23(2) *Ratio Juris* 258–273.

Bielby, Phillip (2008) *Competence and Vulnerability in Biomedical Research* (Springer).

Biggs, Hazel (2007) '"Taking Account of the Views of the Patient", but only if the Clinician (and the Court) Agrees – *R (Burke) v General Medical Council*' 19 *Child & Family Law Quarterly* 225–238.

Bowcott, Owen (2014) 'High Court Judge is First to be Formally Addressed as Ms Justice' *The Guardian*, 21 May, www.theguardian.com/law/2014/may/21/high-court-judge-ms-justice

Boylan, Michael (ed) (1999) *Gewirth: Critical Essays on Action, Rationality and Community* (Rowman & Littlefield).

Boyle, Joseph (2004) 'Medical Ethics and Double Effect: The Case of Terminal Sedation' 25(1) *Theoretical Medicine and Bioethics* 51–60.

Brazier, Margaret (1987) 'Patient Autonomy and Consent to Treatment: The Role of the Law?' 7 *Legal Studies* 169–193.

Brazier, Margaret and Glover, Nicola (2000) 'Does Medical Law Have a Future?' in David Hayton (ed) *Law's Future* (Hart), 371–388.

Brazier, Margaret and Lobjoit, Mary (1999) 'Fiduciary Relationship: An Ethical Approach and a Legal Concept' in Rebecca Bennett and Charles Erin (eds) *HIV and AIDS: Testing, Screening and Confidentiality* (Oxford University Press), 179–199.

Brems, Eva (ed) (2012) *Diversity and European Human Rights: Rewriting Judgments of the ECHR* (Cambridge University Press).

Brown, Stephen (2004) 'Alan Gewirth: An Obituary' *Studies in Social and Political Thought* 88–95.

Brown, Stephen (2016) 'A Dialectically Necessary Approach to the Sociological Understanding of Power and Real Interests' in Per Bauhn (ed) *Gewirthian Perspectives on Human Rights* (Routledge), 82–95.

Buchanan, Allan (1988) 'Advance Directives and the Personal Identity Problem' 17 *Philosophy and Public Affairs* 277–302.

Burns, JH and Hart, HLA (eds) (1970) *The Collected Works of Jeremy Bentham: An Introduction to the Principles of Morals and Legislation* (University of London, The Athlone Press).

Burns, JH and Hart, HLA (eds) (1977) *The Collected Works of Jeremy Bentham: A Comment on the Commentaries and A Fragment of Government* (Clarendon).

Campbell, David (2007) 'Relational Contract and the Nature of Private Ordering: A Comment on Vincent-Jones' 14(2) *Indiana Journal of Global Legal Studies* 279–300.

Capps, Benjamin (2017) 'Public Goods in the Ethical Reconsideration of Research Innovation' in Patrick Capps and Shaun D Pattinson (eds) *Ethical Rationalism and the Law* (Hart Publishing), 149–169.

Capps, Patrick M (2009) *Human Dignity and the Foundations of International Law* (Hart Publishing).

Capps, Patrick M and Pattinson, Shaun D (eds) (2017a) *Ethical Rationalism and the Law* (Hart Publishing).

Capps, Patrick M and Pattinson, Shaun D (2017b) 'The Past, Present and Future of Ethical Rationalism' in Patrick Capps and Shaun D Pattinson (eds) *Ethical Rationalism and the Law* (Hart Publishing), 1–16.

Castañeda, Hector-Neri (1979) 'Intentionality and Identity in Human Action and Philosophical Method' 13 *Noûs* 235–260.

Cave, Emma (2009) 'Adolescent Consent and Confidentiality in the UK' 16 *European Journal of Health Law* 309–331.

176 *Bibliography*

Cave, Emma (2013) 'Competence and Authority: Adolescent Treatment Refusals for Physical and Mental Health Conditions' 8(2) *Contemporary Social Science* 92–103.

Cave, Emma (2014) 'Goodbye Gillick? Identifying and Resolving Problems with the Concept of Child Competence' 34(1) *Legal Studies* 103–122.

Cave, Emma (2015) 'Determining Capacity to Make Medical Treatment Decisions: Problems Implementing the Mental Capacity Act 2005' 36(1) *Statute Law Review* 86–106.

Cave, Emma and Wallbank, Julie (2012) 'Minors' Capacity to Refuse Treatment: A Reply to Gilmore and Herring' 20(3) *Medical Law Review* 423–449.

Cerminara, Kathy L (2010) 'The *Schiavo* Maelstrom's Potential Impact on the Law of End-of-Life Decision Making' in Kenneth W Goodman (ed) *The Case of Terri Schiavo* (Oxford University Press), 78–100.

Christman, John (2004) 'Relational Autonomy, Liberal Individualism, and the Social Constitution of Selves' 117 *Philosophical Studies* 143–164.

Claassen, Rutger and Düwell, Marcus (2013) 'The Foundations of Capability Theory: Comparing Nussbaum and Gewirth' 16(3) *Ethical Theory and Moral Practice* 493–510.

Clucas, B (2006) 'The Sheffield School and Discourse Theory: Divergences and Similarities in Legal Idealism/Anti-Positivism' 19(2) *Ratio Juris* 230–244.

Clucas, B and O'Donnell, Kath (2002) 'Conjoined Twins: The Cutting Edge' 5 *Web Journal of Current Legal Issues*, www.bailii.org/uk/other/journals/WebJCLI/2002/issue5/clucas5.html

Coggon, John (2007) 'Varied and Principled Understandings of Autonomy in English Law: Justifiable Inconsistency or Blinkered Moralism?' 15 *Health Care Analysis* 235–255.

Corazzol, Martina, et al (2017) 'Restoring Consciousness with Vagus Nerve Stimulation' 27(18) *Current Biology* R979–R1001.

Cornock, Marc and Montgomery, Heather (2011) 'Children's Rights In and Out of the Womb' (2011) 19 *International Journal of Children's Rights* 3–19.

Cruse, Damian, et al (2011) 'Bedside Detection of Awareness in the Vegetative State: A Cohort Study' 378 *The Lancet* 2088–2094.

Department for Constitutional Affairs (2007) *Mental Capacity Act: Code of Practice* (The Stationery Office).

Devlin, Patrick (1985) *Easing the Passing: The Trial of Dr John Bodkin Adams* (Bodley Head).

DH (Department of Health) (2000) *Stem Cell Research: Medical Progress with Responsibility. A Report from the Chief Medical Officer's Expert Group Reviewing the Potential of Developments in Stem Cell Research and Cell Nuclear Replacement to Benefit Human Health* (DH).

Dickson, Brice (1999) 'The Lords of Appeal and Their Work 1967–1996' in Paul Carmichael and Brice Dickson (eds) *The House of Lords: Its Parliamentary and Judicial Roles* (Hart Publishing), 127–154.

Dobson, Lynn (2006) *Supranational Citizenship* (Manchester University Press).

Donnelly, Mary (2010) *Healthcare Decision-Making and the Law* (Cambridge University Press).

Donohoe, Margaret M (1996) 'Our Epidemic of Unnecessary Caesarean Sections: The Role of the Law in Creating It, the Role of the Law in Stopping It' 11 *Wisconsin Women's Law Journal* 197–241.

Douglas, Benedict (2018) 'Too Attentive to Our Duty: The Fundamental Conflict Underlying Human Rights Protection in the UK' *Legal Studies*, https://doi.org/10.1017/lst.2017.25

Douglas, Gillian (1992) 'The Retreat from *Gillick*' 55 *Modern Law Review* 569–576.

Bibliography 177

Dresser, Joshua (2013) 'Reflections on *Dudley and Stephens* and Killing the Innocent: Taking a Wrong Conceptual Path' in Dennis J Baker and Jeremy Horder (eds) *The Sanctity of Life and the Criminal Law: The Legacy of Glanville Williams* (Cambridge University Press), 126–147.

Dresser, Rebecca (1995) 'Dworkin on Dementia: Elegant Theory, Questionable Policy' 25 *Hastings Center Report* 32–38.

Düring, Dascha and Düwell, Marcus (2017) 'Hope, Agency, and Aesthetic Sensibility: A Response to Beyleveld's Account of Kantian Hope' in Patrick Capps and Shaun D Pattinson (eds) *Ethical Rationalism and the Law* (Hart Publishing), 55–71.

Duxbury, Neil (2008) *The Nature and Authority of Precedent* (Cambridge University Press).

Dworkin, Gerald (1988) *The Theory and Practice of Autonomy* (Cambridge University Press).

Dworkin, Ronald (1978) *Taking Rights Seriously* (Harvard University Press, revised edn, original edn published 1977).

Dworkin, Ronald (1985) *A Matter of Principle* (Harvard University Press).

Dworkin, Ronald (1986) *Law's Empire* (Hart Publishing).

Dyer, Clare (1997) 'Hillsborough Survivor Emerges from Permanent Vegetative State' 314 *British Medical Journal* 993.

Eekelaar John (1986) 'The Emergence of Children's Rights' 6(2) *Oxford Journal of Legal Studies* 161–182.

Egli, Dieter and Chia, Gloryn (2014) 'A Protocol for Embryonic Stem Cell Derivation by Somatic Cell Nuclear Transfer into Human Oocytes' *Protocol Exchange*, www.nature.com/protocolexchange/protocols/3117#/procedure

Faludi, Susan (1992) *Backlash: The Undeclared War Against Women* (Chatto & Windus).

Finlay, Ilora (2009) 'The Art of Medicine: Dying and Choosing' 373 *The Lancet* 1840–1841.

Finnis, John (1990) 'Natural Law and Legal Reasoning' 38 *Cleveland State Law Review* 1–13.

Finnis, John (1993) '*Bland*: Crossing the Rubicon?' 109 *Law Quarterly Review* 329–337.

Finnis, John (1995a) 'A Philosophical Case Against Euthanasia' in John Keown (ed) *Euthanasia Examined* (Cambridge University Press), 23–35.

Finnis, John (1995b) 'The Fragile Case for Euthanasia: A Reply to John Harris' in John Keown (ed) *Euthanasia Examined* (Cambridge University Press), 46–55.

Finnis, John (1995c) 'Misunderstanding the Case Against Euthanasia: Response to Harris's First Reply' in John Keown (ed) *Euthanasia Examined* (Cambridge University Press), 62–71.

Fortin, Jane (2011) 'The *Gillick* Decision – Not Just a High-water Mark' in Stephen Gilmore, Jonathan Herring and Rebecca Probert (eds) *Landmark Cases in Family Law* (Hart Publishing), 199–223.

Foster, Charles (2011) '*Airedale NHS Trust v Bland* [1993]' in Stephen Gilmore, Jonathan Herring and Rebecca Probert (eds) *Landmark Cases in Family Law* (Hart Publishing), 83–110.

Foster, Charles, et al (2011) 'The Double Effect' 20(1) *Cambridge Quarterly of Healthcare Ethics* 56–72.

Foster, Peggy (1998) 'Informed Consent in Practice' in Sally Sheldon and Michael Thomson (eds) *Feminist Perspectives on Health Care Law* (Cavendish), 53–72.

Fox, Marie and Moreton, Kirsty (2015) '*Re MB (An Adult: Medical Treatment)* [1997] and *St George's Healthcare NHS Trust v S* [1998]: The Dilemma of the "Court-Ordered"

178 *Bibliography*

Caesarean' in Jonathan Herring and Jesse Wall (eds) *Landmark Cases in Medical Law* (Hart Publishing), 145–174.

Freeman, Michael (2000) 'The Future of Children's Rights' 14 *Children & Society* 277–293.

Freeman, Michael (2005) 'Rethinking *Gillick*' 13 *International Journal of Children's Rights* 201–217.

Freeman, Michael (2007) 'Why It Remains Important to Take Children's Rights Seriously' 15 *International Journal of Children's Rights* 5–23.

Freeman, Michael (2014) *Lloyd's Introduction to Jurisprudence* (Sweet & Maxwell).

Fuller, Lon (1949) 'The Case of the Speluncean Explorers' 62 *Harvard Law Review* 616–645.

Fuller, Lon (1967) *Legal Fictions* (Stanford University Press).

Fuller, Lon (1969) *The Morality of Law* (Yale University Press).

Gee, Henry (1999) 'Dolly Is Not Quite a Clone' *Nature*, 31 August, www.nature.com/news/1999/990831/full/news990902-5.html

Gewirth, Alan (1978) *Reason and Morality* (Chicago University Press).

Gewirth, Alan (1981) 'Are There Any Absolute Rights?' 31 *Philosophical Quarterly* 1–16.

Gewirth, Alan (1988) 'Human Rights and Concepts of the Self' 18 *Philosophia* 129–149.

Gewirth, Alan (1996) *The Community of Rights* (Chicago University Press).

Gewirth, Alan (1999) 'Replies to my Colleagues' in Michael Boylan (ed) *Gewirth: Critical Essays on Action, Rationality, and Community* (Rowman & Littlefield), 191–213.

Gillick, Victoria (1989) *A Mother's Tale* (Hodder and Stoughton).

Gillon, Raanan (2001) 'Editorial: Imposed Separation of Conjoined Twins—Moral Hubris by the English Courts' 27 *Journal of Medical Ethics* 3–4.

Gillon, Raanan (2004) 'Why the GMC is Right to Appeal over Life Prolonging Treatment' 329 *British Medical Journal* 810–811.

Gilmore, Stephen and Herring, Jonathan (2011a) '"No" is the Hardest Word: Consent and Children's Autonomy' 23 *Child and Family Law Quarterly* 3–25.

Gilmore, Stephen and Herring, Jonathan (2011b) 'Children's Refusal of Medical Treatment: Could Re W be Distinguished?' 41(7) *Family Law* 715–718.

Gilmore, Stephen and Herring, Jonathan (2012) 'Children's Refusal of Medical Treatment: The Debate Continues?' 41(7) *Family Law* 973–978.

Glazebrook, Peter (2013) 'Glanville Llewelyn Williams 1911–1997: A Biographical Note' in Dennis J Baker and Jeremy Horder (eds) *The Sanctity of Life and the Criminal Law: The Legacy of Glanville Williams* (Cambridge University Press), 1–25.

GMC (General Medical Council) (2002) *Withholding and Withdrawing Life-prolonging Treatments: Good Practice in Decision-making*.

GMC (2010) *Treatment and Care Towards the End of Life*.

Grace, John (1999) 'Should the Foetus Have Rights in Law?' 67(2) *Medico-Legal Journal* 57–67.

Grubb, Andrew (1993a) 'Treatment Decisions: Keeping It in the Family' in Andrew Grubb (ed) *Choices and Decisions in Heath Care* (Wiley), 37–96.

Grubb, Andrew (1993b) 'Treatment Without Consent: Adult: *Re T (Adult: Refusal of Treatment)*' 1(1) *Medical Law Review* 84–87.

Grubb, Andrew (1994) 'The Doctor as Fiduciary' 47(2) *Current Legal Problems* 311–340.

Grubb, Andrew (2002a) 'Infertility Treatment: Posthumous Use of Sperm and Withdrawal of Consent: *The Centre for Reproductive Medicine v U*' 10(2) *Medical Law Review* 204–206.

Grubb, Andrew (2002b) 'Regulating Cloned Embryos?' 118 *Law Quarterly Review* 358–363.

Grubb, Andrew (2004) 'Consent to Treatment: The Competent Patient' in Andrew Grubb (ed) *Principles of Medical Law* (2nd edn, Oxford University Press), 131–203.

Bibliography 179

Gunn, MJ, et al (1999) 'Decision-Making Capacity' 7(3) *Medical Law Review* 269–306.

Hagger, Lynn (2009) *The Child as Vulnerable Patient: Protection and Empowerment* (Ashgate).

Hall, Marion H and Bewley, Susan (1999) 'Maternal Mortality and Mode of Delivery' 354 *The Lancet* 776.

Halliday, Samantha (2016) *Autonomy and Pregnancy: A Comparative Analysis of Compelled Obstetric Intervention* (Routledge).

Halliday, Simon, Formby, Adam and Cookson, Richard (2015) 'An Assessment of the Court's Role in the Withdrawal of Clinically Assisted Nutrition and Hydration from Patients in the Permanent Vegetative State' 23(4) *Medical Law Review* 556–587.

Hardcastle, Rohan (2007) *Law and the Human Body: Property Rights, Ownership and Control* (Hart Publishing).

Harris, BV (2002) 'Final Appellate Courts Overruling Their Own "Wrong" Precedents: The Ongoing Search for Principle' 118 *Law Quarterly Review* 408–427.

Harris, John (1985) *The Value of Life: An Introduction to Medical Ethics* (Routledge).

Harris, John (1995a) 'Euthanasia and the Value of Life' in John Keown (ed) *Euthanasia Examined* (Cambridge University Press), 6–22.

Harris, John (1995b) 'The Philosophical Case Against the Philosophical Case Against Euthanasia' in John Keown (ed) *Euthanasia Examined* (Cambridge University Press), 36–45.

Harris, John (1995c) 'Final Thoughts on Final Acts' in John Keown (ed) *Euthanasia Examined* (Cambridge University Press), 56–61.

Harris, John (1998) *Clones, Genes and Immortality: Ethics and the Genetic Revolution* (Oxford University Press).

Harris, John (2001) 'Human Beings, Persons and Conjoined Twins: An Ethical Analysis of the Judgment in *Re A*' n9(3) *Medical Law Review* 221–236.

Hart, HLA (1955) 'Are There Any Natural Rights?' 64(2) *Philosophical Review* 175–191.

Hastings, Geraldine (2010) '*Re A (Children) (Conjoined Twins: Surgical Separation)*' in Rosemary Hunter, Clare McGlynn and Erika Rackley (eds) *Feminist Judgments: From Theory to Practice* (Hart Publishing), 139–146.

Herbert, Alan Patrick (1932) *Misleading Cases in the Common Law* (Methuen).

Hernández, Gleider I (2014) *The International Court of Justice and the Judicial Function* (Oxford University Press).

Herring, Jonathan and Wall, Jesse (eds) (2015) *Landmark Cases in Medical Law* (Hart Publishing).

Hewson, Barbara (2013) '"Neither Midwives nor Rainmakers" – Why DL is Wrong' *Public Law* 451–459.

Hill, James F (1984) 'Are Marginal Agents "Our Recipients"?' in Edward Regis (ed) *Gewirth's Ethical Rationalism: Critical Essays with a Reply by Gewirth* (Chicago University Press), 180–191.

Hohfeld, Wesley Newcomb (1923) *Fundamental Legal Conceptions: As Applied in Judicial Reasoning and Other Legal Essays* (ed Walter Wheeler Cook) (Yale University Press).

Holm, Søren and Coggon, John (2008) 'A Cautionary Note Against "Precautionary Reasoning" in Action Guiding Morality' 22(2) *Ratio Juris* 295–309.

Hoppe, Nils and Miola, José (2014) *Medical Law and Medical Ethics* (Cambridge University Press).

House of Lords Select Committee (1994) *Report of the Select Committee on Medical Ethics Volume I—Report* (Session 1993-1994) (HMSO).

180 *Bibliography*

Hübenthal, Christoph (2016) 'Gewirth's Moral Philosophy and the Foundation of Catholic Social Thought' in Per Bauhn (ed) *Gewirthian Perspectives on Human Rights* (Routledge), 96–110.

Hunter, Rosemary, McGlynn, Clare and Rackley, Erika (eds) (2010a) *Feminist Judgments: From Theory to Practice* (Hart Publishing).

Hunter, Rosemary, McGlynn, Clare and Rackley, Erika (2010b) 'Feminist Judgments: An Introduction' in Rosemary Hunter, Clare McGlynn and Erika Rackley (eds) *Feminist Judgments: From Theory to Practice* (Hart Publishing), 3–29.

Huxtable, Richard (2000) '*Re M (Medical Treatment: Consent)* – Time to Remove the "Flak Jacket"?' 12(1) *Child and Family Law Quarterly* 83–88.

Huxtable, Richard (2012) *Law, Ethics and Compromise at the Limits of Life: To Treat or not to Treat?* (Routledge).

Jackson, Emily (2012) 'In Favour of Legalisation of Assisted Dying' in Emily Jackson and John Keown, *Debating Euthanasia* (Hart Publishing), 1–82.

Jennett, Bryan (1999) 'Should Cases of Permanent Vegetative State Still Go to Court? Britain Should Follow Other Countries and Keep the Courts for Cases of Dispute' 319 *British Medical Journal* 796–797.

Jennett, Bryan (2002) 'The Vegetative State' 73 *Journal of Neurology, Neurosurgery and Psychiatry* 355–357.

Jennett, Bryan and Plum, Fred (1972) 'Persistent Vegetative State after Brain Damage' 1 *The Lancet* 734–737.

Kalbian, Aline H (2005) 'Narrative *ARTi*fice and Women's Agency' 19(2) *Bioethics* 93–111.

Kaplan, Robert M (2009) *Medical Murder: Disturbing Cases of Doctors Who Kill* (Allen & Unwin).

Keene, Alex Ruck (2015) 'Capacity is Not an Off-Switch', *Mental Capacity Law and Policy blog*, 1 October, www.mentalcapacitylawandpolicy.org.uk/capacity-is-not-an-off-switch

Kennedy, Ian (1988) *Treat Me Right: Essays in Medical Law and Ethics* (Oxford University Press).

Kennedy, Ian (1992) 'Consent to Treatment: The Capable Person' in C Dyer (ed) *Doctors, Patients and the Law* (Blackwell), ch 3.

Kennedy, Ian (1996) 'The Fiduciary Relationship and its Application to Doctors' in P Birks (ed) *Wrongs and Remedies in the Twenty-first Century* (Clarendon Press), 111–140.

Kennedy, Ian and Grubb, Andrew (1994) *Medical Law: Text with Materials* (2nd edn, Oxford University Press).

Kennedy, Ian and Grubb, Andrew (2000) *Medical Law: Text with Materials* (3rd edn, Oxford University Press).

Keown, John (1997) 'Restoring Moral and Intellectual Shape to the Law after *Bland*' 113 *Law Quarterly Review* 482–503.

Keown, John (2000) 'Beyond *Bland*: A Critique of the BMA Guidance on Withholding and Withdrawing Medical Treatment' 20(1) *Legal Studies* 66–84.

Keown, John (2002) *Euthanasia, Ethics and Public Policy* (Cambridge University Press).

Keown, John (2006) 'Restoring the Sanctity of Life and Replacing the Caricature: A Reply to David Price' 26(1) *Legal Studies* 109–119.

Keown, John (2012) 'Against Decriminalising Euthanasia; for Improving Care' in Emily Jackson and John Keown, *Debating Euthanasia* (Hart Publishing), 83–174.

Kitzinger, Celia and Kitzinger, Jenny (2015) 'Why Are Patients in Permanent Comas Routinely Kept Alive?' *The Conversation*, 18 June, http://theconversation.com/why-are-patients-in-permanent-comas-routinely-kept-alive-43365

Bibliography 181

Kronman, Anthony T (1990) 'Precedent and Tradition' 99 *Yale Law Review* 1029–1068.

Laing, Jacqueline (2002) '"Vegetative" State – The Untold Story' 152 *New Law Journal* 1272.

Laudreys, Steven (2000) 'Human Rights Act Does Not Affect the Law on PVS' 321 *British Medical Journal* 916.

Laurie, Graeme (2006) 'The Autonomy of Others: Reflections on the Rise and Rise of Patient Choice in Contemporary Medical Law' in SAM Mclean (ed) *First Do No Harm* (Ashgate), 131–149.

Law Commission (1974) *Report on Injuries to Unborn Children* (Law Commission Report No 60, Cmnd 5709).

Law Commission (1995) *Mental Incapacity* (Law Commission No 231).

Law Commission (2005) *A New Homicide Act for England and Wales? (Consultation Paper)* [2005] EWLC 177(4) (20 December 2005).

Law, Richard WM and Choong, Kartina A (2018) 'Disorders of Consciousness: Is a Dichotomous Legal Approach Justified?' 25 *European Journal of Health Law* 1–22.

Lee, Simon (1988) *Judging Judges* (Faber and Faber).

Lennings, Nicholas J (2015) 'Forward, *Gillick*: Are Competent Children Autonomous Medical Decision Makers? New Developments in Australia' 2(2) *Journal of Law and the Biosciences* 459–468.

Lewis, Penney (2007) 'Withdrawal of Treatment from a Patient in a Permanent Vegetative State: Judicial Involvement and Innovative "Treatment"' 15(3) *Medical Law Review* 392–399.

Lewis, Penney (2013) 'The Failure of the Defence of Necessity as a Mechanism of Legal Change on Assisted Dying in the Common Law' in Dennis J Baker and Jeremy Horder (eds) *The Sanctity of Life and the Criminal Law: The Legacy of Glanville Williams* (Cambridge University Press), 274–295.

Liu, Zhen, et al (2018) 'Cloning of Macaque Monkeys by Somatic Cell Nuclear Transfer' 172(4) *Cell* 881–887.

Locke, John (1690) *An Essay Concerning Human Understanding*. Reprinted in R Woolhouse (ed) (Penguin Classics, 1997).

MacCormick, Neil (1977) 'Rights in Legislation' in PMS Hacker and J Raz (eds) *Law, Morality and Society: Essays in Honour of HLA Hart* (Clarendon Press), 189–209.

McEwan, Jenny (2001) 'Murder by Design: The "Feel-Good Factor" and the Criminal Law' 9(3) *Medical Law Review* 246–258.

McGee, Andrew (2004) 'Double Effect in the *Criminal Code 1899* (QLD): A Critical Appraisal' 4(1) *QUT Law Review* 46–57.

McGee, Andrew (2013) 'Intention, Foresight and Ending Life: A Reply to Foster, Herring, Melham and Hope' 22(1) *Cambridge Quarterly of Healthcare Ethics* 77–85.

McLean, Sheila AM (2010) *Autonomy, Consent and the Law* (Routledge).

Mackenzie, Catriona and Stoljar, Natalie (2000) 'Introduction: Autonomy Refigured' in Catriona Mackenzie and Natalie Stoljar (eds) *Relational Autonomy: Feminist Perspectives on Autonomy, Agency and the Social Self* (Oxford University Press), 3–34.

Maltz, Earl (1988) 'The Nature of Precedent' 66 *North Carolina Law Review* 367–393.

Martyn, Susan and Bourguignon, Henry J (2000) 'Physicians' Decisions about Patient Capacity' 6 *Psychology Public Policy and Law* 388–401.

Mason, JK (1998) 'Law and Medical Ethics: Have We Learnt Any Lessons?' (unpublished lecture held at Edinburgh Law School, 31 October 1998).

Mason, JK and Laurie, GT (2005) 'Personal Autonomy and the Right to Treatment: A Note on *R (on the application of Burke)* v *General Medical Council*' 9 *Edinburgh Law Review* 123–132.

Bibliography

Matthews, Paul (1983) 'Whose Body? People as Property' 36 *Current Legal Problems* 193–239.

Michalowski, Sabine (1999) 'Court-Authorised Caesarean Sections – The End of a Trend? – *Re MB (An Adult: Medical Treatment)*' 62(1) *Modern Law Review* 115–127.

Michalowski, Sabine (2002) 'Sanctity of Life – Are Some Lives More Sacred than Others?' 22(3) *Legal Studies* 377–397.

Mill, John Stuart (1835) 'Professor Sedgwick's Discourse on the Studies of the University of Cambridge' *London Review*, reprinted in *Dissertations and Discussions: Volume 1* (Cosimo, 2008), 95–159.

Montaña, Robert A (2016) 'The Gewirthian Ideal of Self-Fulfillment: Enhancing the Moral Foundations of International Law' in Per Bauhn (ed) *Gewirthian Perspectives on Human Rights* (Routledge), 111–124.

Montgomery, Jonathan, Jones, Caroline and Biggs, Hazel (2014) 'Hidden Lawmaking in the Province of Medical Jurisprudence' 77(3) *Modern Law Review* 343–378.

Monti, MM, et al (2010) 'Willful Modulation of Brain Activity in Disorders of Consciousness' 362 *New England Journal of Medicine* 579–589.

Montrose, L (1958) 'Is Negligence an Ethical or a Sociological Concept?' 21 *Modern Law Review* 259–264.

Morgan, Derek (2001) *Issues in Medical Law and Ethics (Cavendish)*.

Morgan, Derek and Ford, Mary (2004) 'Cell Phoney: Human Cloning after Quintavalle' 30 *Journal of Medical Ethics* 524–526.

Morgan, Derek and Lee, Robert G (1997) 'In the Name of the Father? *Ex parte Blood*: Dealing with Novelty and Anomaly' 60(6) *Modern Law Review* 840–856.

Morgan, Ryan and Devenney, James (2003) 'Mrs U v Centre for Reproductive Medicine' 25 *Journal of Social Welfare and Family Law* 74–83.

Morris, Anne (2002) 'The Angel in the House: Altruism, Competence and the Pregnant Woman' in Anne Morris and Susan Nott (eds) *Well Women: The Gendered Nature of Health Care Provision* (Ashgate), 97–115.

Morton, James (1992) 'Obituary: Lord Devlin' *The Independent*, 11 August, www.independent.co.uk/news/people/obituary-lord-devlin-1539619.html

Munby, James (2010) 'Consent to Treatment: Patients Lacking Capacity and Children' in Andrew Grubb, Judith Laing and Jean McHale (eds) *Principles of Medical Law* (3rd edn, Oxford University Press), 491–581.

Murphy, John (1992) 'W(h)ither Adolescent Autonomy' 14 *Journal of Social Welfare and Family Law* 529–544.

NCOB (Nuffield Council on Bioethics) (2015) *Ideas about Naturalness in Public and Political Debates about Science, Technology and Medicine: Analysis Paper* (November 2015) (NCOB).

Nedelsky, Jennifer (1989) 'Reconceiving Autonomy: Sources, Thoughts and Possibilities' (1989) 1 *Yale Journal of Law and Feminism* 7–36.

Neuberger, Lord (2015) 'Fairness in the Courts: The Best We Can Do' (Address to the Criminal Justice Alliance, 10 April), www.supremecourt.uk/docs/speech-150410.pdf

NHS (2017a) 'Foetal Alcohol Syndrome', 10 January, www.nhs.uk/conditions/foetal-alcohol-syndrome

NHS (2017b) 'Vitamins, Supplements and Nutrition in Pregnancy', 26 January, www.nhs.uk/conditions/pregnancy-and-baby/vitamins-minerals-supplements-pregnant

Olsen, Henrik Palmer (2017) 'Fidelity to International Law: On International Courts and Politics' in Patrick Capps and Shaun D Pattinson (eds) *Ethical Rationalism and the Law* (Hart Publishing), 191–211.

Bibliography 183

Olsen, Henrik Palmer and Toddington, Stuart (1999) *Law in Its Own Right* (Hart Publishing).

Ormerod, David and Laird, Karl (2015) *Smith and Hogan's Criminal Law* (14th edn, Oxford University Press).

Oshana, Marina OL (1998) 'Personal Autonomy and Society' 29(1) *Journal of Social Philosophy* 81–102.

Ost, Suzanne (2017) 'Judgment 1 – *Re A (Conjoined Twins: Surgical Separation)* [2001] Fam 147' in Stephen W Smith et al (eds) *Ethical Judgments: Re-Writing Medical Law* (Hart Publishing), 11–17.

Palmer, Henry (1957) 'Dr Adam's Trial for Murder' *Criminal Law Review* 365–377.

Parfit, Derek (1984) *Reason and Persons* (Clarendon Press).

Parkinson, Patrick (1986) 'The *Gillick* Case – Just What Has It Decided?' 16 *Family Law* 11–14.

Paterson, Alan (1982) *The Law Lords* (Macmillan).

Pattinson, Shaun D (2002a) *Influencing Traits Before Birth* (Ashgate).

Pattinson, Shaun D (2002b) 'Undue Influence in the Context of Medical Treatment' 5(4) *Medical Law International* 305–317.

Pattinson, Shaun D (2002c) 'Reproductive Cloning: Can Cloning Harm the Clone?' 10(3) *Medical Law Review* 295–307.

Pattinson, Shaun D (2005) 'Some Problems Challenging the UK's Human Fertilisation and Embryology Authority' 24 *Medicine and Law* 391–401.

Pattinson, Shaun D (2006) *Medical Law and Ethics* (1st edn, Sweet & Maxwell).

Pattinson, Shaun D (2009a) 'Consent and Informational Responsibility' 35(3) *Journal of Medical Ethics* 176–179.

Pattinson, Shaun D (2009b) *Medical Law and Ethics* (2nd edn, Sweet & Maxwell).

Pattinson, Shaun D (2011) 'Directed Donation and Ownership of Human Organs' 31(3) *Legal Studies* 392–410.

Pattinson, Shaun D (2014) *Medical Law and Ethics* (4th edn, Sweet & Maxwell).

Pattinson, Shaun D (2015a) 'The Human Rights Act and the Doctrine of Precedent' 35(1) *Legal Studies* 142–164.

Pattinson, Shaun D (2015b) 'Contemporaneous and Advance Requests: The Fight for Rights at the End of Life' in Jonathan Herring and Jesse Wall (eds) *Landmark Cases in Medical Law* (Hart Publishing), 651–723.

Pattinson, Shaun D (2017a) 'Advance Refusals and the Personal Identity Objection' in Patrick Capps and Shaun D Pattinson (eds) *Ethical Rationalism and the Law* (Hart Publishing), 91–108.

Pattinson, Shaun D (2017b) *Medical Law and Ethics* (5th edn, Sweet & Maxwell).

Pattinson, Shaun D (2017c) 'Some Comments on Developmental Thresholds and Their Moral and Policy Significance' in Nuffield Council on Bioethics (ed) *In Human Embryo Culture* (NCOB), 81–83.

Pattinson, Shaun D and Caulfield, Timothy (2004) 'Variations and Voids: The Regulation of Human Cloning Around the World' 5 *BMC Medical Ethics* 9, www.biomedcentral.com/1472-6939/5/9

Pattinson, Shaun D and Kind, Vanessa (2017) 'Using a Moot to Develop Students' Understanding of Human Cloning and Statutory Interpretation' 17(3) *Medical Law International* 111–133.

Phillipson, Gavin and Williams, Alexander (2011) 'Horizontal Effect and the Constitutional Constraint' 74(6) *Modern Law Review* 878–910.

Plomer, Aurora (2002) 'Beyond the HFE Act 1990: The Regulation of Stem Cell Research in the UK' (2002) 10(2) *Medical Law Review* 132–164.

184 *Bibliography*

Pluhar, Evelyn B (1995) *Beyond Prejudice: The Moral Significance of Human and Nonhuman Animals* (Duke University Press).

Price, David (1997) 'Euthanasia, Pain Relief and Double Effect' 17(2) *Legal Studies* 323–342.

Price, David (2001) 'Fairly Bland: An Alternative View of a Supposed New "Death Ethic" and the BMA Guidelines' 21(4) *Legal Studies* 618–643.

Price, David (2007) 'My View of the Sanctity of Life: A Rebuttal of John Keown's Critique' 27(4) *Legal Studies* 549–565.

Price, David (2009) *Human Tissue in Transplantation and Research: A Model Legal and Ethical Donation Framework* (Cambridge University Press).

Purshouse, Craig (2018) 'Utilitarianism as Tort Theory: Countering the Caricature' 38(1) *Legal Studies* 24-41.

Rachels, James (1979) 'Killing and Starving to Death' 54 *Philosophy* 159–171.

Rackley, Erika (2010) 'The Art and Craft of Writing Judgments: Notes on the Feminist Judgments Project' in Rosemary Hunter, Clare McGlynn and Erika Rackley (eds) *Feminist Judgments: From Theory to Practice* (Hart Publishing), 44–56.

Rae, Maggie (1992) 'Consent to Medical Treatment' 142 *New Law Journal* 1574.

RCP (Royal College of Physicians) (2013) *Prolonged Disorders of Consciousness: National Clinical Guidelines* (RCP).

Regis, Edward (ed) (1984) *Gewirth's Ethical Rationalism: Critical Essays with a Reply by Alan Gewirth* (Chicago University Press).

Robertson, David (1998) *Judicial Discretion in the House of Lords* (Clarendon Press).

Robertson, John A (1983) 'Procreative Liberty and the Control of Conception, Pregnancy and Childbirth' 69 *Virginia Law Review* 405–464.

Rodrigues, H Catarina ML and van den Berg, Paul P (2012) 'Morally and Procedurally Justified Argument for the Moral Obligations of Physicians toward Pregnant Women (and Fetuses) in the Context of Maternal-Fetal Surgery: A Gewirthian Precautionary Approach' 12(2) *Medical Law International* 142–155.

Ross, Lainie Friedman (1998) *Children, Families and Health Care Decision-Making* (Oxford University Press).

Samar, Vincent J (2016) 'A Gewirthian Framework for Protecting the Basic Human Rights of Lesbian, Gay, Bisexual, and Transgender (LGBT) People' in Per Bauhn (ed) *Gewirthian Perspectives on Human Rights* (Routledge), 157–173.

Sample, Ian (2014) 'Stem Cell Therapy Success in Treatment of Sight Loss from Macular Degeneration' *The Guardian*, 15 October, www.theguardian.com/science/2014/oct/15/stem-cell-success-in-treating-macular-degeneration.

Schauer, Frederick (1987) 'Precedent' 39 *Stanford Law Review* 571–605.

Scott, Rosamund (2004) 'The English Fetus and the Right to Life' 11 *European Journal of Health Law* 347–364.

Scott, Rosamund, et al (2012) 'Donation of "Spare" Fresh or Frozen Embryos to Research: Who Decides that an Embryo Is "Spare" and How Can We Enhance the Quality and Protect the Validity of Consent?' 20 *Medical Law Review* 255–303.

Scottish Law Commission (1995) *Report on Incapable Adults* (Scottish Law Commission No 151).

Seale, C (2009) 'End-of-life Decisions in the UK Involving Medical Practitioners' 23 *Palliative Medicine* 198–204.

Singer, Peter (1993) *Practical Ethics* (2nd edn, Cambridge University Press).

Skegg, PDG (1973) 'Consent to Medical Procedures on Minors' 36(4) *Modern Law Review* 370–381.

Smith, JC (1986) 'Comment on *Gillick*' *Criminal Law Review* 113–118.

Smith, JC (1989) *Justification and Excuse in the Criminal Law* (Stevens & Sons).

Smith, Stephen A (2004) *Contract Theory* (Oxford University Press).

Smith, Stephen W, et al (eds) (2017) *Ethical Judgments: Re-Writing Medical Law* (Hart Publishing).

Spence, Edward (2006) *Ethics Within Reason: A Neo-Gewirthian Approach* (Lexington Books).

Spencer, JR (1997) 'Obituary: Professor Glanville Williams' *The Independent*, 17 April, www.independent.co.uk/news/people/obituary-professor-glanville-williams-1267628.html

Stavropoulos, Nicos (2017) 'The Debate that Never Was' 130 *Harvard Law Review* 2082–2095.

Steavenson, Wendell (2015) 'Jonathan Sumption: The Brain of Britain' *The Guardian*, 6 August, www.theguardian.com/law/2015/aug/06/jonathan-sumption-brain-of-britain

Stefan, Susan (1993) 'Silencing the Different Voice: Competency Feminist Theory and Law' 47 *University of Miami Law Review* 736–815.

Stevenson, Miriam (2016) 'Gewirthian Philosophy and Young Adults Who Have Down Syndrome: Towards a Human Rights-Based Model of Community Engagement for Young People Living with an Intellectual Disability' in Per Bauhn (ed) *Gewirthian Perspectives on Human Rights* (Routledge), 191–211.

Stoljar, Natalie (2000) 'Autonomy and Feminist Intuition' in Catriona Mackenzie and Natalie Stoljar (eds) *Relational Autonomy: Feminist Perspectives on Autonomy, Agency and the Social Self* (Oxford University Press), 94–111.

Sykes, Nigel and Thorns, Andrew (2003) 'The Use of Opioids and Sedatives at the End of Life' 4(5) *Lancet Oncology* 312–318.

Tang, Shu-Mei and Yen, Shang-Yung (2016) 'Confucianism and Gewirthian Human Rights in a Taiwanese Context' in Per Bauhn (ed) *Gewirthian Perspectives on Human Rights* (Routledge), 111–124.

Teff, Harvey (1994) *Reasonable Care: Legal Perspectives on the Doctor-Patient Relationship* (Clarendon Press).

Thorns, Andrew and Sykes, Nigel (2000) 'Opioid Use in the Last Week of Life and Implications for End of Life Decision-making' 356 *The Lancet* 398–399.

Thornton, Rosy (1992) 'Multiple Keyholders – Wardship and Consent to Medical Treatment' 51(1) *Cambridge Law Journal* 34–37.

Todd, Stephen (2017) 'Actions Arising from Birth' in Andrew Grubb, Judith Laing and Jean McHale (eds) *Principles of Medical Law* (4th edn, Oxford University Press), 236–296.

Toddington, Stuart (1993) *Rationality, Social Action and Moral Judgment* (Edinburgh University Press).

Townend, David (2017) 'Privacy, Politeness and the Boundary between Theory and Practice in Ethical Rationalism' in Patrick Capps and Shaun D Pattinson (eds) *Ethical Rationalism and the Law* (Hart Publishing), 171–190.

Trounson, Alan and DeWitt, Natalie D (2013) 'Pluripotent Stem Cells from Cloned Human Embryos: Success at Long Last' 12(6) *Cell Stem Cell* 636–638.

Wade, Katherine (2013) 'Refusal of Emergency Caesarean Section in Ireland: A Relational Approach' 21(1) *Medical Law Review* 1–25.

Wade, Katherine (2017) 'Caesarean Section Refusal in the Irish Courts: *Health Service Executive v B*' 25(3) *Medical Law Review* 494–504.

Waldron, Jeremy (1984) 'Introduction' in Jeremy Waldron (ed) *Theories of Rights* (Oxford University Press), 1–20.

186 *Bibliography*

Walters, Gregory J and Morley, Marie Constance (2016) 'Thomas Piketty and Alan Gewirth: Is a Global Community of Rights Possible in the Twenty-First Century' in Per Bauhn (ed) *Gewirthian Perspectives on Human Rights* (Routledge), 140–154.

Warnock, Mary, et al (1984) *The Report of the Committee of Inquiry into Human Fertilisation and Embryology (HMSO)*.

Westphal, Kenneth R (2017) 'Identifying and Justifying Moral Norms: Necessary Basics' in Patrick Capps and Shaun D Pattinson (eds) *Ethical Rationalism and the Law* (Hart Publishing), 37–53.

Wheeler, Robert (2006) 'Gillick or Fraser? A Plea for Consistency over Competence in Children' 332 *British Medical Journal* 807.

Wicks, Elizabeth (2017) 'The Legal Definition of Death and the Right to Life' in Shane McCorristine (ed) *Interdisciplinary Perspectives on Mortality and its Timings: When Is Death?* (Palgrave MacMillan), 119–131.

Wijdicks, Eelco FM (2014) *The Comatose Patient* (2nd edn, Oxford University Press).

Wilkinson, Stephen (2000) 'Palliative Care and the Doctrine of Double Effect' in Donna Dickenson, Malcolm Johnson and Jeanne Samson Katz, *Death, Dying and Bereavement* (2nd edn, Sage), 299–302.

Williams, Glanville (1958) *The Sanctity of Life and the Criminal Law* (Faber and Faber).

Williams, Glanville (1961) *Criminal Law: The General Part* (Stevens & Sons).

Williams, Glanville (1977) 'A Commentary on *R v Dudley and Stephens*' 8 *Cambrian Law Review* 94–99.

Williams, Glanville (1985) 'The Gillick Saga – II' 135 *New Law Journal* 1179–1182.

Williams, Glanville (1987) 'Oblique Intention' 46(3) *Cambridge Law Journal* 417–438.

Williams, Glanville (1994) 'The Fetus and the "Right to Life"' 53(1) *Cambridge Law Journal* 71–88.

Williams, Glenys (2001) 'The Principle of Double Effect and Terminal Sedation' 9 *Medical Law Review* 41–53.

Williams, Glenys (2007) *Intention and Causation in Medical Non-killing: The Impact of Criminal Law Concepts on Euthanasia and Assisted Suicide* (Routledge-Cavendish).

Wilmut, I, et al (1997) 'Viable Offspring Derived from Fetal and Adult Mammalian Cells' 385 *Nature* 810–813.

Wolf, Don P, et al (2017) 'Concise Review: Embryonic Stem Cells Derived by Somatic Cell Nuclear Transfer: A Horse in the Race?' 35(1) *Stem Cells* 26–34.

Index

The cross-references below are to subheadings where the relevant concepts are mentioned. Bold is used, where appropriate, to indicate the principal discussion of the relevant concept.

abortion 2.3, 2.4, 2.7, 3.3.2, 3.3.4, 3.4.1, 3.6, 5.2.3, 5.4.2, 5.6
agents
  defined 1.3.1 (n 76), 1.3.3
  free will 1.3.1 (n 80), 3.4.1
  ostensible agents **1.3.3**, 2.5, 3.4.1, 3.4.2, 4.3, 5.4.2, 6.4.3, 6.4.4
  potential 1.3.3, 5.4.2

best interests *see* incapacity

caesarean sections 3.5, 5.1, 5.2ff, 5.3, 5.4.1, 5.4.2, 5.6
capacity
  defined **3.1**, 5.1 (n 3), 5.2.1
  Gillick test **3.2.1**, 3.3.1, 3.3.2, 3.3.3
  Mental Capacity Act (adult) test **3.3.2**, 3.3.3, 5.2.1
  risk-relativity, and **5.2.1**, 5.4.1
  see also competence, incapacity
charitable interpretation *see* principle of charitable interpretation
cloning 6.4.3
communitarianism 3.4.1
competence
  defined **3.1**, 3.3.3, **3.4.2**, 5.1 (n 3), 5.2.1
  reflective v unreflective will 3.4.2
  risk-relativity, and 3.4.2, 3.5, 5.2.1, 5.4.1
  see also capacity
conscientious objection 3.4.1, 6.4.2 (n 63)
consent *see* capacity, competence, incapacity

criterion of
  avoidance of more probable harm **1.3.3**, 1.3.4, 4.3, 5.4.2, 6.4.1
  degrees of needfulness for action **1.3.3**, 1.3.4, 2.5, 2.6, 4.3, 5.4.2, 6.4.1

dialectically contingent *see* PGC
dialectically necessary *see* PGC
double effect *see* principle of doctrine of double effect

end of life decisions
  assisted suicide (requesting assistance to die) 2.2, 2.3, 2.4.1, 2.5, 2.6, 5.1, **5.2.2**
  life-shortening (lethal) interventions 2.2, 2.5, 4.3, 6.4.1
  palliative care 2.2, 2.3, 2.4.1, 6.4.4
  refusing life-prolonging treatment 3.3.1, 3.3.2, 3.3.3, 3.4.1, 5.2.1
  requesting life-prolonging treatment 6.4.4
  see also principle of double effect, sanctity of life
European Convention of Human Rights 1.3.2, 6.1 (n 11)
European Court of Human Rights 1.3.2, 4.2.3, 6.4.4

feminism *see* gender, relational autonomy

188 *Index*

gender 1.5, 3.4.1, 6.2.1, 6.3
gender reassignment 3.3.4, 3.4.2
generic rights *see* PGC

Hercules 1.1, 1.2, **1.2.1**, 1.2.2, 1.4,
  1.5, 2.6, 3.6, 4.5, 6.1
human dignity 1.3.2, 3.3.1, 3.4.1, 5.3,
  6.1, 6.4.4
Human Fertilisation and Embryology
  Authority 1.1.1, 6.4.3
Human Tissue Authority 1.1.1

idealised judgments
  Adams 2.7
  Bland 4.5
  Burke 6.4.4
  Gillick 3.6
  Quintavalle 6.4.3
  Re A 6.4.1
  Re MB 5.6
  U 6.4.2
  Yearworth 6.4.5
incapacity
  best interests test 2.4, 3.2.2, 3.2.3,
    3.3.1, 3.3.3, 3.4.2, 3.5, 4.1, 4.2.1,
    4.2.2, 4.2.3, 4.5, 5.1, 5.2.4, 5.2.5,
    5.6, 6.4.1, 6.4.4,
  overall interests test 4.1, **4.5**, 5.5,
    5.6, 6.3
  substituted judgment test 3.1, **5.2.4**,
    5.5, **5.6**, 6.3, 6.3.1, 6.4.4
  see also capacity, competence
intuition 3.4.1, 3.4.2
inviolability of life *see* sanctity of life

jurisdictions 1.1, 2.4.1, 3.3.4, 4.2.4, 5.3
  Australia 3.3.4
  Canada 2.4.1, 3.3.4, 5.2.3
  Germany 5.3
  India 4.2.4
  Ireland 4.2.4, 5.3
  Israel 4.2.4
  Italy 4.2.4
  New Zealand 2.4.1, 4.2.4
  Northern Ireland 4.2.4
  Scotland 4.2.4
  US 2.4.1, 3.3.4, 3.6, 4.2.4, 5.3,
    5.4.2, 5.6

law as integrity (Dworkin) 1.1, 1.1.2, 1.2,
  1.2.1, 1.2.2, 1.4, 2.6, 6.2, 6.5
legal fictions 2.4, 2.6, 3.3.3, 3.4.2,
  4.2.1, 4.2.2, 4.4, 4.5, 5.5, 6.3
legal idealism 1.2, 1.2.2, 1.3, 6.1
legal positivism 1.2, 1.2.1, 1.2.2, 1.3

moral relativism 3.4.1
moral status of
  embryos/fetus, the 5.2.3, **5.4.2**
  newborn baby, a 1.3.3
  other humans 1.3.3, 4.3, 6.4.1,
    6.4.4
  vegetative state, those in a 4.3

natural law *see* legal idealism

PGC (principle of generic
  consistency)
  compared with utilitarianism 2.6
  dialectically contingent method
    1.3.2, 3.4.1
  dialectically necessary method **1.3.1**,
    1.3.2, 1.3.3, 1.3.4, 3.4.1
  direct application **1.3.3**, 1.3.4, 2.5, 4.3
  generic rights (rights to the generic
    conditions) 1.3.1, 1.3.2, **1.3.3**,
    1.3.4, 1.4, 2.5, 3.4, 3.4.1, 3.4.2,
    3.5, 4.3, 5.4.1, 5.4.2, 6.2, 6.3,
    6.3.1, 6.4.2, 6.4.3, 6.4.4, 6.4.5
    additive rights 1.3.3, 1.3.4
    basic rights 1.3.3, 1.3.4, 2.5, 3.4.1,
      3.4.2, 4.3, 5.4.1, 5.4.2, 6.4.1,
      6.4.3
    nonsubtractive rights 1.3.3
  indirect application **1.3.4**, 2.5, 6.2,
    6.4.3, 6.5
  positive rights **1.3.1**, 3.4.1, 3.4.2,
    4.3, 5.4.2
  see also criterion of . . . and principle
    of . . .
precautionary reasoning *see* principle of
  precaution
precedent 1.1, 1.2.1, 1.5, 2.2, 2.6, 3.1,
  5.2.4 (n 89), **6.2**
principle of
  avoidance of more probable harm
    see criterion of avoidance of more
    probable harm
  charitable interpretation 1.2.2 (n 70),
    2.3, **6.5**
  competence-based capacity 3.4.1,
    3.4.2, **3.6**, 5.2.1, 5.4.1, **5.6**,
    6.3, 6.3.1
  degrees of needfulness for action *see*
    criterion of degrees of needfulness
    for action
  double effect 2.1, 2.2, **2.3**, 2.4,
    2.4.1, 2.5, 2.6, 2.7, 3.6,
    6.3, 6.4.1
  generic consistency *see* PGC
  intervening action 2.5 (n 79)

Index 189

the lesser of two evils 2.2, 2.6, 2.7, 3.3.2, 3.6, 4.3, 4.4, 4.5, 6.3, 6.3.1, 6.4.1
limited/proportional status 1.3.3, 4.3, **4.5**, 5.2.3, 5.4.2, **5.6**, 6.3, 6.3.1, 6.4.1, 6.4.3
precaution **1.3.3**, 3.4.1, 3.4.2, 4.3, 5.2.1, 5.4.2, 6.4.1
proportionality under precaution *see* principle of precaution
substituted judgment 5.5, 5.6, 6.3, 6.4.4
sui generis status 4.5, 5.2.3, 6.3, 6.3.1, 6.4.1

relational autonomy **3.4.1**, 3.4.2, 6.4.2
religion
Born Again Christians 5.6
Catholicism 2.3, 3.1, 6.4.1
Jehovah's Witnesses 3.3.1, 3.3.2, 3.3.4, 5.6

rights
generic rights *see* PGC
interest-rights (interest conception of rights) 1.3.2, 1.3.3, 2.5, 4.3, 5.4.2
positive rights/duties 1.3.3, 3.4.1, 3.4.2, 4.3, 5.3, 5.4.2, 6.4.4
will-rights (will conception of rights) 1.3.2, 1.3.3, 2.5, 3.4.1, 4.3, 5.4.2

sanctity of life **2.3**, 2.5, 4.2.1, 4.3, 4.5, 6.4.4

utilitarianism 2.6, 4.3, 6.1 (n 10)

vegetative state
persistent v permanent 4.1, 4.4
recover from 4.2.2, 4.3
virtue ethics 3.4.1

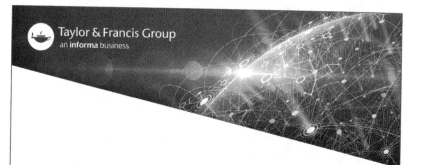